THE COMPLETE WORKS

OF

GEORGE SAVILE

MARQUESS OF HALIFAX

Emery Walker Ph. sc.

George Savile, Marquess of Halifax

From the portrait by Sir Peter Lely
belonging to the Duke of Devonshire at Hardwicke Hall

THE
COMPLETE WORKS
OF *GEORGE SAVILE*
FIRST MARQUESS OF
HALIFAX

Edited with an Introduction

By WALTER RALEIGH

OXFORD
AT THE CLARENDON PRESS
1912

HENRY FROWDE
PUBLISHER TO THE UNIVERSITY OF OXFORD
LONDON, EDINBURGH, NEW YORK
TORONTO AND MELBOURNE

PRINTED IN ENGLAND.

CONTENTS.

INTRODUCTION.

IT would have given no displeasure to Sir George Savile, First Marquess of Halifax, to think that by later generations of his countrymen he should be almost forgotten. Statesmen are easily forgotten. A prosperous lie made Titus Oates immortal; but the man who was the practical genius of the English Revolution, and the acutest critical genius among English politicians, is now little more than a name. What is most commonly remembered about him is that he was called the 'Trimmer'. The nickname was put upon him angrily by his contemporaries, and was worn proudly by himself. The imputation it conveyed was, no doubt, that he trimmed his sails to the varying breezes of opinion ; but in his famous pamphlet, the noise of which still echoes distantly in the public ear, he changed the metaphor. A boat, he said, goes ill, and is in danger of capsizing, if the people in it weigh it down all on one side, or all on the other. But there is a kind of men ' who conceive that it would do as well if the boat went even, without endangering the passengers '. And it is hard to imagine, he adds, how it should come to be a fault, or a heresy, to attempt to trim the boat.

He calls it a boat (he never uses magnificent or extravagant language), but what he means is the ship of State, that ship on whose seaworthiness the lives even of the mutineers depend. Halifax was a pilot for the greater part of his responsible life, and his chief care was always the State. His reputation has none of that glamour which shines upon heroic folly. The leader of a forlorn hope excites a ready enthusiasm ; the martyr for an idea, the rebel who will have his own way or nothing, the stickler for principle, who cares little to stay in a world where his

darling

darling creed is not to prevail—all these are easily made into heroes, and worshipped for their courage. But the pilot, to whom danger and difficulty are not heroic crises, but the very material of his craft, or the engine-driver, who has had the care of a thousand lives in his sole charge, goes home unnoticed, and takes his modest wage. On his constancy and judgement the safety of humanity depends; his faith and skill have made it possible for the thoughtless passengers to dream in peace and to warm their imagination with the admirable deeds of fiction. Life would be a poorer thing than it is if work of this kind were rewarded by monuments and testimonials and public fame. The old Roman way is better : expect the best from your political servants, and try them for treason if they give you less.

Not many men have written books on the practical business of their lives. Statesmen have commonly been content to make laws, or treaties, leaving it to philosophers to expound the principles of politics. It is the fascination of the writings of Halifax that they were suggested by his experience of life, and are crammed with the lessons drawn directly from that experience. Here are no flights of the imagination, no ingenious ornaments of style, no beautiful vanities of authorship. He quotes none of those fallacious historical precedents which are dear to the mind of the academic scholar; his writings are bare of classical allusion. What he has to tell is what he has found out for himself in the course of his traffic with the world; but he tells it with so much wit and irony, with such acuteness of observation and pungency of phrasing, that he runs some risk of losing the esteem of those who think that wise men must needs be dull. Moreover, books have failed, from time immemorial, to convey the lessons of experience; and the wisdom of life can be bought only by the expenditure of life itself. Old men would be very glad to to tell what they know, but they cannot hope to be understood. If they are wise, they say little; if they are foolish, they babble pleasantly enough, but have nothing to tell. Halifax has much to tell, but a beginner is not likely to learn it. On the other hand, a man who has served on a jury, or has stood an election, or has been responsible for the management of any business, will feel a thrill of pleasure when his own experience is brought home to him again in that brilliant epigrammatic dress. English literature is very rich; only a very rich literature could have afforded to neglect so distinguished a writer. But it is not rich in practical wisdom; and the neglect of Halifax is a thing to be regretted and amended.

His writings are strangely modern, and, withal, are wholly English. The politics of this country have altered very little, one would say, since the days of the Exclusion Bill. Indeed it is one of the chief attractions of Seventeenth-Century history that there is hardly a live question to-day which was unknown to the men of that time. It is something to feel that we are not more fantastic or absurd than our ancestors. Any one who reads the pamphlets which contain Halifax's reflections on the controversies of his own time will find himself, almost against his will, applying these reflections to the matter of to-day. No violence is required to make the application; page after page of the pamphlets might have been written yesterday for all the evidence that they show of bygone modes. It is a fashion nowadays to decry the Party system in politics. Once upon a time (so the argument runs) Party names stood for something real; they marked fundamental and irreconcilable differences of opinion on essential questions. But now they have become empty of meaning, the pretexts of competitors for power and reward. Such an account of the Party system is not good history. Swift, who lived when the succession to
the

the Crown was a Party question, made light of Whig and
Tory, and here, at the very birth of the system, is Halifax,
its most destructive critic. The names of Whig and Tory
do not occur in his works. He disliked devotion in a conventicle, and loyalty in a drunken Club. He was troubled
to see men of all sides sick of a calenture. He knew that
men, though they forget much, never forget themselves; and
that the World is nothing but Vanity cut out into several
shapes. His remarks *Of Parties* in his *Political Thoughts and
Reflections* are the severest things ever said about Party :

' It turneth all Thought into talking instead of doing.
Men get a habit of being unuseful to the Publick by turning in a Circle of Wrangling and Railing, which they
cannot get out of.'

' Ignorance maketh most Men go into a Party, and
Shame keepeth them from getting out of it.'

The fact is that the rigours of Party, which are easily
maintained, with all their consequences, by logicians,
journalists, and theorists, will not suffer the practical test.
Men exalt themselves on their principles, and glory in the
partition which separates the sheep from the goats, who
prove, after all, to be only the other sheep. But the
English have a genius for government, and when government is the business in hand, this separatist method has
no value. Men who differ rabidly on principles will find
that the lessons they learn from experience have a tendency
to be the same. Then, if they change their course, or
modify the policy which has been so bravely announced,
they are accused of being false. The charge is true ; they
have been false ; but it was their thinking and talking
that was false, not their corrected action. The melodrama
of their boastful creed would not bear translation into the
life of this world. They have been the dupes of literature ;
all that is heroic in literature is simple and straightfor-
ward, but then, the hero is prepared to die. Society is not

                                                    prepared

prepared to die for a creed, and politics is a vast complex network of means to an end, the end being the continued life and comfort of mankind. It is the irony of the states-man's position that while his work is very like the work of a good housekeeper, the literary deceits and fictions incident to the process of persuasion invite us to regard him as a hero of romance, a lone figure on a mountain peak, silhouetted against the moon. 'I think it's the novels', said the old lady quoted by Mr. Bagehot, 'that make my girls so *heady*.'

The old political families of England, who have borne a hand for generations in the government of the country, are often exempt from these errors. They are not easily intoxicated by public duties, which have been their matter-of-fact business for centuries. You may call them Whig or Tory, it makes little difference ; some third name, more fundamental in its implications, is needed to describe them. They look at things instinctively from the point of view of the administration. The fervours of the pulpit and the platform do not much delight them. It was the great advantage of George Savile that he was born into such a family, and was connected by kinship, or by the accidents of life, with many of the most influential persons of that age. Sir Henry Savile, wit and scholar, Warden of Merton College, Oxford, and Provost of Eton, perhaps the most learned Greek scholar of Elizabethan England, was his distant kinsman. The Lord Keeper Coventry was his grandfather. The great Earl of Strafford was his father's uncle. Anthony Ashley Cooper, first Earl of Shaftesbury, who vies with one other claimant for the credit of being the first Whig, was his uncle by marriage, his colleague, and, in the end, his rival. Lady Dorothy Sidney, Waller's 'Sacharissa', was his wife's mother. More notable still, the famous Earl of Chesterfield was his grandson. In short, he was intimately connected with most of those
whose

whose names fill the pages of English History during the latter half of the Seventeenth Century, and was a witness of the events of that history from a position of extraordinary vantage. His family, moreover, though staunchly Royalist, managed to keep possession of its estates, and in 1643, when his father, Sir William Savile, after loyal service rendered to the King, died at the age of thirty-one, the young George Savile had the ball at his feet. Concerning his youth and education we know next to nothing. He was born in 1633, and was brought up under the control of his widowed mother, who was a woman of strong character. When she died, in 1662, her son was already married, settled on his estate of Rufford, in Nottinghamshire, and prominent in public life.[1] He was described, later, by Evelyn the diarist, as ' a very rich man, very witty, and in his younger days somewhat positive'. His wit and his riches he kept throughout life ; his opinions became less positive. His wit was perhaps his chief fault ; he could not keep it under, or refuse himself a pointed jest. 'One great argument', says a contemporary account, ' of the prodigious depth and quickness of his sense is, that many of his observations and wise sayings were on the sudden, when talking to a friend or going from him.' The spontaneity and freedom of his talk was ill taken by Clarendon and other cautious and explanatory persons, and Savile was reputed to be void of all sense of religion—which he certainly was not. Later, among his *Moral Thoughts and Reflections*, he says, ' There is so much Danger in Talking, that a Man strictly wise can hardly be called a sociable Creature.' This was a

lesson

---

[1] All who concern themselves with Halifax must acknowledge their great debt to the careful and exhaustive work of Miss Foxcroft, *The Life and Letters of Sir George Savile, Bart., First Marquis of Halifax, &c., with a new edition of his works now for the first time collected and revised* by H. C. Foxcroft. Two volumes, Longmans, 1898.

lesson that he learned but slowly, if indeed he ever learned it. His conduct of business was discreet almost to a fault ; his letters are so prudent and reserved that they are amazingly dull to read ; but he indemnified himself for these restraints by the freedom of his intimate conversation. The writings in which he has allowed himself most of this freedom were either non-political, like his *Advice to a Daughter,* or were posthumously published, like his *Character of King Charles the Second : and Political, Moral and Miscellaneous Thoughts and Reflections.* These are the best of his works. That prudence and discretion which keeps a man safe and sequestered in life conceals him also from the notice of later generations ; the same caution which delivers him from malicious gossip, puts him beyond the reach of posthumous sympathy. Halifax, the author, appeals to our interest because he says many things which politicians know and do not say. To avoid even paltry enmities may be the clear duty of a statesman. ' It is a Misfortune ', Halifax remarks, ' for a Man not to have a Friend in the World, but for that reason he shall have no Enemy.'

The events of his public life, as parliamentary leader, as Minister under Charles II, as President of the Council under James II, and as Lord Privy Seal under William III, are written broad on the history of England, and cannot be recorded here. He bore a hand in all the chief events of the time, from the Restoration onwards, to his death, in 1695. His importance may be well measured by this, that it never depended on the office that he held. He was respected, consulted, and feared in opposition no less than when he was chief Minister of the Crown. The greatest of his achievements, it will probably be agreed, was the rejection of the Exclusion Bill in 1680 by the House of Lords. No record remains of the speeches made ; but the severity and brilliancy of his duel with Shaftesbury is attested by

many

many contemporaries. He stood up to Shaftesbury, and answered him every time he spoke. He carried the House, in the end, triumphantly with him. It was a triumph not so much of argument as of intelligence and insight. He understood the temper of the people of England as Shaftesbury never did, and he knew that the ebullitions of popular enthusiasm are no safe index to that temper. Monmouth was adored by the people ; the Duke of York was neither liked nor loved. Shaftesbury thought to earn the nation's gratitude by offering them Monmouth in place of York. He miscalculated cruelly ; the people did not fear a new King ; but they did fear a Kingmaker. The whole edifice of constitutional monarchy was designed not for the protection of bad kings, but for the humiliation of arrogant ministers. This Halifax understood ; so he became the guardian of the Constitution, and later, when James II had set himself to break the Constitution, the guiding spirit of the Revolution. His politics are our politics ; his political creed remains in the Twentieth Century what it was in the Seventeenth Century, the creed of John Bull. But the rare delight is to find John Bull a wit ! Wit is commonly employed in extremes, where it works most easily. To satirize novelty, and ridicule all that is unfamiliar ; or, reversing the process, to ridicule all that is familiar, to deny the truth of proverbs and to flout the sayings that embody general opinion—these devices furnish wit with a simple and effective mechanism. But Halifax employs the subtlest resources of wit in defence of the practical expedient, the middle course, the reasonable compromise.

Dryden pays tribute, in *Absalom and Achitophel,* not only to the wit of Halifax, but to his courage and eloquence :

> *Jotham* of piercing Wit and pregnant Thought,
> Endew'd by nature and by learning taught

To

To move Assemblies, who but onely tri'd
The worse a while, then chose the better side ;
Nor chose alone, but turned the Balance too ;
So much the weight of one brave man can do.

Indeed, for all that he is called the Trimmer, Halifax has
been very generally recognized for an upright and honourable man. He was promoted, by steady gradation, to high
honours and high offices, yet no one has been found foolish
enough to pretend that he was a self-seeker. Macaulay,
who expresses some distrust of him in the *Essays*, and
introduces him, in the *History*, as one who was not sufficiently indifferent to titles of honour, makes amends, in
a later passage, by a full and generous eulogy :

' What distinguishes him from all other English states-
men is this, that, through a long public life, and through
frequent and violent revolutions of public feeling, he almost
invariably took that view of the great questions of his
time which history has finally adopted. He was called
inconstant, because the relative position in which he stood
to the contending factions was perpetually varying. As
well might the pole-star be called inconstant because it is
sometimes to the east and sometimes to the west of the
pointers. To have defended the ancient and legal constitution of the realm against a seditious populace at one
conjunction, and against a tyrannical government at
another ; to have been the foremost champion of order in
the turbulent Parliament of 1680, and the foremost
champion of liberty in the servile Parliament of 1685 ;
to have been just and merciful to Roman Catholics in the
days of the Popish plot, and to Exclusionists in the days
of the Rye House plot ; to have done all in his power to
save both the head of Stafford and the head of Russell ;
this was a course which contemporaries, heated by passion,
might not unnaturally call fickle, but which deserves a very
different name from the later justice of posterity.'

One stain, and one only, Macaulay finds on his memory,
that in the reign of William III he stooped to hold com-
munication with the exiled Court of St. Germain. The
fact is not disputed, but a wise judgement on the fact asks
for

for a more active and careful imagination than is usually brought to it. The black-and-white school of moralists are not valuable critics of the politics of the Seventeenth Century. They would be better employed in writing laudatory biographies of the authors of *Histriomastix* and Εἰκὼν βασιλική. For many years it was not certain who was King of England. It was not certain whether England was to be a monarchy or a commonwealth. Many patriotic Englishmen had been driven abroad, and hardly a man of note had not relatives in France. In these civil conflicts, which divide families, the law of treason must needs be humanely interpreted; and the offence proved against Halifax amounts only to misprision of treason; that is to say, he did not cut off all confidential relations with his friends and acquaintance on the other side.

This, at any rate, is certain, he never for one moment sought any other end than the security and greatness of England. He very early recognized that one portentous question was beginning to obscure the whole political horizon. ' The Greatness of France,' wrote the English Envoy at Lisbon, ' as I have heard your Lordship observe, hath made all old politics useless.' So, in 1668, he welcomed the Triple Alliance between England, Holland, and Sweden, to hold Louis XIV in check. So far, his politics were the politics of William of Orange. But William of Orange was a European statesman and general; Halifax was purely an Englishman. He was glad to have the help of alliances, but he did not like to have to trust to them. Real friendships between nations are things of very slow and difficult growth; while friendships between governments are subject to the dangers and disadvantages of friendships between two bodies of trustees representing different interests. If such friendships are immutable, they are dishonest. Halifax was not deceived by them.

In

In a letter to Sir William Temple, written shortly before the Triple Alliance was concluded, he discusses the possibility of a French invasion, and concludes : ' We must rely upon the Oak and Courage of England to do our Business, there being small Appearance of anything to help us from abroad.'

Many fine things have been said of England by Englishmen ; none of them more sincere and moving than the things said by Halifax. He is a quiet writer, critical and sceptical, keenly aware of the absurdity of enthusiasm. He keeps his feelings so well in hand that he has the reputation of a cynic. But this is how he writes of England :

' Our *Trimmer* is far from Idolatry in other things, in one thing only he cometh near it, his Country is in some degree his Idol; he doth not Worship the Sun, because 'tis not peculiar to us, it rambles about the World, and is less kind to us than others ; but for the Earth of *England,* tho perhaps inferior to that of many places abroad, to him there is Divinity in it, and he would rather dye, than see a spire of *English* Grass trampled down by a Foreign Trespasser : He thinketh there are a great many of his mind, for all plants are apt to taste of the Soyl in which they grow, and we that grow here, have a Root that produceth in us a Stalk of English Juice, which is not to be changed by grafting or foreign infusion ; and I do not know whether any thing less will prevail, than the Modern Experiment, by which the Blood of one Creature is transmitted into another ; according to which, before the *French* blood can be let into our Bodies, every drop of our own must be drawn out of them.'

When these words were written England stood in greater danger of invasion than she has known at any later time, unless it were in the time of Napoleon. Halifax had seen the Navy driven off the sea by the Dutch, and the shipping in the Thames burnt, yet the people were slow to awake to their danger. In the pamphlet entitled *A Rough Draught of a New Model at Sea,* which was published in 1694, but was probably written earlier, he tries to awaken them. He knew the difficulty of the attempt.

'A

'A Nation is a great while', he observes, 'before they can see, and generally they must feel first before their Sight is quite cleared. This maketh it so long before they can see their *Interest*, that for the most part it is too late for them to pursue it : If Men must be supposed always to follow their true *Interest*, it must be meant of a New Manufactory of Mankind by God Almighty ; there must be some new *Clay*, the old *Stuff* never yet made any such infallible Creature.'

Yet the means to safety was clear, and he puts it in the forefront of his argument :

'I will make no other Introduction to the following Discourse, than that as the Importance of our being strong at *Sea*, was ever very great, so in our present Circumstances it is grown to be much greater ; because, as formerly our Force of Shipping contributed greatly to our *Trade* and Safety ; so now it is become indispensibly necessary to our very *Being*.

'It may be said now to *England, Martha, Martha*, thou art busy about many things, but one thing is necessary. To the Question, What shall we do to be saved in this World ? there is no other Answer but this, Look to your Moate.

'The first Article of an *English-man's* Political Creed must be, That he believeth in the Sea, *&c.* without that there needeth no General Council to pronounce him incapable of Salvation here.'

This is all very modern, and so also are his recommendations in the matter of commissions in the Navy. It is perhaps no bad vindication of his opinions that they are in complete agreement with the best practice of the Navy from that time to this. There were those who held that all naval officers should be gentlemen born, as there were others who held that they should all be *tarpaulins*—that is, men who had been bred from boyhood to the rough work of practical seamen. He discusses the merits and faults of both sorts of officer, and rejects both proposals as evil extremes. There must be a mixture, he holds, of the two classes, in a proportion to be determined by experiment and circumstance ; and the dangers that may attend

attend the mixture are to be avoided by one main precaution :

' The *Gentlemen* shall not be capable of bearing Office
at *Sea*, except they be *Tarpaulins* too ; that is to say,
except they are so trained up by a continued habit of living
at *Sea*, that they may have a Right to be admitted free
Denizens of *Wapping*.'

There must be an end of sending idle young noblemen
to sea in positions of authority.

' When a *Gentleman* is preferr'd at *Sea*, the *Tarpaulin* is
very apt to impute it to Friend or Favour : But if that
Gentleman hath before his Preferment passed through all
the Steps which lead to it, so that he smelleth as much of
Pitch and *Tar*, as those that were *Swadled* in *Sail-Cloath* ;
his having an *Escutcheon* will be so far from doing him
harm, that it will set him upon the advantage Ground : It
will draw a real Respect to his Quality when so supported,
and give him an Influence and Authority infinitely superior
to that which the *meer Sea man* can ever pretend to.'

A sailor can never be fit to command till he has learned
to obey ; nor can he be trusted to inflict punishments to
which he has never been liable.

' When the undistinguish'd *Discipline* of a Ship hath
tamed the young Mastership, which is apt to arise from
a *Gentleman's* Birth and Education, he then groweth
Proud in the right place, and valueth himself first upon
knowing his Duty, and then upon doing it.'

The experience of the two wars with Holland had plenti-
fully illustrated the evils of which Halifax speaks ; it was
his own knowledge of human nature which directed him so
clearly to the remedy.

The works of Halifax all belong to the last ten years or
so of his life. The earliest of them, *The Character of a
Trimmer*, is a complete handbook to the politics of the
closing years of Charles the Second's reign. The *Letter to
a Dissenter* and *The Anatomy of an Equivalent*, which
followed it within a few months, are directed against
James the Second's famous attempt to buy off the
hostility

hostility of the Dissenters by including them in his project of toleration. None of these tracts, when first printed, bore the author's name. The naval tract mentioned above, and the tract entitled *Some Cautions Offered to the Consideration of Those who are to Chuse Members to Serve for the Ensuing Parliament*, are also anonymous, and are his latest writings. When the ensuing Parliament came to be elected he had been six months dead. All his worldly wisdom shines in this last tract, which, again, applies almost without change to the circumstances of to-day. The last satirical injunction has a strangely familiar ring :

' In the mean time, after having told my Opinion, Who ought not to be Chosen :

' If I should be ask'd, Who ought to be, my Answer must be, Chuse *Englishmen* ; and when I have said that, to deal honestly, I will not undertake that they are easy to be found.'

In some ways his *Advice to a Daughter*, which, alone among the writings published during his lifetime, seems to have been carefully prepared by his own hand for the press, is the most attractive of his works. It was written for his daughter Elizabeth, who became the wife of the third Earl of Chesterfield, and the mother of a famous son. The habit of giving advice to the younger generation would appear to have been hereditary in the family. But Halifax's social maxims are more profound than Chesterfield's, as his political maxims are more profound than Bolingbroke's. The book was immensely popular ; it ran through some twenty-five editions, and held the field for almost a century, to be superseded at last by Dr. Gregory's *Father's Legacy* and Mrs. Chapone's *Letters on the Improvement of the Mind*. The *Advice* is somewhat melancholy in tone. The author sets before his daughter no ideas of self-advancement, and indulges her with scant hopes of happiness. There is too little room in his scheme for the holiday virtues, and the free play of impulse. ' Whilst you are

playing

playing full of Innocence, the spitefull World will bite,
except you are guarded by your *Caution.*' His words are
a prophylactic against the inevitable ills of life. His
section on a Husband is devoted mainly to considerations
which may palliate a husband's faults and vices. His commandments are commandments without promise. There
is to be no relaxation ; life is one long fencing-bout. ' You
are to have as strict a Guard upon yourself amongst your
Children, as if you were amongst your *Enemies.*' This is
a wise remark, but it does not make home seem a place
of warmth and ease. The same cold good sense and
discernment govern his thinking on such topics as Religion
and Friendship. He is judicious, sane, and balanced, but
he does not think of the world as a cheerful place.

Yet, with all this, there is something very moving in
his solicitude. His high principles of conduct and his deep
affection for his daughter peep out unwittingly here and
there. It is small wonder that the book was cherished by
her, and lay always upon her table. The calm of the
perfectly well-bred style forbids all direct expression of the
emotions, but the impression it makes is all the greater.
' When my *Fears* prevail, I shrink as if I was struck, at the
Prospect of *Danger,* to which a young Woman must be
expos'd.' His concluding advice on the article of marriage
has a pathos of its own :

' That you would, as much as Nature will give you
leave, endeavour to forget the great *Indulgence* you have
found at home. After such a gentle Discipline as you have
been under, every thing you dislike will seem the harsher
to you. The tenderness we have had for you, *My Dear,*
is of another nature, peculiar to kind Parents, and differing from that which you will meet with first in any Family
into which you shall be transplanted ; and yet they may
be very kind too, and afford no justifiable reason to you
to complain. You must not be frighted with the first
Appearances of a *differing Scene* ; for when you are used
to it, you may like the House you go to, better than that
you

you left ; and your *Husband's* Kindness will have so much advantage of ours, that we shall yield up all *Competition*, and as well as we love you, be very well contented to Surrender to such a *Rival.*'

Something of the same fragrance makes itself felt in the worldly wisdom of his advice concerning Censure :

' The Triumph of *Wit* is to make your *good Nature* subdue your *Censure* ; to be quick in *seeing Faults*, and slow in *exposing* them. You are to consider, that the invisible thing called a *Good Name*, is made up of the Breath of Numbers that speak well of you ; so that if by a *disobliging Word* you silence the *meanest*, the *Gale* will be less strong which is to bear up your *Esteem*. And though nothing is so vain as the eager pursuit of *empty Applause*, yet to be well thought of, and to be kindly used by the World, is like a *Glory* about a Womans *Head* ; 'tis a Perfume she carrieth about with her, and leaveth wherever she goeth ; 'tis a Charm against *Ill-will*. *Malice* may empty her Quiver, but cannot wound ; the Dirt will not stick, the Jests will not take ; Without the consent of the World a *Scandal* doth not go deep ; it is only a slight stroak upon the injured Party and returneth with the greater force upon those that gave it.'

The *Character of King Charles II* is a masterpiece. Perhaps no such intimate portrait of an English King, drawn by a contemporary, is to be found in the whole course of our history. It makes us regret that Halifax has left us so few descriptions of the persons whom he knew. The tendency to aphorism and epigram is strong, and the *Character* is full of brilliant sentences. ' Men given to dissembling are like Rooks at play, they will cheat for shillings, they are so used to it.' ' Mistresses are in all Respects craving Creatures.' But the dispassionate analysis of the King's character and motives ; the account given of the effect of his early misfortune on his disposition ; and the incidental pictures, for those who read between the lines, of the daily life of the Court ;—all these are as convincing as a scientific demonstration. The King's

ruling

ruling passion, the love of ease, was never so vividly drawn. Nothing to him was worth purchasing at the price of a difficulty. We see him surrounded by a crowd of importunate beggars of both sexes ; he would walk fast to avoid being engaged by them. ' He would slide from an asking Face, and could guess very well.' When he was brought to bay, he would buy off his tormentors by large concessions for the sake of present ease. In this way ' the King was made the Instrument to defraud the Crown, which is somewhat extraordinary.' It is plain to see, for all the delicacy with which the Royal foibles are described, that Lord Halifax was not perfectly happy in the familiar company that the King kept about him. ' His Mistresses were such as did not care that Wit of the best kind should have the Precedence in their Apartments.' The King delighted in broad allusions, and made fun of those who would not join in. He had a good memory, but told stories too often, and at too great length. He appreciated wit, but (and here is a cry from the soul) ' of all Men that ever *liked* those who *had Wit,* he could the best *endure* those who had *none*'. Yet the natural amiability and sweetness of Charles's temper shines through all the description. There is a certain attractiveness in his impatience of the formalities of his position ; his tendency to relapse into Charles Stuart and so regain the freedom of a private estate. The closing eulogy on this unfortunate and gentle Prince is a sincere and true testimony from a competent witness :

' A Prince neither sharpened by his Misfortunes whilst Abroad, nor by his Power when restored, is such a shining Character, that it is a Reproach not to be so dazzled with it, as not to be able to see a Fault in its full Light. . . . He is under the Protection of common Frailty, that must engage Men for their own sakes not to be too severe, where they themselves have so much to answer.'

The *Political, Moral and Miscellaneous Thoughts and*
Reflections

Reflections is the most notable English collection of Maxims, the nearest parallel and rival to the work of La Roche-foucauld and La Bruyère. Popular proverbs, it has often been remarked, are not very generous in their treatment of humanity ; and a writer of aphorisms, which are pro-verbs coined in a private mint, is open to the same charge. An aphorism is an act of judgement, and so can pretend to no higher merit than justice, which is not the greatest of human virtues. The beauties of human character are vague and living things ; the deformities lend themselves more readily to be outlined by a decisive pencil. Yet the aphorisms of Halifax never sacrifice sense to wit, and always provoke thought. His political reflections, especially, could only have been written by a statesman of experience. He is often severe, but he is no cynic. ' Men must be saved in this World ', he says, ' by their Want of Faith ' ; but he was not so foolish as to deny the existence of un-selfishness. ' It is a Mistake to say a Friend can be bought.' In his *Character of King Charles II*, commenting on the insatiability of the King's followers, he falls into the same vein of argument :

' I am of an Opinion, in which I am every Day more confirmed by Observation, that Gratitude is one of those things that cannot be bought. It must be born with Men, or else all the Obligations in the World will not create it. An outward Shew may be made to satisfy Decency, and to prevent Reproach ; but a real Sense of a kind thing is a Gift of Nature, and never was, nor can be acquired.'

Yet even sincere Friendship has its weaknesses. ' Those Friends who are above Interest are seldom above Jealousy.' The aphorisms of Halifax are a better guide to the world as it is than all the brilliancies of his epigrammatic French contemporaries. His satire bears no trace of disappointed ambition or poisoned egotism. Some of his sayings are condensed treatises in their weight of thought. Why is it that

that popularity is so often suspect ?   He puts his finger
at once on the answer. ' Popularity is a Crime from the
Moment it is sought ; it is only a Virtue where Men have
it whether they will or no.'   Who has ever defined a Fool
better than in these few words : ' A Fool hath no Dialogue
within himself, the first Thought carrieth him without the
Reply of a second ' ?   How could the verdict of mankind
on plaintive persons be more truly expressed than in
the sentences on *Complaint* ?—

' Complaining is a Contempt upon ones self :
' It is an ill Sign both of a Man's Head and of his Heart.
' A Man throweth himself down whilst he complaineth ;
and when a Man throweth himself down, no body careth
to take him up again.'

There is very little mention made of Halifax in the
writings of his contemporaries.   Though he held a con-
spicuous station, he seems to have passed through life
observing rather than observed.   A fascinating sketch of
him is given in Burnet's *History of His Own Time*, as he
appeared to that prelate of unbounded energy and coarse
perceptions.   Virtue may win over vice ; but intelligence
cannot make a convert of stupidity.   Burnet, whose
power in the State came late in Halifax's career, is a good
example of the bluff, hot-headed partisan, to whom it is
impossible to doubt that right is all on one side.   Halifax,
we are told by a contemporary, ' was never better pleased
than when he was turning Bishop Burnet and his politics
into ridicule.'   Burnet's verdict on Halifax will not mislead
those who have heard the Trimmer speak for himself :

' He was a man of a great and ready wit ; full of life,
and very pleasant ; much turned to satire.   He let his
wit run much on matters of religion, so that he passed for
a bold and determined atheist ; though he often protested
to me he was not one ; and said, he believed there was not
one in the world : he was a Christian in submission : he
believed as much as he could and he hoped that God would
not

not lay it to his charge, if he could not digest iron, as an ostrich did, nor take into his belief things that must burst him : if he had any scruples, they were not sought for, nor cherished by him ; for he never read an atheistical book. In a fit of sickness I knew him very much touched with a sense of religion. I was then often with him. He seemed full of good purposes, but they went off with his sickness. He was always talking of morality and friendship. He was punctual in all payments, and just in all his private dealings. But, with relation to the public, he went backwards and forwards, and changed sides so often, that in conclusion no side trusted him. He seemed full of commonwealth notions, yet he went into the worst part of King Charles's reign.'

He is the last of the long line of statesmen who found it possible to govern England without paying allegiance to party. Their day is past ; and the party system is stronger now than it was in the time of the Jacobites and Hanoverians. No better method has ever been devised for the peaceful settlement of differences of opinion on domestic questions. The nation is not prepared to revive the custom of impeaching unpopular ministers. Englishmen sometimes rail at party, as they rail at cricket and football, but they know that there is no escape from it. It deceives vainglorious partisans, no doubt, and it offends righteous philosophers ; but it suits the national temper. Yet there is no need to be duped by it ; and any one who tries to think clearly on politics must be a very wise man, or a very foolish one, if he gets no help from the writings of the Marquess of Halifax.

It remains to say a few words on the text of Halifax. The present edition is based on the two volumes which together contain the works of Halifax, namely, the volume of *Miscellanies*, first published in 1700, and the volume entitled *A Character of King Charles the Second : and Political, Moral and Miscellaneous Thoughts and Reflections*, published

published in 1750. For these last two pieces the 1750 volume is the sole authority. It was printed from material supplied by Lady Burlington, Halifax's grand-daughter, and seems to be virtually free from mistakes. The *Advice to a Daughter*, which is included in the *Miscellanies*, is likewise a good and careful text. Some few variations occur among the many editions of this piece, but they are of very little importance.

Of the political tracts there are of course many separate editions earlier than the *Miscellanies*. These tracts were most of them first circulated in manuscript, and I cannot convince myself that any one of them, when it came to be printed, was overseen by the author. It may be, as Miss Foxcroft suggests, that he corrected the proofs of *The Anatomy of an Equivalent*, but against this it must be said that men of quality rarely corrected proofs, and that *The Character of a Trimmer*, a much more important and personal document, appeared in print again and again, during his lifetime, full of nonsensical mistakes, which varied from edition to edition, but did not diminish in number. There is no authoritative edition of any of the controversial writings. But the variations in the earlier editions of the shorter tracts are unimportant, and the obvious blunders are comparatively few.

The only serious textual difficulties are presented by *The Character of a Trimmer*. This piece seems, from the first, to have been the plaything of copyists and printers. Miss Foxcroft, in her admirable edition, has collated the various printed texts, and has compared them in detail with four manuscript copies. But the manuscripts are not more trustworthy, or less corrupt, than the printed editions, so that the result is disappointing. Some of the best emendations in her text are suggested by herself; some are borrowed from the manuscripts. I desire to express my obligation for the readings which I owe to her edition,

notably

notably ' discountenance ' for ' distinct name ' (*infra*, p. 52, l. 21), and (best of all) ' spire of *English* Grass ' for ' piece of *English* Glass ' (p. 97, l. 18). This last emendation has restored its highest touch of imagination to the finest passage in the tract. I have resisted the temptation to suggest important emendations. Once only I have yielded to it; and have read ' landlord ' for ' language ' on p. 84, l. 20. The reading ' language ' would leave to the sentence a possible meaning, but would make nonsense of the argument. It is a significant fact that this reading, which I take to be an obvious blunder, is found in all the editions, and in all the manuscripts.

Miss Foxcroft has taken a hint from the manuscripts, and has restored the inflection -*eth*, or -*th*, in the third person singular of the present tense. In this I have followed her example. There is no doubt that the termination in -*es*, or -*s*, was substituted by the printers for the old-fashioned usage, which was preferred by Halifax in his authoritative works, and which is necessary for the cadence of his sentences.

I have followed my printed originals in the matter of capitals and italics. I have also preserved the old punctuation, correcting it only in those few instances where it seemed to be wrong judged by its own principles. The modern usage in all these matters sacrifices everything to naked logic; and substitutes bare outline for the delicate emotional shading of the older fashion.

WALTER RALEIGH.

OXFORD, 1912.

THE WORKS OF

HALIFAX

Miscellanies

BY

The Right Noble LORD,
The Late Lord Marquess

O F

HALIFAX.

V I Z.

I. *Advice to a* DAUGHTER.
II. *The Character of a* TRIMMER.
III. *The Anatomy of an* EQUIVALENT.
IV. *A Letter to a* DISSENTER.
V. *Cautions for Choice of* PARLIA-
MENT MEN.
VI. *A Rough Draught of a* NEW MO-
DEL *at* SEA.
VII. *Maxims of* STATE, *&c.*

LONDON:
Printed for *Matt. Gillyflower* at the *Spread-
Eagle* in *Westminster-Hall.* 1700.

A

CHARACTER

OF

KING *CHARLES*

THE SECOND:

AND

POLITICAL, MORAL *and* MISCELLANEOUS
THOUGHTS *and* REFLECTIONS.

By *GEORGE SAVILE*,

MARQUIS of HALIFAX.

LONDON:

Printed for J. and R. TONSON and S. DRAPER
in the *Strand.* MDCCL.

THE
Lady's New-Year's-Gift:
OR,
ADVICE
TO A
DAUGHTER

Dear Daughter,

I Find, that even our most pleasing Thoughts *will* be unquiet; they *will* be in motion; and the *Mind* can have no rest whilst it is possess'd by a darling Passion. *You* are at present the chief Object of my *Care,* as well as of my *Kindness,* which sometimes throweth me into *Visions* of your being happy in the World, that are better suited to my partial *Wishes,* than to my reasonable *Hopes* for you. At other times, when my *Fears* prevail, I shrink as if I was struck, at the Prospect of *Danger,* to which a young Woman must be expos'd. But how much the more *Lively,* so much the more *Liable* you are to be hurt; as the finest Plants are the soonest nipped by the *Frost.* Whilst you are playing full of Innocence, the spitefull World will bite, except you are guarded by your *Caution.* Want of *Care* therefore, my dear Child, is never to be excus'd; since, as to *this* World, it hath the same effect as want of *Vertue.* Such an early sprouting Wit requireth so much the more to be sheltred by some *Rules,* like something strew'd on tender Flowers to preserve them from being blasted. You must take it well to be prun'd by so kind a Hand as that of a *Father.*

B   There

There may be some bitterness in meer Obedience: The natural Love of *Liberty* may help to make the Commands of a Parent harder to go down: Some inward resistance there will be, where *Power* and not *Choice* maketh us move. But when a *Father* layeth aside his Authority, and persuadeth only by his Kindness, you will never answer it to Good Nature, if it hath not weight with you.

A great part of what is said in the following *Discourse* may be above the present growth of your Understanding; but that becoming every day taller, will in a little time reach up to it, so as to make it easie to you. I am willing to begin with you before your *Mind* is quite form'd, that being the time in which it is most capable of receiving a *Colour* that will last when it is mix'd with it. Few things are well learnt, but by early *Precepts*: Those well infus'd, make them *Natural*; and we are never sure of retaining what is valuable, till by a continued *Habit* we have made it a Piece of us.

Whether my skill can draw the Picture of a fine Woman, may be a question: but it can be none, That I have drawn that of a kind *Father*: If you will take an exact Copy, I will so far presume upon my workmanship, as to undertake you shall not make an ill *Figure*. Give me so much Credit as to try, and I am sure that neither your Wishes nor mine shall be disappointed by it.

RELIGION.

THe first thing to be considered, is *Religion*. It must be the chief Object of your Thoughts, since it would be a vain thing to direct your *Behaviour* in the World, and forget that which you are to have towards him who made it.

In a strict sense, it is the only thing necessary: you must take it into your *Mind*, and from thence throw it into your *Heart*, where you are to embrace it so close as never to lose the

Possession

Possession of it. But then it is necessary to distinguish between the *Reality* and the *Pretence*.

Religion doth not consist in believing the Legend of the *Nursery*, where Children with their *Milk* are fed with the Tales of Witches, Hobgoblins, Prophecies, and Miracles. We suck in so greedily these early *Mistakes*, that our riper *Understanding* hath much ado to cleanse our *Minds* from this kind of *Trash*: The Stories are so entertaining, that we do not only believe them, but relate them; which makes the discovery of the *Truth* somewhat grievous, when it makes us lose such a Field of Impertinence, where we might have diverted our selves, besides the throwing some shame upon us for having ever received them. This is making the *World* a *Jest*, and imputing to God Almighty, That the Province he assigneth to the Devil, is to play at Blindmans-buff, and shew Tricks with Mankind; and is so far from being *Religion*, that it is not *Sense*, and hath right only to be call'd that kind of Devotion, of which *Ignorance* is the undoubted *Mother*, without competition or dispute. These Mistakes are therefore to be left off with your Hanging sleeves; and you ought to be as much out of countenance to be found with them about you, as to be seen playing with Babies at an *Age* when other things are expected from you.

The next thing to be observ'd to you, is, That *Religion* doth as little consist in loud Answers and devout Convulsions at Church, or Praying in an extraordinary manner. Some Ladies are so extream stirring at *Church*, that one would swear the *Worm* in their *Conscience* made them so unquiet. Others will have such a Divided Face between a *Devout Goggle* and an *Inviting Glance*, that the unnatural Mixture maketh even the *best Looks* to be at that time *ridiculous*. These affected *Appearances* are ever suspected, like very strong Perfumes, which are generally thought no very good Symptoms in those that make use of them. Let your earnestness therefore be reserv'd for your *Closet*, where you may have God Almighty to your self: In *Publick* be still and calm, neither undecently *Careless*, nor *Affected* in the other Extream.

It is not true Devotion, to put on an angry *Zeal* against those

B 2

who

who may be of a differing Persuasion. *Partiality* to our selves makes us often mistake it for a *Duty,* to fall hard upon others in that case ; and being push'd on by *Self-conceit,* we strike without mercy, believing that the *Wounds* we give are *Meritorious,* and that we are fighting God Almighty's Quarrel ; when the truth is, we are only setting out our selves. Our *Devotion* too often breaketh out into that *Shape* which most agreeth with our particular *Temper.* The *Cholerick* grow into a hardned Severity against all who dissent from them ; snatch at all the Texts of Scripture that suit with their *Complexion* ; and because God's Wrath was some time kindled, they conclude, That *Anger* is a Divine Vertue ; and are so far from imagining their ill natur'd *Zeal* requireth an *Apology,* that they value themselves upon it, and triumph in it. *Others,* whose Nature is more Credulous than ordinary, admit no Bounds or Measure to it ; they grow as proud of extending their *Faith,* as Princes are of enlarging their *Dominions* ; not considering that our *Faith,* like our Stomach, is capable of being over-charg'd ; and that as the last is destroy'd by taking in more than it can digest, so our *Reason* may be extinguish'd by oppressing it with the weight of too many strange things ; especially if we are forbidden to chew what we are commanded to swallow. The *Melancholy* and the *Sullen* are apt to place a great part of their *Religion* in dejected or ill-humour'd *Looks,* putting on an unsociable Face, and declaiming against the Innocent Entertainments of *Life,* with as much sharpness as they could bestow upon the greatest *Crimes.* This generally is only a *Vizard,* there is seldom any thing real in it. No other thing is the better for being *Sowre* ; and it would be hard that *Religion* should be so, which is the best of things. In the mean time it may be said with truth, That this *surly* kind of *Devotion* hath perhaps done little less hurt in the World, by frighting, than the most scandalous *Examples* have done by infecting it.

Having told you, in these few Instances, to which many more might be added, what is not true *Religion* ; it is time to describe to you, what is so. The ordinary *Definitions* of it are no more like it, than the common Sign-posts are like the Princes they
would

would represent. The unskilful *Dawbers* in all Ages have generally laid on such ill *Colours,* and drawn such harsh *Lines,* that the Beauty of it is not easily to be discerned : They have put in all the forbidding Features that can be thought of; and in the first place, have made it an irreconcilable Enemy to *Nature;* when, in reality, they are not only *Friends,* but *Twins,* born together at the same time; and it is doing violence to them both, to go about to have them separated. Nothing is so kind and so inviting as true and *unsophisticated Religion* : Instead of imposing unnecessary Burdens upon our *Nature,* it easeth us of the greater weight of our *Passions* and *Mistakes* : Instead of subduing us with *Rigour,* it redeemeth us from the *Slavery* we are in to our selves, who are the most severe Masters, whilst we are under the Usurpation of our *Appetites* let loose and not restrain'd.

Religion is a chearful thing, so far from being always at *Cuffs* with *Good Humour,* that it is inseparably united to it. Nothing unpleasant belongs to it, though the *Spiritual Cooks* have done their unskilful part to give an ill *Relish* to it. A wise *Epicure* would be *Religious* for the sake of *Pleasure;* Good Sense is the Foundation of both; and he is a *Bungler* who aimeth at true *Luxury,* but where they are join'd.

Religion is exalted *Reason,* refin'd and sifted from the grosser parts of it : It dwelleth in the upper Region of the *Mind,* where there are fewest *Clouds* or *Mists* to darken or offend it : It is both the Foundation and the Crown of all Vertues : It is *Morality* improv'd and rais'd to its height, by being carried nearer *Heaven,* the only place where *Perfection* resideth. It cleanseth the *Understanding,* and brusheth off the Earth that hangeth about our *Souls.* It doth not want the *Hopes* and the *Terrors* which are made use of to support it; neither ought it to descend to the borrowing any Argument out of it self, since there we may find every thing that should invite us. If we were to be hired to *Religion,* it is able to out-bid the corrupted World, with all it can offer to us, being so much the *Richer* of the two, in every thing where *Reason* is admitted to be a Judge of the Value.

Since

Since this is so, it is worth your pains to make *Religion* your choice, and not make use of it only as a *Refuge*. There are Ladies, who finding by the too visible decay of their good Looks, that they can shine no more by that *Light*, put on the *Varnish* of an affected Devotion, to keep up some kind of Figure in the World. They take Sanctuary in the *Church*, when they are pursued by growing *Contempt*, which will not be stopt, but followeth them to the *Altar*. Such late penitence is only a disguise for the tormenting grief of being no more handsome. That is the killing thought which draweth the sighs and tears, that appear outwardly to be applied to a better end.

There are many who have an *Aguish Devotion*, Hot and Cold Fits, long Intermissions, and violent Raptures. This unevenness is by all means to be avoided. Let your method be a steady course of good *Life*, that may run like a smooth Stream, and be a perpetual Spring to furnish to the continued *Exercise* of *Vertue*. Your *Devotion* may be earnest, but it must be unconstrained; and like other Duties, you must make it your *Pleasure* too, or else it will have very little efficacy. By this *Rule* you may best judge of your own Heart. Whilst those *Duties* are *Joys*, it is an Evidence of their being sincere; but when they are a *Penance*, it is a sign that your *Nature* maketh some resistance; and whilst that lasteth, you can never be entirely secure of your self.

If you are often unquiet, and too nearly touch'd by the cross Accidents of *Life*, your *Devotion* is not of the right *Standard*; there is too much *Allay* in it. That which is right and unmixt, taketh away the *Sting* of every thing that would trouble you: It is like a healing *Balm*, that extinguisheth the sharpness of the Bloud; so this softeneth and dissolveth the *Anguish* of the *Mind*. A devout *Mind* hath the Privilege of being free from *Passions*, as some Climates are from all venomous kind of Creatures. It will raise you above the little *Vexations* to which others for want of it, will be expos'd, and bring you to a *Temper*, not of stupid *Indifference*, but of such a wise *Resignation*, that you may live in the *World*, so as it may hang about you like a loose Garment, and not tied too close to you.

Take

Take heed of running into that common *Error*, of applying God's Judgments upon particular Occasions. Our Weights and Measures are not competent to make the Distribution either of his *Mercy* or his *Justice* : He hath thrown a Veil over these things, which makes it not only an *Impertinence*, but a kind of *Sacrilege*, for us to give Sentence in them without his *Commission*.

As to your particular *Faith*, keep to the *Religion* that is grown up with you, both as it is the best in it self, and that the reason of staying in it upon that Ground is somewhat stronger for your *Sex*, than it will perhaps be allow'd to be for ours; in respect that the Voluminous enquiries into the *Truth*, by Reading, are less expected from you. The *Best* of *Books* will be direction enough to you not to change; and whilst you are fix'd and sufficiently confirm'd in your own *Mind*, you will do best to keep vain *Doubts* and *Scruples* at such a distance that they may give you no disquiet.

Let me recommend to you a Method of being rightly in-form'd, which can never fail : It is in short this. Get *Under-standing*, and practise *Vertue*. And if you are so *Blessed* as to have those for your *Share*, it is not surer that there is a *God*, than it is, that by him all *Necessary Truths* will be revealed to you.

HUSBAND.

THAT which challengeth the next place in your Thoughts, is how to live with a *Husband*. And though that is so large a Word, that few *Rules* can be fix'd to it which are unchange-able, the *Methods* being as various as the several *Tempers* of *Men* to which they must be suited ; yet I cannot omit some *General Observations*, which, with the help of your own may the better direct you in the part of your Life upon which your *Happiness* most dependeth.

It is one of the *Disadvantages* belonging to your *Sex*, that young Women are seldom permitted to make their own *Choice*;
their

their Friends Care and Experience are thought safer Guides to them, than their own *Fancies*; and their *Modesty* often forbiddeth them to refuse when their Parents recommend, though their *inward Consent* may not entirely go along with it. In this case there remaineth nothing for them to do, but to endeavour to make that easie which falleth to their *Lot*, and by a wise use of every thing they may dislike in a *Husband*, turn that by degrees to be very supportable, which, if neglected, might in time beget an *Aversion*.

You must first lay it down for a Foundation in general, That there is *Inequality* in the *Sexes*, and that for the better Oeconomy of the World, the *Men*, who were to be the Lawgivers, had the larger share of *Reason* bestow'd upon them; by which means your Sex is the better prepar'd for the *Compliance* that is necessary for the better performance of those *Duties* which seem to be most properly assign'd to it. This looks a little uncourtly at the first appearance; but upon Examination it will be found, that *Nature* is so far from being unjust to you, that she is partial on your side. She hath made you such large *Amends* by other Advantages, for the seeming *Injustice* of the first Distribution, that the Right of Complaining is come over to our Sex. You have it in your power not only to free your selves, but to subdue your Masters, and without violence throw both their *Natural* and *Legal Authority* at your Feet. We are made of differing *Tempers*, that our *Defects* may the better be mutually supplied: Your *Sex* wanteth our *Reason* for your *Conduct*, and our *Strength* for your *Protection*: Ours wanteth your *Gentleness* to soften, and to entertain us. The first part of our Life is a good deal subjected to you in the *Nursery*, where you Reign without Competition, and by that means have the advantage of giving the first *Impressions*. Afterwards you have stronger Influences, which, well manag'd, have more force in your behalf, than all our *Privileges* and *Jurisdictions* can pretend to have against you. You have more strength in your *Looks*, than we have in our *Laws*, and more power by your *Tears*, than we have by our *Arguments*.

It is true, that the *Laws* of *Marriage*, run in a harsher stile towards

towards your *Sex*. *Obey* is an ungenteel word, and less easie to be digested, by making such an unkind distinction in the Words of the Contract, and so very unsuitable to the excess of *Good Manners*, which generally goes before it. Besides, the *universality* of the Rule seemeth to be a *Grievance*, and it appeareth reasonable, that there might be an *Exemption* for extraordinary Women, from ordinary Rules, to take away the just Exception that lieth against the false measure of *general Equality*.

It may be alledged by the *Counsel* retained by your Sex, that as there is in all other Laws, an Appeal from the *Letter* to the *Equity*, in Cases that require it, it is as reasonable, that some *Court* of a larger *Jurisdiction* might be erected, where some *Wives* might resort and plead *specially*. And in such instances where Nature is so kind, as to raise them above the *level* of their own *Sex*, they might have *Relief*, and obtain a *Mitigation* in their own particular, of a *Sentence* which was given generally against *Woman kind*. The causes of *Separation* are now so very coarse, that few are confident enough to buy their *Liberty* at the price of having their Modesty so exposed. And for *disparity of Minds*, which above all other things requireth a *Remedy*, the *Laws* have made no *provision*; so little refin'd are numbers of Men, by whom they are compil'd. This and a great deal more might be said to give a colour to the Complaint.

But the Answer to it, in short is, That the *Institution* of *Marriage* is too sacred to admit a *Liberty* of *objecting* to it; That the supposition of yours being the weaker *Sex*, having without all doubt a good Foundation, maketh it reasonable to subject it to the *Masculine Dominion*; That no *Rule* can be so *perfect*, as not to admit some *Exceptions*; But the Law presumeth there would be so few found in this Case, who would have a sufficient Right to such a Privilege, that it is safer some *Injustice* should be *conniv'd* at in a very few Instances, than to break into an Establishment, upon which the Order of Humane Society doth so much depend.

You are therefore to make your best of what is *settled* by *Law* and *Custom*, and not vainly imagine, that it will be *changed*
for

for your sake. But that you may not be discouraged, as if you lay under the weight of an *incurable Grievance*, you are to know, that by a *wise* and *dexterous* Conduct, it will be in your power to *relieve* your self from any thing that looketh like a disadvantage in it. For your better direction, I will give a hint of the most ordinary *Causes* of *Dissatisfaction* between Man and Wife, that you may be able by such a *Warning* to live so upon your *Guard*, that when you shall be married, you may know how to *cure* your Husband's *Mistakes*, and to *prevent* your own.

First then, you are to consider, you live in a time which hath rendred some kind of Frailties so habitual, that they lay claim to large *Grains* of *Allowance*. The World in this is somewhat unequal, and our Sex seemeth to play the *Tyrant* in distinguishing *partially* for our selves, by making that in the utmost degree *Criminal* in the *Woman*, which in a *Man* passeth under a much *gentler Censure*. The Root and the Excuse of this Injustice is the *Preservation* of Families from any *Mixture* which may bring a Blemish to them: And whilst the *Point* of *Honour* continues to be so plac'd, it seems unavoidable to give your *Sex*, the greater share of the Penalty. But if in this it lieth under any *Disadvantage*, you are more than recompens'd, by having the *Honour* of *Families* in your keeping. The Consideration so great a Trust must give you, maketh full amends; and this Power the World hath lodged in you, can hardly fail to restrain the Severity of an *ill* Husband, and to improve the Kindness and Esteem of a *good* one. This being so, remember, That next to the danger of *committing* the Fault your self, the greatest is that of *seeing* it in your *Husband*. Do not seem to look or hear that way: If he is a Man of Sense, he will reclaim himself; the Folly of it, is of it self sufficient to cure him: if he is not so, he will be provok'd, but not reform'd. To expostulate in these Cases, looketh like declaring War, and preparing Reprisals; which to a *thinking Husband* would be a dangerous Reflexion. Besides, it is so coarse a Reason which will be assign'd for a Lady's too great Warmth upon such an occasion, that Modesty no less than Prudence ought to restrain her; since

such

such an undecent Complaint makes a Wife much more ridiculous, than the Injury that provoketh her to it.   But it is yet worse, and more unskilful, to *blaze it* in the World, expecting it should rise up in Arms to take her part : Whereas she will find, it can have no other Effect, than that she will be served up in all Companies, as the *reigning Jest* at that time ; and will continue to be the common Entertainment, till she is rescu'd by some *newer Folly* that cometh upon the Stage, and driveth her away from it.   The Impertinence of such Methods is so plain, that it doth not deserve the pains of being laid open.   Be assur'd, that in these Cases your *Discretion* and *Silence* will be the most *prevailing Reproof*.   An *affected Ignorance,* which is seldom a *Vertue,* is a great one here : And when your *Husband* seeth how unwilling you are to be uneasie, there is no stronger Argument to perswade him not to be unjust to you.   Besides, it will naturally make him more *yielding* in other things : And whether it be to *cover* or redeem his *Offence,* you may have the good Effects of it whilst it lasteth, and all that while have the most reasonable Ground that can be, of presuming, such a Behaviour will at last entirely convert him.   There is nothing so glorious to a *Wife,* as a Victory so gain'd : A Man so re-claim'd, is for ever after subjected to her *Vertue* ; and her *bearing* for a time, is more than rewarded by a Triumph that will continue as long as her Life.

The next thing I will suppose, is, That your *Husband* may love *Wine* more than is convenient.   It will be granted, That though there are Vices of a deeper dye, there are none that have greater *Deformity* than this, when it is not restrain'd : But with all this, the same Custom which is the more to be lamented for its being so general, should make it less uneasie to every one in particular who is to suffer by the Effects of it : So that in the first place, it will be no new thing if you should have a *Drunkard* for your *Husband* ; and there is by too frequent Examples evidence enough, that such a thing may happen, and yet a *Wife* may live too without being miserable.   *Self-love* dictateth aggravating words to every thing we feel ; *Ruine* and *Misery* are the Terms we apply to whatever we do not like, forgetting

forgetting the Mixture allotted to us by the Condition of Human Life, by which it is not intended we should be quite exempt from trouble. It is fair, if we can escape such a degree of it as would oppress us, and enjoy so much of the pleasant part as may lessen the ill taste of such things as are unwelcome to us. Every thing hath two Sides, and for our own ease we ought to direct our Thoughts to that which may be least liable to exception. To fall upon the *worst side* of a *Drunkard,* giveth so unpleasant a prospect, that it is not possible to dwell upon it. Let us pass then to the more *favourable part,* as far as a *Wife* is concern'd in it.

I am tempted to say (if the Irregularity of the Expression could in strictness be justified) That a *Wife* is to thank God her *Husband* hath *Faults.* Mark the seeming Paradox my Dear, for your own Instruction, it being intended no further. A *Husband* without *Faults* is a dangerous Observer; he hath an Eye so piercing, and seeth every thing so plain, that it is expos'd to his full Censure. And though I will not doubt but that your *Vertue* will disappoint the sharpest Enquiries; yet few Women can bear the having all they say or do *represented* in the clear Glass of an Understanding without *Faults.* Nothing softneth the *Arrogance* of our *Nature,* like a Mixture of some *Frailties.* It is by them we are best told, that we must not strike too hard upon others, because we our selves do so often deserve Blows : They pull our Rage by the Sleeve, and whisper Gentleness to us in our Censures, even when they are rightly applied. The *Faults* and *Passions* of *Husbands* bring them down to you, and make them content to live upon less unequal Terms, than Faultless Men would be willing to stoop to; so haughty is Mankind till humbled by common Weaknesses and Defects, which in our corrupted State contribute more towards the reconciling us to one another, than all the *Precepts* of the *Philosophers* and *Divines.* So that where the *Errors* of our *Nature* make amends for the *Disadvantages* of yours it is more your part to make use of the *Benefit,* than to quarrel at the *Fault.*

Thus in case a *Drunken Husband* should fall to your share,

if

if you will be *wise* and *patient,* his *Wine* shall be of your side; it will throw a *Veil* over your Mistakes, and will set out and improve every thing you do, that he is pleased with. Others will like him less, and by that means he may perhaps like you the more. When after having dined too well, he is received at home without a *Storm,* or so much as a *reproaching Look,* the *Wine* will naturally work out all in Kindness, which a *Wife* must encourage, let it be wrapped up in never so much Impertinence. On the other side it would boil up into *Rage,* if the mistaken *Wife* should treat him roughly, like a certain thing called a *kind Shrew,* than which the World, with all its Plenty, cannot shew a more Senseless, ill-bred, forbidding Creature. Consider, that where the Man will give such frequent Intermissions of the use of his *Reason,* the *Wife* insensibly getteth a Right of *Governing* in the Vacancy, and that raiseth her *Character* and *Credit* in the Family, to a higher pitch than perhaps could be done under a *sober Husband,* who never putteth himself into an Incapacity of holding the *Reins.* If these are not intire *Consolations,* at least they are *Remedies* to some Degree. They cannot make *Drunkenness* a *Vertue,* nor a *Husband* given to it a *Felicity*; but you will do your self no ill office in the endeavouring, by these means, to make the best of such a *Lot,* in case it should happen to be yours, and by the help of a wise Observation, to make that very supportable, which would otherwise be a *Load* that would oppress you.

The next Case I will put is that your *Husband* may be *Cholerick* or *Ill-humour'd.* To this it may be said, That *passionate* Men generally make amends at the Foot of the Account. Such a Man, if he is angry one day without any *Sense,* will the next day be as kind without any *Reason.* So that by marking how the *Wheels* of such a Man's Head are used to move, you may easily bring over all his *Passion* to your Party. Instead of being struck down by his Thunder, you shall direct it where and upon whom you shall think it best applied. Thus are the *strongest Poisons* turn'd to the *best Remedies*; but then there must be *Art* in it, and a *skilful Hand,* else the least *bungling* maketh it mortal. There is a great
deal

deal of nice Care requisite to deal with a Man of this Complexion. *Choler* proceedeth from *Pride,* and maketh a Man so partial to himself that he swelleth against Contradiction ; and thinketh he is lessened if he is opposed. You must in this Case take heed of *increasing the Storm* by an *unwary Word,* or *kindling the Fire* whilst the Wind is in a Corner which may blow it in your Face : You are dextrously to yield every thing till he beginneth to cool, and then by slow degrees you may rise and gain upon him : Your *Gentleness* well timed, will, like a Charm, dispel his Anger ill placed ; a *kind Smile* will *reclaim,* when a *shrill pettish Answer* would *provoke* him ; rather than fail upon such occasions, when other *Remedies* are too weak, a little *Flattery* may be admitted, which by being necessary, will cease to be Criminal.

If *Ill-Humour* and *Sullenness,* and not open and sudden Heat is his Disease, there is a way of treating that too, so as to make it a Grievance to be endured. In order to it, you are first to know, that naturally *good Sense* hath a mixture of *surly* in it : and there being so much *Folly* in the World, and for the most part so triumphant, it giveth frequent Temptations to raise the *Spleen* of Men who think right. Therefore that which may generally be call'd *Ill-Humour,* is not always a Fault ; it becometh one when either it is wrong applied, or that it is continued too long, when it is not so : For this Reason you must not too hastily fix an ill name upon that which may perhaps not deserve it ; and though the Case should be, that your *Husband* might too sowerly resent any thing he disliketh, it may so happen, that more Blame shall belong to your *Mistake,* than to his *Ill-Humour.* If a *Husband* behaveth himself sometimes with an *Indifference* that a *Wife* may think offensive, she is in the wrong to put the worst sence upon it, if by any Means it will admit a better. Some *Wives* will call it *Ill-humour* if their Husbands change their *Style* from that which they used whilst they made their first Addresses to them : Others will allow no *Intermission* or *Abatement* in the Expressions of Kindness to them, not enough distinguishing Times, and forgetting that it is impossible for Men to keep themselves up all

their

their Lives to the height of some *extravagant Moments.* A Man may at some times be less careful in little things, without any cold or disobliging Reason for it; as a *Wife* may be too expecting in smaller matters, without drawing upon her-self the inference of being *unkind.* And if your *Husband* should be really sullen, and have such frequent Fits, as might take away the excuse of it, it concerneth you to have an Eye prepared to discern the first Appearances of Cloudy Weather, and to watch when the Fit goeth off, which seldom lasteth long if it is let alone. But whilst the Mind is sore, every thing galleth it, and that maketh it necessary to let the *Black Humour* begin to spend it self, before you come in and venture to undertake it.

If in the Lottery of the World you should draw a *Covetous Husband,* I confess it will not make you proud of your *good Luck;* yet even such a one may be endured too, though there are few Passions more untractable than that of *Avarice.* You must first take care that your *Definition* of *Avarice* may not be a Mistake. You are to examine every Circumstance of your *Husband*'s Fortune, and weigh the Reason of every thing you expect from him before you have right to pronounce that sentence. The Complaint is now so general against all *Husbands,* that it giveth great suspicion of its being often ill-grounded; it is impossible they should all deserve that Censure, and therefore it is certain, that it is many times misapplied. He that *spareth* in every thing is an *inexcusable Niggard;* he that *spareth* in nothing is as *inexcusable a Madman.* The *mean* is, to spare in what is least necessary, to lay out more liberally in what is most required in our several circumstances. Yet this will not always satisfie. There are *Wives* who are impatient of the Rules of Oeconomy, and are apt to call their *Husband*'s Kindness in question, if any other measure is put to their expence than that of their own Fancy. Be sure to avoid this dangerous Error, such a partiality to your Self, which is so offensive to an understanding Man, that he will very ill bear a *Wife*'s giving her self such an injurious *preference* to all the *Family,* and whatever belongeth to it.

But to admit the worst, and that your *Husband* is really a

Close-

Close-handed Wretch, you must in this, as in other Cases, endeavour to make it less afflicting to you; and first you must observe *seasonable hours* of speaking. When you offer any thing in opposition to this reigning Humour, a *third hand* and a *wise Friend,* may often prevail more than you will be allowed to do in your own Cause. Sometimes you are dexterously to go along with him in things, where you see that the niggardly part of his Mind is most predominant, by which you will have the better opportunity of perswading him in things where he may be more indifferent. Our *Passions* are very unequal, and are apt to be raised or lessened, according as they work upon different Objects ; they are not to be *stopped* or *restrained* in those things where our Mind is more particularly engaged. In other matters they are more tractable, and will sometimes give Reason a hearing, and admit a fair Dispute. More than that, there are few Men, even in this instance of *Avarice,* so intirely abandoned to it, that at some hours, and upon some occasions, will not forget their natures, and for that time turn Prodigal. The same Man who will *grudge* himself what is *necessary,* let his *Pride* be raised and he shall be *profuse* ; at another time his *Anger* shall have the same effect ; a fit of *Vanity, Ambition,* and sometimes of *Kindness,* shall open and inlarge his *narrow Mind* ; a Dose of Wine will work upon this tough humor, and for the time dissolve it. Your business must be, if this Case happeneth, to watch these *critical moments,* and not let one of them slip without making your advantage of it ; and a *Wife* may be said to want *skill,* if by these means she is not able to secure her self in a good measure against the Inconveniences this scurvy quality in a *Husband* might bring upon her, except he should be such an incurable *Monster,* as I hope will never fall to your share.

The last supposition I will make, is, That your *Husband* should be *weak* and *incompetent* to make use of the Privileges that belong to him. It will be yielded, that such a one leaveth room for a great many Objections. But God Almighty seldom sendeth a *Grievance* without a *Remedy,* or at least such a Mitigation as taketh away a great part of the sting, and the

smart

smart of it. To make such a *Misfortune* less heavy, you are first to bring to your Observation, That a *Wife* very often maketh the better Figure, for her *Husband*'s making no great one : And there seemeth to be little reason, why the same *Lady* that chuseth a *Waiting-Woman* with *worse Looks*, may not be content with a *Husband* with *less Wit*; the Argument being equal from the advantage of the Comparison. If you will be more ashamed in some Cases, of such a *Husband*, you will be less afraid than you would perhaps be of a wise one. His *Unseasonable Weakness* may no doubt sometimes grieve you, but then set against this, that it giveth you the *Dominion*, if you will make the right use of it. It is next to his being dead, in which Case the *Wife* hath right to Administer; therefore, be sure, if you have such an Idiot, that none, except your self, may have the benefit of the forfeiture ; Such a Fool is a dangerous Beast, if others have the keeping of him ; and you must be very undexterous if when your *Husband* shall resolve to be an *Ass*, you do not take care he may be *your Ass*. But you must go skilfully about it, and above all things, take heed of distinguishing in publick, what kind of *Husband* he is : Your inward thoughts must not hinder the outward payment of the consideration that is due to him : Your *slighting* him in *Company*, besides that it would, to a discerning By stander, give too great encouragement for the making nearer applications to you, is in it self such an undecent way of assuming, that it may provoke the tame Creature to break loose, and to shew his *Dominion* for his Credit, which he was content to forget for his Ease. In short, the surest and the most approved method will be to do like a wise *Minister* to an easie *Prince* ; first give him the Orders you afterwards receive from him.

With all this, that which you are to pray for, is a *Wise Husband*, one that by knowing how to be a *Master*, for that very reason will not let you feel the weight of it; one whose Authority is so soften'd by his Kindness, that it giveth you ease without abridging your *Liberty*; one that will return so much tenderness for your *Just Esteem* of him, that you will never want *power*, though you will seldom care to use it. Such a

Husband is as much above all the other Kinds of them, as a *rational subjection* to a Prince, great in himself, is to be preferr'd before the disquiet and uneasiness of *Unlimited Liberty.*

Before I leave this Head, I must add a little concerning your *Behaviour* to your *Husband's Friends*, which requireth the most refined part of your Understanding to acquit your self well of it. You are to study how to live with them with more care than you are to apply to any other part of your Life ; especially at first, that you may not stumble at the first setting out. The *Family* into which you are grafted will generally be apt to expect, that like a Stranger in a Foreign Country, you should conform to their Methods, and not bring in a new Model by your own Authority. The *Friends* in such a Case are tempted to rise up in Arms as against an unlawful Invasion, so that you are with the utmost Caution to avoid the least appearances of any thing of this Kind. And that you may with less difficulty afterwards give your Directions, be sure at first to receive them from your *Husband's* Friends. Gain them to you by early applying to them, and they will be so satisfied, that as nothing is more thankful than Pride, when it is complied with, they will strive which of them shall most recommend you ; and when they have helped you to take Root in your *Husband's* good Opinion, you will have less dependence upon theirs, though you must not neglect any reasonable means of preserving it. You are to consider, that a Man govern'd by his *Friends*, is very easily inflamed by them ; and that one who is not so, will yet for his own sake expect to have them consider'd. It is easily improved to a point of Honour in a *Husband*, not to have his *Relations* neglected ; and nothing is more dangerous, than to raise an Objection, which is grounded upon *Pride* : It is the most stubborn and lasting Passion we are subject to, and where it is the first cause of the *War*, it is very hard to make a secure *Peace.* Your *Caution* in this is of the last importance to you.

And that you may the better succeed in it, carry a strict Eye upon the *Impertinence* of your *Servants* ; take heed that their *Ill-humour* may not engage you to take Exceptions, or

their

their too much assuming in small matters, raise Consequences which may bring you under great Disadvantage. Remember that in the case of a *Royal Bride,* those about her are generally so far suspected to bring in a Foreign Interest, that in most Countries they are insensibly reduced to a very small number, and those of so low a Figure, that it doth not admit the being *Jealous* of them. In little and in the Proportion, this may be the Case of every *New married Woman,* and therefore it may be more adviseable for you, to gain the *Servants* you find in a Family, than to tie your self too fast to those you carry into it.

You are not to overlook these small Reflections, because they may appear low and inconsiderable; for it must be said, that as the *greatest streams* are made up of the *small drops* at the head of the Springs from whence they are derived, so the *greater circumstances* of your Life, will be in some degree directed by these seeming *trifles,* which having the advantage of being the first acts of it, have a greater effect than singly in their own nature they could pretend to.

I will conclude this Article with my Advice, That you would, as much as Nature will give you leave, endeavour to forget the great *Indulgence* you have found at home. After such a gentle Discipline as you have been under, every thing you dislike will seem the harsher to you. The tenderness we have had for you, *My Dear,* is of another nature, peculiar to kind Parents, and differing from that which you will meet with first in any Family into which you shall be transplanted; and yet they may be very kind too, and afford no justifiable reason to you to complain. You must not be frighted with the first Appearances of a *differing Scene;* for when you are used to it, you may like the House you go to, better than that you left; and your *Husband*'s Kindness will have so much advantage of ours, that we shall yield up all *Competition,* and as well as we love you, be very well contented to Surrender to such a *Rival.*

HOUSE,

HOUSE, FAMILY, and CHILDREN.

YOU must lay before you, *My Dear*, there are degrees of
Care to recommend your self to the World in the several
parts of your Life. In many things, though the doing them well
may raise your *Credit* and *Esteem*, yet the omission of them
would draw no immediate reproach upon you : In others, where
your duty is more particularly applyed, the *neglect* of them is
amongst those Faults which are not forgiven, and will bring
you under a *Censure*, which will be a much heavier thing than
the trouble you would avoid. Of this kind is the *Government*
of your *House, Family*, and *Children*, which since it is the
Province allotted to your Sex, and that the *discharging it well*,
will for that reason be expected from you, if you either desert
it out of *Laziness*, or manage it ill for *want of skill*, instead of
a *Help* you will be an *Incumbrance* to the *Family* where you
are placed.

I must tell you, that no *respect* is lasting, but that which is
produced by our being in some degree useful to those that pay
it. Where that faileth, the Homage and the Reverence go
along with it, and fly to others where something may be expected in exchange for them. And upon this principle the
respects even of the *Children* and the *Servants* will not stay
with one that doth not think them worth their Care, and the
old *House-keeper* shall make a better Figure in the Family, than
the *Lady* with all her fine Cloaths, if she wilfully relinquishes
her Title to the *Government*. Therefore take heed of carrying
your *good Breeding* to such a height, as to be good for nothing,
and to be proud of it. Some think it hath a great Air to be
above troubling their thoughts with such ordinary things as
their *House* and *Family* ; others dare not admit *Cares* for fear
they should hasten *Wrinkles* ? mistaken *Pride* maketh some
think they must keep themselves up, and not descend to these
Duties, which do not seem enough refined for great *Ladies* to
be imploy'd in ; forgetting all this while, that it is more than
the

the greatest *Princes* can do, at once to preserve respect, and to neglect their Business. No *Age* ever erected *Altars* to *insignificant Gods*; they had all some quality applied to them to draw *worship* from *Mankind*; this maketh it the more unreasonable for a *Lady* to expect to be consider'd, and at the same time resolve not to deserve it. *Good looks* alone will not do; they are not such a lasting *Tenure*, as to be relied upon; and if they should stay longer than they usually do, it will by no means be safe to depend upon them: For when time hath abated the violence of the first liking, and that the *Napp* is a little worn off, though still a good degree of kindness may remain, Men recover their sight which before might be dazell'd, and allow themselves to object as well as to admire.

In such a Case, when a *Husband* seeth an empty airy thing sail up and down the House to no kind of purpose, and look as if she came thither only to make a Visit; when he findeth that after her *Emptiness* hath been extreme busie about some very senseless thing, she eats her Breakfast half an hour before Dinner, to be at greater liberty to afflict the Company with her Discourse; then calleth for her Coach, that she may trouble her Acquaintance, who are already cloy'd with her: And having some *proper Dialogues* ready to display her *Foolish Eloquence* at the top of the Stairs, she setteth out like a Ship out of the Harbour, laden with trifles and cometh back with them: at her return she repeateth to her faithful waiting-Woman, the *Triumphs* of that day's *Impertinence*; then wrap'd up in Flattery and clean Linen, goeth to Bed so satisfied, that it throweth her into pleasant Dreams of her own Felicity. Such a one is seldom serious but with her *Taylor*; her *Children* and Family may now and then have a random thought, but she never taketh aim but at something very Impertinent. I say, when a *Husband*, whose Province is without Doors, and to whom the Oeconomy of the House would be in some degree Indecent, findeth no *Order* nor *Quiet* in his *Family*, meeteth with *Complaints* of all kinds springing from this Root; The *Mistaken Lady*, who thinketh to make *amends* for all this, by having a well-chosen *Petty-Coat*, will at last be convinced of

her

her *Error*, and with grief be forced to undergo the Penalties that belong to those who are willfully *Insignificant*. When this scurvy hour cometh upon her, she first groweth *Angry*; then when the time of it is past, would perhaps grow *wiser*, not remembring that we can no more have *Wisdom* than *Grace*, whenever we think fit to call for it. There are Times and Periods fix'd for both; and when they are too long neglected, the Punishment is, that they are *Irrecoverable*, and nothing remaineth but an useless *Grief* for the Folly of having thrown them out of our power. You are to think what a mean Figure a Woman maketh, when she is so degraded by her own Fault; whereas there is nothing in those Duties which are expected from you, that can be a lessening to you, except your want of *Conduct* makes it so. You may love your *Children* without living in the *Nursery*, and you may have a *competent* and *discreet care* of them, without letting it break out upon the Company, or exposing your self by turning your Discourse that way, which is a kind of *Laying Children* to the *Parish*, and it can hardly be done any where, that those who hear it will be so forgiving, as not to think they are overcharged with them. A Woman's *tenderness* to her *Children* is one of the least deceitful Evidences of her Vertue; but yet the way of expressing it, must be subject to the Rules of *good Breeding*: And though a *Woman* of *Quality* ought not to be less kind to them, than *Mothers* of the *Meanest Rank* are to theirs, yet she may distinguish her self in the *manner*, and avoid the coarse Methods, which in Women of a lower size might be more excusable. You must begin early to make them *love* you, that they may *obey* you. This Mixture is no where more necessary than in Children. And I must tell you, that you are not to expect Returns of Kindness from yours, if ever you have any, without Grains of Allowance; and yet it is not so much a *defect* in their *good Nature*, as a *shortness of Thought* in them. Their first *Insufficiency* maketh them lean so entirely upon their *Parents* for what is *necessary*, that the *habit* of it maketh them continue the same *Expectations* for what is *unreasonable*; and as often as they are *denied*, so often they think they are *injured*: and

whilst

whilst their *Desires* are strong, and their *Reasons* yet in the Cradle, their *Anger* looketh no farther than the thing they long for and cannot have; And to be *displeased* for their *own good*, is a *Maxim* they are very slow to understand: So that you may conclude, the first Thoughts of your *Children* will have no small Mixture of Mutiny; which being so natural, you must not be angry, except you would increase it. You must deny them as seldom as you can, and when there is no avoiding it, you must do it *gently*; you must flatter away their ill Humour, and take the next Opportunity of pleasing them in some other thing, before they either ask or look for it: This will strengthen your *Authority*, by making it soft to them; and confirm their *Obedience*, by making it their Interest. You are to have as strict a Guard upon your self amongst your *Children*, as if you were amongst your *Enemies*. They are apt to make wrong Inferences, to take Encouragement from half Words, and mis-apply what you may say or do, so as either to lessen their *Duty*, or to extend their *Liberty* farther than is convenient. Let them be more in awe of your *Kindness* than of your *Power*. And above all, take heed of supporting a *Favourite Child* in its Impertinence, which will give Right to the rest of claiming the same Privilege. If you have a divided Number, leave the *Boys* to the *Father*'s more peculiar Care, that you may with the greater Justice pretend to a more immediate Jurisdiction over those of your own *Sex*. You are to live so with them, that they may never chuse to avoid you, except when they have *offended*; and then let them tremble, that they may distinguish: But their Penance must not continue so long as to grow too *sowre* upon their *Stomachs*, that it may not *harden* in stead of *correcting* them: The kind and severe Part must have their several *turns* seasonably applied; but your *Indulgence* is to have the broader mixture, that *Love*, rather than *Fear*, may be the Root of their *Obedience*.

Your *Servants* are in the next place to be considered; and you must remember not to fall into the mistake of thinking, that because they receive Wages, and are so much *Inferiour* to you, therefore they are *below* your Care to know how to manage them.

them. It would be as good Reason for a *Master Workman* to despise the *Wheels* of his *Engines*, because they are made of *Wood*. These are the *Wheels* of your *Family*; and let your Directions be never so faultless, yet if these *Engines* stop or move wrong, the whole Order of your *House* is either at a stand, or discomposed. Besides, the *Inequality* which is between you, must not make you forget, that *Nature* maketh no such distinction, but that *Servants* may be looked upon as *humble Friends*, and that *Returns* of *Kindness* and *good Usage* are as much due to such of them as deserve it, as their *Service* is due to *us* when we require it. *A foolish haughtiness* in the Style of *speaking*, or in the manner of *commanding* them, is in it self very undecent; besides that it begetteth an *Aversion* in them, of which the least ill Effect to be expected, is, that they will be *slow* and *careless* in all that is injoyned them: And you will find it true by your Experience, that you will be so much the more *obeyed* as you are less *Imperious*. Be not *too hasty* in giving your *Orders*, nor *too angry* when they are not altogether *observed*; much less are you to be loud, and too much disturbed: An *evenness* in distinguishing when they do well or *ill*, is that which will make your *Family* move by a Rule, and without Noise, and will the better set out your Skill in conducting it with Ease and Silence, that it may be like a well disciplin'd Army, which knoweth how to anticipate the *Orders* that are fit to be given them. You are never to neglect the Duty of the *present Hour*, to do another thing, which though it may be better in it self, is not to be unseasonably preferred. Allot well chosen Hours for the Inspection of your *Family*, which may be so distinguished from the rest of your Time, that the *necessary Cares* may come in their proper Place, without any Influence upon your good Humour, or Interruption to other things. By these Methods you will put your self in possession of being valued by your Servants, and then their *Obedience* will naturally follow.

I must not forget one of the greatest *Articles* belonging to a *Family*, which is the *Expence*. It must not be such, as by failing either in the Time or measure of it, may rather draw
Censure

Censure than gain *Applause.* If it was well examined, there is more Money given to be laughed at, than for any one thing in the World, though the Purchasers do not think so. A well-stated Rule is like the *Line,* when that is once pass'd we are under another *Pole* ; so the first *straying* from a *Rule,* is a step towards making that which was before a *Vertue,* to change its Nature, and to grow either into a *Vice,* or at least an *Impertinence.* The Art of laying out Money wisely, is not attained to without a great deal of thought ; and it is yet more difficult in the Case of a *Wife,* who is accountable to her *Husband* for her mistakes in it. It is not only his *Money,* his *Credit* too is at Stake, if what lyeth under the *Wife*'s Care is managed, either with undecent *Thrift,* or too loose *Profusion.* You are therefore to keep the *Mean* between these two *Extremes,* and it being hardly possible to hold the Balance exactly even, let it rather incline towards the *Liberal* side as more suitable to your *Quality,* and less subject to *Reproach.* Of the two a little *Money* mispent is sooner *recovered,* than the *Credit* which is lost by having it unhandsomely *saved* ; and a Wise *Husband* will less forgive a shameful piece of *Parcimony,* than a little *Extravagance,* if it be not too often repeated. His *Mind* in this must be your chief *Direction* ; and his *Temper,* when once known, will in great measure justifie your part in the management, if he is pleased with it.

In your *Clothes* avoid too much Gaudy ; do not value your self upon an *Imbroidered Gown* ; and remember, that a *reasonable Word,* or an *obliging Look,* will gain you more respect, than all your *fine Trappings.* This is not said to restrain you from a *decent Compliance* with the World, provided you take the wiser, and not the foolisher part of your Sex for your Pattern. Some *distinctions* are to be allowed, whilst they are well suited to your *Quality* and *Fortune,* and in the distribution of the Expence, it seemeth to me that a *full Attendance,* and *well chosen Ornaments* for your House, will make you a better Figure, than *too much glittering* in what you wear, which may with more ease be imitated by those that are below you. Yet this must not tempt you to starve every thing but your own

Appartment ;

Appartment; or in order to more abundance there, give just cause to the least Servant you have, to complain of the Want of what is necessary. Above all, fix it in your thoughts, as an unchangeable *Maxim*, That nothing is *truly fine* but what is *fit*, and that just so much as is proper for your *Circumstances* of their several kinds, is much finer than all you can add to it. When you once break through these bounds, you launch into a wide Sea of *Extravagance*. Every thing will become necessary, because you have a mind to it; and you have a mind to it, not because it is *fit* for you, but because some body else *hath it*. This *Lady's Logick* setteth *Reason* upon its Head, by carrying the *Rule from* things to *Persons*, and appealing from what is *right* to every Fool that is in the *wrong*. The word *necessary* is miserably applyed, it disordereth *Families*, and overturneth *Governments* by being so abused. Remember that *Children* and *Fools* want every thing because they want Wit to distinguish: and therefore there is no stronger Evidence of a *Crazy Understanding*, than the making too large a Catalogue of things necessary, when in truth there are so very few things that have a right to be placed in it. Try every thing first in your *Judgment*, before you allow it a place in your *Desire*; else your *Husband* may think it as necessary for him to deny, as it is for you to *have* whatever is unreasonable; and if you shall too often give him that advantage, the habit of *refusing* may perhaps reach to things that are not unfit for you.

There are unthinking *Ladies*, who do not enough consider, how little their own Figure agreeth with the *fine things* they are so proud of. Others when they have them will hardly allow them to be *visible*; they cannot be seen without *Light*, and that is many times so sawcy and so prying, that like a too forward *Gallant* it is to be forbid the *Chamber*. Some, when you are ushered into their *Dark Ruelle*, it is with such solemnity, that a Man would swear there was something in it, till the *Unskilful Lady* breaketh silence, and beginneth a Chat, which discovereth it is a Puppet-play with Magnificent Scenes. Many esteem things rather as they are hard to be gotten, than that they are worth getting: This looketh as if they had an Interest
to

to pursue that Maxim, because a great part of their own *value* dependeth upon it. Truth in these Cases would be often *unmannerly*, and might derogate from the *Prerogative*, great *Ladies* would assume to them selves, of being distinct Creatures from those of their Sex which are inferiour and of less difficult access.

In other things too, your Condition must give the rule to you, and therefore it is not a Wife's part to aim at more than a bounded *Liberality* ; the farther extent of that *Quality* (otherwise to be commended) belongeth to the *Husband*, who hath better means for it. *Generosity* wrong placed becometh a *Vice*. It is no more a *Vertue* when it groweth into an *Inconvenience*, *Vertues* must be inlarged or restrained according to differing Circumstances. A *Princely Mind* will undo a *private Family* : Therefore things must be suited, or else they will not deserve to be Commended, let them in themselves be never so valuable : And the Expectations of the World are best answered when we acquit our selves in that manner which seemeth to be prescribed to our several Conditions, without usurping upon those Duties, which do not so particularly belong to us.

I will close the consideration of this *Article* of *Expence*, with this short word. Do not *fetter* your self with such a *Restraint* in it as may make you *Remarkable* ; but remember that *Vertue* is the greatest *Ornament*, and good *Sence* the *best Equipage*.

BEHAVIOUR and *CONVERSATION*.

IT is time now to lead you out of your *House* into the *World*. A Dangerous step ; where your Vertue alone will not secure you, except it is attended with a great deal of *Prudence*. You must have *both* for your *Guard*, and not stir without them. The Enemy is abroad, and you are sure to be taken, if you are found stragling. Your *Behaviour* is therefore to incline strongly towards the *Reserved part* ; your *Character* is to be im-

moveably

moveably fixed upon that Bottom, not excluding a mixture of greater freedom, as far as it may be innocent and well timed. The *Extravagancies* of the Age have made *Caution* more necessary; and by the same reason that the too great Licence of ill Men hath by Consequence in many things restrained the Lawful Liberty of those who did not abuse it, the unjustifiable Freedoms of some of your Sex have involved the rest in the Penalty of being reduced.   And though this cannot so alter the Nature of things, as to make that *Criminal*, which in it self is *Indifferent*; yet if it maketh it *dangerous*, that alone is sufficient to justifie the *Restraint*.   A *close behaviour* is the fittest to receive *Vertue* for its constant *Guest*, because there, and there only, it can be secure.   Proper *Reserves* are the Outworks, and must never be deserted by those who intend to keep the Place; they keep off the possibilities not only of being *taken*, but of being *attempted*; and if a Woman seeth Danger, tho at never so remote a Distance, she is for that time to shorten her *Line* of *Liberty*.   She who will allow her self to go to the *utmost Extent* of every thing that is *Lawful*, is so very near going farther, that those who lie at watch, will begin to count upon her.

Mankind, from the double temptation of *Vanity* and *Desire*, is apt to turn every thing a *Woman* doth to the *hopeful side*; and there are few who dare make an impudent Application, till they discern something which they are willing to take for an *Encouragement*.   It is safer therefore to prevent such *Forwardness*, than to go about to *cure* it.   It gathereth Strength by the first *allowances*, and claimeth a Right from having been at any time suffered with Impunity.   Therefore nothing is with more care to be avoided, than such a kind of *Civility* as may be mistaken for *Invitation*; and it will not be enough for you to keep your self free from any criminal *Engagements*; for if you do that which either raiseth *Hopes* or createth *Discourse*, there is a Spot thrown upon your Good Name; and those kind of Stains are the harder to be taken out, being dropped upon you by the *Man*'s *Vanity*, as well as by the *Woman*'s *Malice*.

Most Men are in one sence *Platonick Lovers*, though they are not willing to own that *Character*.   They are so far
Philosophers,

Philosophers, as to allow, that the greatest part of Pleasure lieth in the *Mind*; and in pursuance of that *Maxim,* there are few who do not place the Felicity more in the Opinion of the World, of their being *prosperous Lovers,* than in the *Blessing* it self, how much soever they appear to value it. This being so, you must be very cautious not to gratifie these *Cameleons* at the price of bringing a *Cloud* upon your *Reputation,* which may be deeply wounded, tho your *Conscience* is unconcerned.

Your own Sex too will not fail to help the least Appearance that giveth a *Handle* to be ill-turned. The best of them will not be displeased to improve their own Value, by laying others under a *Disadvantage,* when there is a fair Occasion given for it. It distinguisheth them still the more : their own *Credit* is more exalted, and, like a Picture set off with Shades, shineth more when a *Lady,* either less *Innocent,* or less *Discreet,* is set near, to make them appear so much the brighter. If these lend their Breath to blast such as are so unwary as to give them this Advantage, you may be sure there will be a stronger Gale from those, who, besides *Malice* or *Emulation,* have an *Interest* too, to strike hard upon a Vertuous Woman. It seemeth to them, that their Load of Infamy is lessened, by throwing part of it upon others : So that they will not only improve it when it lieth in their way, but take pains to find out the least mistake an *Innocent Woman* committeth, in Revenge of the Injury she doth in leading a Life which is a Reproach to them. With these you must be extreme *wary,* and neither provoke them to be *angry,* nor invite them to be *Intimate.*

To the *Men* you are to have a *Behaviour* which may secure you, without offending them. No ill-bred affected *Shyness,* nor a *Roughness,* unsuitable to your *Sex,* and unnecessary to your *Vertue*; but a way of Living that may prevent all coarse *Railleries* or *unmannerly Freedoms* ; *Looks* that forbid without *Rudeness,* and oblige without *Invitation,* or leaving room for the sawcy Inferences Men's Vanity suggesteth to them upon the least Encouragements. This is so very nice, that it must engage you to have a perpetual *Watch* upon your *Eyes,* and to remember, that one careless *Glance* giveth more advantage than

a

a *hundred Words* not enough considered; the *Language* of the *Eyes* being very much the most *significant*, and the most *observed*.

Your *Civility*, which is always to be preserved, must not be carried to a *Compliance*, which may betray you into irrecoverable Mistakes. This *French* ambiguous word *Complaisance* hath led your Sex into more blame, than all other things put together. It carrieth them by degrees into a certain thing called a *good kind* of *Woman*, an easie *Idle Creature*, that doth neither *Good* nor *Ill* but by *chance*, hath no *Choice*, but leaveth that to the Company she keepeth. *Time*, which by degrees addeth to the signification of *Words*, hath made her, according to the Modern Stile, little better than one who thinketh it a *Rudeness* to deny when civilly required, either her *Service in Person*, or her *friendly Assistance*, to those who would have a *meeting*, or want a *Confident*. She is a certain thing always at hand, an easie *Companion*, who hath ever great *Compassion* for *distressed Lovers*: She censureth nothing but *Rigor*, and is never without a *Plaister* for a *wounded Reputation*, in which chiefly lieth her Skill in *Chirurgery*; She seldom hath the Propriety of any *particular Gallant*, but liveth upon *Brokage*, and waiteth for the Scraps her Friends are content to leave her.

There is another *Character* not quite so *Criminal*, yet not less *Ridiculous*; which is that of a *good-humour'd Woman*, one who thinketh she must always be in a *Laugh*, or a broad *Smile*, because *Good humour* is an obliging Quality; thinketh it less ill-manners to talk *Impertinently*, than to be silent in Company. When such a prating *Engine* rideth *Admiral*, and carrieth the *Lantern*, in a *Circle of Fools*, a *cheerful Coxcomb* coming in for a *Recruit*, the *Chattering* of *Monkeys* is a better noise than such a *Concert* of *senceless Merriment*. If she is applauded in it, she is so encouraged, that, like a *Ballad singer*, who if commended, breaketh his Lungs, she letteth her self loose, and overfloweth upon the Company. She conceiveth that Mirth is to have no intermission, and therefore she will carry it about with her, though it be to a *Funeral*; and if a Man should put a familiar Question, she doth not know very well how to be angry, for then she would be no more that pretty thing called a *Good humour'd humour'd Woman.* This necessity of appearing at all times to be so infinitely pleased is a grievous mistake; since in a *handsom Woman* that *Invitation* is unnecessary; and in one who is not so, *ridiculous*. It is not intended by this, that you should forswear *Laughing*; but remember, that Fools being always painted in that posture, it may fright those who are wise from doing it too frequently, and going too near a Copy which is so little inviting, and much more from doing it *loud*, which is an unnatural Sound and looketh so much like another Sex, that few things are more offensive. That *boisterous* kind of *Jollity* is as contrary to *Wit* and *Good Manners*, as it is to *Modesty* and *Vertue*. Besides, it is a coarse kind of quality, that throweth a Woman into a lower Form, and degradeth her from the Rank of those who are more refined. Some *Ladies* speak *loud* and make a *noise* to be the more minded, which looketh as if they beat their *Drums* for *Volunteers*, and if by misfortune none come in to them, they may, not without reason, be a good deal out of Countenance.

There is one thing, yet more to be avoided, which is the *Example* of those who intend nothing farther than the Vanity of *Conquest*, and think themselves secure of not having their Honour tainted by it. Some are apt to believe their *Vertue* is too *Obscure*, and not *enough known*, except it is exposed to a *broader Light*, and set out to its best advantage, by some publick Trials. These are dangerous experiments, and generally fail, being built upon so weak a foundation, as that of a too great *Confidence* in our selves. It is as safe to play with *Fire*, as to dally with *Gallantry*. *Love* is a Passion that hath Friends in the Garrison, and for that reason must by a Woman be kept at such a distance, that she may not be within the danger of doing the most usual thing in the World, which is conspiring against her Self: Else the humble Gallant, who is only admitted as a Trophy, very often becometh the Conquerour; he putteth on the style of victory, and from an *Admirer* groweth into a *Master*, for so he may be called from the moment he is in Possession. The first Resolutions of stopping at good Opinion and Esteem, grow weaker by degrees against the Charms of

Courtship

Courtship skilfully applied. A Lady is apt to think a Man speaketh so much reason whilst he is *Commending* her, that she hath much ado to believe him in the wrong when he is making Love to her : And when besides the natural Inducements your Sex hath to be merciful, she is bribed by well-chosen *Flattery,* the poor Creature is in danger of being caught like a Bird listening to the Whilstle of one that hath a Snare for it. *Conquest* is so tempting a thing, that it often maketh Women mistake Men's *Submissions*; which with all their fair Appearance, have generally less *Respect* than *Art* in them. You are to remember, that Men who say extreme fine things, many times say them most for their own sakes ; and that the vain Gallant is often as well pleased with his own *Compliments,* as he could be with the *kindest answer*. Where there is not that *Ostentation* you are to suspect there is *Design*. And as strong *perfumes* are seldom used but where they are necessary to smother an unwelcome *scent*; so *Excessive good Words* leave room to believe they are strewed to cover something, which is to gain admittance under a Disguise. You must therefore be upon your Guard, and consider, that of the two, *Respect* is more dangerous than *Anger*. It puts even the best Understandings out of their place for the time, till their second thoughts restore them ; it stealeth upon us insensibly, throweth down our *Defences,* and maketh it too late to resist, after we have given it that advantage. Whereas railing goeth away in sound ; it hath so much noise in it, that by giving warning it bespeaketh Caution. *Respect* is a slow and a sure *Poison,* and like *Poison* swelleth us within our selves. Where it prevaileth too much, it groweth to be a kind of *Apoplexie* in the Mind, turneth it quite round, and after it hath once seized the understanding, becometh *mortal* to it. For these reasons, the safest way is to treat it like a sly Enemy, and to be perpetually upon the watch against it.

I will add one *Advice* to conclude this head, which is that you will let every seven years make some alteration in you towards the *Graver* side, and not be like the *Girls* of Fifty, who resolve to be always *Young,* whatever *Time* with his Iron Teeth hath determined to the contrary. Unnatural things carry a

Deformity

Deformity in them never to be *Disguised*; the *Liveliness* of *Youth* in a riper Age, looketh like a *new patch* upon an *old Gown*; so that a *Gay Matron*, a cheerful *old Fool* may be reasonably put into the List of the *Tamer* kind of *Monsters*. There is a certain Creature call'd a *Grave Hobby-Horse*, a kind of a she *Numps*, that pretendeth to be pulled to a Play, and must needs go to *Bartholomew Fair*, to look after the young Folks, whom she only seemeth to make her care, in reality she taketh them for her excuse. Such an old *Butterfly* is of all *Creatures* the most ridiculous, and the soonest found out. It is good to be early in your Caution, to avoid any thing that cometh within distance of such despicable Patterns, and not like some *Ladies*, who defer their *Conversion*, till they have been so long in possession of being laughed at, that the World doth not know how to change their style, even when they are reclaimed from that which gave the first occasion for it.

The advantages of being *reserved* are too many to set down, I will only say, that it is a *Guard* to a *good Woman*, and a *Disguise* to an *ill one*. It is of so much use to both, that those ought to use it as an *Artifice*, who refuse to practise it as a *Vertue*.

FRIENDSHIPS.

I Must in a particular manner recommend to you a strict Care in the Choice of your *Friendships*. Perhaps the best are not without their *Objections*, but however, be sure that yours may not stray from the Rules which the wiser part of the World hath set to them. The Leagues *Offensive* and *Defensive*, seldom hold in *Politicks*, and much less in *Friendships*. The violent *Intimacies*, when once broken, of which they scarce ever fail, make such a *Noise*; the Bag of Secrets untied, they fly about like Birds let loose from a Cage, and become the *Entertainment* of the *Town*. Besides, these great *Dearnesses* by degrees grow *Injurious* to the rest of your *Acquaintance*, and throw them off from you. There is such an *Offensive* Distinction when the *Dear Friend* cometh into the Room, that it is *flinging Stones* at the *Company*, who are not apt to forgive it.

Do not lay out your *Friendship* too *lavishly* at first, since it will, like other things, be so much the sooner spent ; neither let it be of too sudden a *growth* ; for as the Plants which shoot up too *fast* are not of that *continuance*, as those which take more time for it ; so too swift a Progress in pouring out your *Kindness*, is a certain Sign that by the Course of Nature it will not be *long lived*. You will be responsible to the World, if you pitch upon such *Friends* as at the time are under the weight of any *Criminal Objection*. In that case you will bring your self under the disadvantages of their *Character*, and must bear your part of it. *Chusing* implieth *Approving* ; and if you fix upon a *Lady* for your *Friend* against whom the World shall have given Judgment, 'tis not so well natur'd as to believe you are altogether *averse* to her way of *living*, since it doth not discourage you from Admitting her into your *Kindness*. And *Resemblance* of *Inclinations* being thought none of the least Inducements to *Friendship*, you will be looked upon at least as a Well-wisher if not a *Partner* with her in her Faults. If you can forgive them in another, it may be presumed you will not be less gentle to your self ; and therefore you must not take it ill, if you are reckoned a *Croupiere*, and condemned to pay an equal Share with such a Friend of the *Reputation* she hath lost.

If it happeneth that your *Friend* should fall from the State of *Innocence* after your Kindness was engaged to her, you may be slow in your belief in the beginning of the Discovery : But as soon as you are convinced by a *Rational Evidence*, you must, without breaking too *roughly*, make a far and a quick *Retreat* from such a *Mistaken Acquaintance* : Else by moving *too slowly* from one that is so tainted, the Contagion may reach you so far as to give you part of the *Scandal*, though not of the *Guilt*. This Matter is so nice, that as you must not be too hasty to *joyn* in the *Censure* upon your *Friend* when she is *accused*, so you are not on the other side to *defend* her with too much warmth ; for if she should happen to deserve the
Report

Report of *Common Fame,* besides the Vexation that belongeth to such a mistake, you will draw an *ill appearance* upon your self, and it will be thought you pleaded for her not without some *Consideration* of your self. The *Anger* which must be put on to vindicate the *Reputation* of an *injured Friend,* may incline the Company to suspect you would not be so *zealous,* if there was not a possibility that the Case might be your own. For this reason you are not to carry your *dearness* so far, as absolutely to lose your Sight where your Friend is concerned. Because *Malice* is too quick sighted, it doth not follow, that *Friendship* must be *blind*: There is to be a *Mean* between these two *Extremes,* else your Excess of Good Nature may betray you into a very *ridiculous Figure,* and by degrees who may be preferr'd to such Offices as you will not be proud of. Your *Ignorance* may lessen the *Guilt,* but will improve the *Jest* upon you, who shall be kindly sollicitous to procure a Meeting, and innocently contribute to the *ills* you would avoid : Whilest the *Contriving Lovers,* when they are alone, shall make you the Subject of their *Mirth,* and perhaps (with respect to the Goddess of *Love* be it spoken) it is not the worst part of their *Entertainment,* at least it is the most lasting, to laugh at the *believing Friend,* who was so easily deluded.

Let the good Sence of your *Friends* be a chief Ingredient in your *Choice* of them ; else let your *Reputation* be never so clear, it may be clouded by their *Impertinence.* It is like our Houses being in the Power of a Drunken or a Careless Neighbour ; only so much worse, as that there will be no *Insurance* here to make you amends, as there is in the Case of Fire.

To conclude this Paragraph; If *Formality* is to be allowed in any Instance, it is to be put on to resist the Invasion of such forward Women as shall press themselves into your *Friendship,* where if admitted, they will either be a *Snare* or an *Incumbrance.*

CENSURE.

CENSURE.

I will come next to the Consideration, how you are to manage your *Censure*; in which both Care and skill will be a good deal required. To distinguish is not only *natural* but *necessary*; and the Effect of it is, That we cannot avoid giving Judgment in our Minds, either to *absolve or to condemn* as the Case requireth. The *Difficulty* is, to know when and where it is fit to *proclaim* the *Sentence*. An *Aversion* to what is *Criminal*, a *Contempt* of what is *ridiculous*, are the *inseparable Companions* of Understanding and Vertue; but the letting them go farther than our own *Thoughts*, hath so much danger in it, that though it is neither possible nor fit to *suppress* them intirely, yet it is necessary they should be kept under very great *Restraints*. An *unlimited Liberty* of this kind is little less than sending a *Herald* and proclaiming War to the World, which is an *angry Beast* when so provoked. The Contest will be *unequal*, though you are never so much in the right; and if you begin against such an Adversary, it will tear you in pieces, with this Justification, That it is done in its own defence. You must therefore take heed of *Laughing*, except in Company that is very sure. It is throwing Snow-balls against Bullets; and it is the *disadvantage* of a Woman, that the Malice of the World will help the Brutality of those who will throw a *slovenly Untruth* upon her. You are for this Reason to suppress your *Impatience* for Fools; who besides that they are too strong a Party to be unnecessarily provoked, are of all others, the most dangerous in this Case. A *Blockhead* in his *Rage* will return a *dull Jest* that will lie heavy, though there is not a *Grain* of *Wit* in it. Others will do it with more Art, and you must not think your self secure because your *Reputation* may perhaps be out of the reach of *Ill-will*; for if it findeth that part *guarded*, it will seek one which is more *exposed*. It flieth, like a corrupt Humour in the Body, to the *weakest* Part. If you have a *tender Side*, the World will be sure to find it, and to put the worst *Colour* upon all you say or do, give an *Aggravation*

to

to every thing that may lessen you, and a *spiteful turn* to every thing that might recommend you. *Anger* laieth open those Defects which *Friendship* would not see, and *Civility* might be willing to forget. *Malice* needeth no such *Invitation* to encourage it, neither are any *Pains* more superfluous than those we take to be ill spoken of. If *Envy,* which never dyeth, and seldom sleepeth, is content sometimes to be in a *Slumber,* it is very unskilful to make a noise to *awake* it.

Besides, your *Wit* will be misapplied if it is wholly directed to discern the *Faults* of *others,* when it is so necessary to be often used to *mend* and *prevent your own.* The sending our *Thoughts* too much abroad, hath the same Effect, as when a *Family* never stayeth at home; *Neglect* and *Disorder* naturally followeth; as it must do within our selves, if we do not frequently turn our Eyes inwards, to see what is amiss with us, where it is a sign we have an *unwelcome Prospect,* when we do not care to *look* upon it, but rather seek our *Consolations* in the *Faults* of those we converse with.

Avoid being the first in fixing a *hard Censure,* let it be confirmed by the *general Voice,* before you give into it; Neither are you then to give Sentence like a *Magistrate,* or as if you had a *special Authority* to bestow a *good* or *ill Name* at your discretion. Do not dwell too long upon a *weak Side,* touch and go away; take pleasure to stay longer where you can commend, like Bees that fix only upon those Herbs out of which they may extract the Juice of which their Honey is composed. A *Vertue* stuck with *Bristles* is too rough for this Age; it must be adorned with some *Flowers,* or else it will be unwillingly entertained; so that even where it may be fit to strike, do it like a *Lady,* gently; and assure your self, that where you care to do it, you will wound others more, and hurt your self less, by *soft Strokes,* than by being *harsh* or *violent.*

The Triumph of *Wit* is to make your *good Nature* subdue your *Censure;* to be quick in *seeing Faults,* and slow in *exposing* them. You are to consider, that the invisible thing called a *Good Name,* is made up of the Breath of Numbers that speak well of you; so that if by a *disobliging Word* you silence the
meanest,

meanest, the *Gale* will be less strong which is to bear up your *Esteem.* And though nothing is so vain as the eager pursuit of *empty Applause,* yet to be well thought of, and to be kindly used by the World, is like a *Glory* about a Womans *Head*; 'tis a Perfume she carrieth about with her, and leaveth where-ever she goeth; 'tis a Charm against *Ill-will.* *Malice* may empty her Quiver, but cannot wound; the Dirt will not stick, the Jests will not take; Without the consent of the World a *Scandal* doth not go deep; it is only a slight stroak upon the injured Party and returneth with the greater force upon those that gave it.

VANITY and AFFECTATION.

I Must with more than ordinary *earnestness* give you Caution against *Vanity,* it being the Fault to which your Sex seemeth to be the most *inclined*; and since *Affectation* for the most part attendeth it, I do not know how to divide them. I will not call them *Twins,* because more properly *Vanity* is the *Mother,* and *Affectation* is the Darling Daughter; *Vanity* is the Sin, and *Affectation* is the Punishment; the first may be called the Root of *Self-Love,* the other the *Fruit.* *Vanity* is never at its full growth till it spreadeth into *Affectation,* and then it is compleat.

Not to dwell any longer upon the definition of them, I will pass to the means and motives to avoid them. In order to it, you are to consider, that the World challengeth the right of distributing Esteem and Applause; so that where any assume by their single Authority to be their own *Carvers,* it groweth angry, and never faileth to seek *Revenge.* And if we may measure a Fault by the greatness of the *Penalty,* there are few of a higher size than *Vanity,* as there is scarce a Punishment which can be heavier than that of being laughed at.

Vanity maketh a Woman tainted with it, so top full of her self, that she spilleth it upon the *Company.* And because her

own

own thoughts are intirely imployed in *Self-Contemplation*; she endeavoureth, by a cruel Mistake, to confine her *Acquaintance* to the same narrow Circle of that which only concerneth her Ladiship, forgetting that she is not of half that *Importance* to the World, that she is to her self, so mistaken she is in her Value, by being her own Appraiser. She will fetch such a Compass in Discourse to bring in her beloved *Self*, and rather than fail, her fine Petty-Coat, that there can hardly be a better Scene than such a Tryal of ridiculous Ingenuity. It is a Pleasure to see her Angle for *Commendations*, and rise so dissatisfied with the Ill-bred *Company*, if they will not *bite*. To observe her throwing her *Eyes* about to fetch in Prisoners, and go about Cruizing like a Privateer, and so out of *Countenance*, if she return without *Booty*, is no ill piece of Comedy. She is so eager to draw respect, that she always misseth it, yet thinketh it so much her due, that when she faileth she groweth *waspish*, not considering, that it is impossible to commit a Rape upon the will; that it must be fairly gained, and will not be taken by *Storm*; and that in this Case, the Tax ever riseth highest by a *Benevolence*. If the World instead of admiring her *Imaginary Excellencies*, taketh the Liberty to laugh at them, she *appealeth* from it to her self, for whom she giveth *Sentence*, and proclaimeth it in all *Companies*. On the other side, if incouraged by a *Civil Word*, she is so obliging, that she will give thanks for being laughed at in good Language. She taketh a *Compliment* for a Demonstration, and setteth it up as an *Evidence*, even against her Looking-Glass. But the good *Lady* being all this while in a most profound *Ignorance* of her self, forgetteth that Men would not let her talk upon them, and throw so many *senseless words* at their head, if they did not intend to put her Person to Fine and Ransom, for her *Impertinence*. Good words of any other Lady, are so many Stones thrown at her, she can by no means bear them, they make her so uneasie, that she cannot keep her *Seat*, but up she riseth and goeth home half burst with *Anger* and *Strait-Lacing*. If by great chance she saith any thing that hath sence in it, she expecteth such an Excessive rate of *Commendations*, that to her

thinking

thinking the Company ever riseth in her *Debt*. She looketh
upon *Rules* as things made for the common People, and not for
Persons of her *Rank*; and this Opinion sometimes tempteth her
to Extend her Prerogative to the dispencing with the commandments.   If by great *Fortune* she happeneth, in spite of her
Vanity, to be honest, she is so troublesome with it, that as far
as in her lieth, she maketh a *scurvy* thing of it.   Her bragging
of her *Vertue*, looketh as if it cost her so much pains to get the
better of her Self, that the *Inferences* are very ridiculous.   Her
good Humour is generally applied to the laughing at *good Sense*.
It would do one good to see how heartily she despiseth any thing
that is fit for her to do.   The greatest part of her *Fancy* is laid
out in chusing her *Gown*, as her *Discretion* is chiefly imploy'd
in *not paying* for it.   She is faithful to the *Fashion*, to which
not only her *Opinion*, but her *Senses* are wholly resigned : so
obsequious she is to it, that she would be ready to be reconciled
even to *Vertue* with all its *Faults*, if she had her Dancing
Master's Word that it was practis'd at Court.

To a Woman so compos'd when *Affectation* cometh in to
improve her *Character*, it is then raised to the highest *Perfection*.   She first setteth up for a *Fine thing*, and for that
Reason will distinguish her self, right or wrong, in every thing
she doth.   She would have it thought that she is made of so
much the *finer Clay*, and so much more *sifted* than ordinary,
that she hath no *common Earth* about her.   To this end she
must neither move nor speak like other Women, because it
would be *vulgar*; and therefore must have a Language of her
own, since *ordinary English* is too coarse for her.   The *Looking-
glass* in the Morning dictateth to her all the *Motions* of the
Day, which by how much the more *studied*, are so much the
more *mistaken*.   She cometh into a Room as if her Limbs were
set on with ill-made Screws, which maketh the Company fear
the pretty thing should leave some of its *artificial Person* upon
the Floor.   She doth not like her self as *God Almighty* made
her, but will have some of *her own* Workmanship; which is so
far from making her a better thing than a *Woman*, that it
turneth her into a worse Creature than a *Monkey*.   She falleth
out

out with *Nature,* against which she maketh War without admitting a *Truce,* those Moments excepted in which her *Gallant* may reconcile her to it. When she hath a mind to be *soft* and *languishing,* there is somthing so unnatural in that *affected Easiness,* that her *Frowns* could not be by many degrees so forbidden. When she would appear unreasonably *humble,* one may see she is so excessively *proud,* that there is no enduring it. There is such an *impertinent Smile,* such a *satisfied Simper,* when she faintly disowneth some fulsom Commendation a Man hapneth to bestow upon her against his Conscience, that her *Thanks* for it are more visible under such a thin *Disguise,* than they could be if she should *print* them. If a *handsomer Woman* taketh any liberty of *Dressing* out of the ordinary Rules the mistaken Lady followeth, without distinguishing the *unequal Pattern,* and maketh her self *uglier* by an example misplaced; either forgetting the Privilege of *good Looks* in *another,* or presuming, without sufficient reason, upon *her own.* Her *Discourse* is a *senseless Chime* of *empty Words,* a heap of *Compliments* so equally applied to differing *Persons,* that they are neither valu'd nor believ'd. Her *Eyes* keep pace with her *Tongue,* and are therefore always in *motion.* One may discern that they generally incline to the *compassionate* side, and that, notwithstanding her pretence to *Vertue,* she is gentle to *distressed Lovers,* and *Ladies* that are *merciful.* She will repeat the tender part of a *Play* so feelingly, that the Company may guess, without Injustice, she was not altogether a *disinterested Spectator.* She thinketh that *Paint* and *Sin* are concealed by railing at them. Upon the latter she is less hard, and being divided between the two opposite Prides of her *Beauty* and her *Vertue,* she is often tempted to give broad Hints that some body is dying for her; and of the two she is less unwilling to let the World think she may be sometimes *profan'd,* than that she is never *worshipped.*

Very great *Beauty* may perhaps so dazle for a time, that Men may not so clearly see the *Deformity* of these *Affectations*; But when the *Brightness* goeth off, and that the *Lover's Eyes* are by that means set at liberty to see things as they are, he will

will naturally return to his Senses, and recover the Mistake
into which the Lady's *good Looks* had at first engaged him,
and being once undeceived, ceaseth to worship that as a
Goddess, which he seeth is only an *artificial Shrine* moved by
Wheels and *Springs,* to delude him. Such Women please only
like the *first Opening* of a *Scene,* that hath nothing to recommend it but the being *new.* They may be compared to *Flies,*
that have pretty shining *Wings* for two or three hot Months,
but the first cold Weather maketh an end of them; so the
latter Season of these *fluttering Creatures* is dismal: From
their nearest Friends they receive a very faint Respect; from
the rest of the World, the utmost degree of contempt.

Let this *Picture* supply the place of any other *Rules* which
might be given to prevent your *resemblance* to it, The *Deformity*
of it, well considered, is *Instruction* enough; from the same
reason, that the sight of a *Drunkard* is a better *Sermon* against
that *Vice,* than the best that was ever preach'd upon that
Subject.

P R I D E.

AFter having said this against *Vanity,* I do not intend to
apply the same *Censure* to *Pride,* well placed, and rightly
defined. It is an *ambiguous Word*; one kind of it is as much
a *Vertue,* as the other is a *Vice*: But we are naturally so apt
to chuse the *worst,* that it is become dangerous to commend the
best side of it.

A Woman is not to be proud of her fine Gown; nor when
she hath less Wit than her Neighbours, to comfort her self that
she hath more Lace. Some Ladies put so much weight upon
Ornaments, that if one could see into their Hearts, it would be
found, that even the Thought of *Death* is made less heavy to
them by the contemplation of their being *laid out* in *State,* and
honourably attended to the *Grave.* One may come a good deal
short of such an *Extream,* and yet still be sufficiently *Impertinent,* by setting a wrong Value upon things, which ought to be
used with more indifference. A Lady must not appear sollicitous
to ingross *Respect* to her self, but be content with a reasonable
                                                    Distribution,

Distribution, and allow it to others, that she may have it returned to her. She is not to be troublesomly *nice,* nor distinguish her self by being too *delicate,* as if ordinary things were too *coarse* for her; this is an *unmannerly* and an *offensive* Pride, and where it is practised, deserveth to be mortified, of which it seldom faileth. She is not to lean too much upon her Quality, much less to despise those who are below it. Some make *Quality* an *Idol,* and then their *Reason* must fall down and Worship it. They would have the World think, that no amends can ever be made for the want of a *great Title,* or an ancient *Coat of Arms*: They imagine, that with these *advantages* they stand upon the *higher Ground,* which maketh them look down upon *Merit* and *Vertue,* as things inferiour to them. This mistake is not only *senseless,* but *criminal* too, in putting a greater Price upon that which is a piece of *good luck,* than upon things which are valuable in themselves. *Laughing* is not enough for such a *Folly*; it must be severely *whipped,* as it justly deserves. It will be confessed, there are frequent *Temptations* given by *pert Upstarts* to be angry, and by that to have our Judgments corrupted in these Cases: But they are to be resisted; and the utmost that is to be allowed, is, when those of a *new Edition* will forget themselves, so as either to brag of their *weak side,* or to endeavour to hide their *Meanness* by their *Insolence,* to cure them by a little seasonable *Raillery,* a little *Sharpness* well placed, without dwelling too long upon it.

These and many other kinds of *Pride* are to be avoided.

That which is to be recommended to you, is an *Emulation* to raise your self to a *Character,* by which you may be distinguished; an Eagerness for precedence in *Vertue,* and all such other things as may gain you a greater share of the good opinion of the World. *Esteem* to *Vertue* is like a *cherishing Air* to *Plants* and *Flowers,* which maketh them blow and prosper; and for that reason it may be allowed to be in some degree the *Cause* as well as the *Reward* of it. That *Pride* which leadeth to a *good End,* cannot be a *Vice,* since it is the beginning of a *Vertue*; and to be pleased with just *Applause,* is so far from a *Fault,* that it would be an *ill Symptom* in a

Woman,

Woman, who should not place the greatest part of her *Satisfaction* in it. *Humility* is no doubt a great *Vertue*; but it ceaseth to be so, when it is afraid to scorn an *ill thing.* Against *Vice* and *Folly* it is becoming your *Sex* to be *haughty*; but you must not carry the *Contempt* of *things* to *Arrogance* towards *Persons,* and it must be done with fitting *Distinctions,* else it may be *Inconvenient* by being unseasonable. A *Pride* that raiseth a little *Anger* to be out-done in any thing that is good, will have so good an *Effect,* that it is very hard to allow it to be a Fault.

It is no easie matter to carry even between these differing kinds so described; but remember that it is safer for a *Woman* to be thought too *proud,* than too familiar.

DIVERSIONS.

THE last thing I shall recommend to you, is a wise and a safe method of using *Diversions.* To be too eager in the pursuit of Pleasure whilst you are *Young,* is dangerous; to catch at it in riper *Years,* is grasping a shadow; it will not be held. Besides that by being less natural it groweth to be indecent. *Diversions* are the most properly applied to ease and relieve those who are *Oppressed* by being too much imployed. Those that are *Idle* have no need of them, and yet they, above all others, give themselves up to them. To unbend our *Thoughts,* when they are too much stretched by our Cares, is not more natural than it is necessary, but to turn our whole Life into a *Holy day,* is not only ridiculous, but destroyeth Pleasure instead of *promoting* it. The *Mind* like the *Body* is tired by being always in one Posture, too serious breaketh, and too diverting looseneth it: It is *Variety* that giveth the Relish; so that *Diversions* too frequently repeated, grow first to be indifferent, and at last tedious. Whilst they are well chosen and well timed, they are never to be blamed; but when they are used to an Excess, though very *Innocent* at first, they often grow to be *Criminal,* and never fail to be *Impertinent.*

Some Ladies are bespoken for Merry Meetings, as *Bessus* was

was for Duels. They are ingaged in a Circle of *Idleness*, where
they turn round for the whole Year, without the *Interruption*
of a serious Hour. They know all the Players Names, and are
Intimately acquainted with all the Booths in *Bartholomew-Fair*.
No Soldier is more *Obedient* to the sound of his Captain's
Trumpet, than they are to that which summoneth them to a
Puppet-Play or a *Monster*. The Spring that bringeth out *Flies*,
and *Fools*, maketh them Inhabitants in *Hide-Park*; in the
Winter they are an Incumbrance to the *Play House*, and the
Ballast of the *Drawing-Room*. The Streets all this while are
so weary of these daily Faces, that *Men's Eyes* are over-laid
with them. The *Sight* is glutted with fine things, as the
Stomach with sweet ones; and when a fair *Lady* will give too
much of her self to the *World*, she groweth luscious, and
oppresseth instead of pleasing. These *Jolly Ladies* do so
continually seek *Diversion*, that in a little time they grow into
a *Jest*, yet are unwilling to remember, that if they were seldomer
seen they would not be so often *laughed at*. Besides they make
themselves *Cheap*, than which there cannot be an *unkinder word*
bestowed upon your *Sex*.

To play sometimes, to entertain *Company*, or to *divert* your
self, is not to be disallowed, but to do it so often as to be called
a *Gamester*, is to be avoided, next to the things that are most
Criminal. It hath Consequences of *several kinds* not to be endured; it will ingage you into a habit of *Idleness* and *ill hours*,
draw you into ill mixed *Company*, make you neglect your
Civilities abroad, and your *Business* at home, and impose into
your *Acquaintance* such as will do you no Credit.

To deep *Play* there will be yet greater *Objections*. It will
give *Occasion* to the World to ask *spiteful Questions*. How
you dare venture to *lose*, and what means you have to *pay* such
great *summs*? If you pay *exactly*, it will be enquired from
whence the *Money* cometh? If you owe, and especially to
a Man, you must be so very *Civil* to him for his forbearance,
that it layeth a ground of having it farther improved, if the
Gentleman is so disposed; who will be thought no unfair
Creditor, if where the *Estate* faileth he seizeth upon the Person.

Besides

Besides if a *Lady* could see her own Face upon an *ill Game,* at a deep Stake, she would certainly forswear any thing that could put her looks under such a *Disadvantage.*

To *Dance* sometimes will not be imputed to you as a fault; but remember that the end of your *Learning* it, was, that you might the better know how to move *gracefully.* It is only an *advantage* so far. When it goeth beyond it, one may call it *excelling* in a Mistake, which is no very great Commendation. It is better for a *Woman* never to *Dance,* because she hath no skill in it, than to do it too often, because she doth it well. The easiest as well as the safest *Method* of doing it, is in *private Companies,* amongst *particular Friends,* and then carelesly, like a *Diversion,* rather than with *Solemnity,* as if it was a business, or had any thing in it to deserve a *Month's preparation* by serious Conference with a *Dancing-Master.*

Much more might be said to all these Heads, and many more might be added to them. But I must restrain my Thoughts, which are full of my Dear Child, and would overflow into a Volume, which would not be fit for a *New-Years-Gift.* I will conclude with my warmest Wishes for all that is good to you. That you may live so as to be an Ornament to your Family, and a Pattern to your Sex. That you may be blessed with a Husband that may value, and with Children that may inherit your Vertue; That you may shine in the World by a true Light, and silence Envy by deserving to be esteemed; That Wit and Vertue may both conspire to make you a great Figure. When they are separated, the first is so empty, and the other so faint, that they scarce have right to be commended. May they therefore meet and never part; let them be your Guardian Angels, and be sure never to stray out of the distance of their joint protection. May you so raise your Character, that you may help to make the next Age a better thing, and leave Posterity in your Debt for the advantage it shall receive by your Example.

Let me conjure you, *My Dearest,* to comply with this kind Ambition of a Father, whose Thoughts are so ingaged in your behalf, that he reckoneth your Happiness to be the greatest part of his own.

THE

THE
CHARACTER
OF A
TRIMMER.

THE
PREFACE.

IT must be more than an ordinary provocation that can tempt a Man to write in an Age over-run with Scribblers, as Egypt was with Flies and Locusts : That worst Vermin of small Authors hath given the World such a Surfeit, that instead of desiring to Write, a Man would be more inclin'd to wish, for his own ease, that he could not Read ; but there are some things which do so raise our passions, that our Reason can make no Resistance ; and when Madmen, in two Extreams, shall agree to make common sense Treason, and joyn to fix an ill Character upon the only Men in the Nation who deserve a good one ; I am no longer Master of my better Resolution to let the World alone, and must break loose from my more reasonable Thoughts, to expose these false Coyners, who would make their Copper Wares pass upon us for good Payment.

Amongst all the Engines of Dissention, there hath been none more powerful in all Times, than the fixing Names upon one another of Contumely and Reproach, and the reason is plain, in respect of the People, who tho' generally they are uncapable of making a Syllogism or forming an Argument, yet they can pronounce a word ; and that serveth their turn to throw it with

their

their dull malice at the Head of those they do not like; such things ever begin in Jest, and end in Blood, and the same word which at first maketh the Company merry, groweth in time to a Military Signal to cut one anothers Throats.

These Mistakes are to be lamented, tho' not easily cured, being suitable enough to the corrupted Nature of Mankind; but 'tis hard, that Men will not only invent ill Names, but they will wrest and misinterpret good ones; so afraid some are even of a reconciling sound, that they raise another noise to keep it from being heard, lest it should set up and encourage a dangerous sort of Men, who prefer Peace and Agreement, before Violence and Confusion.

Were it not for this, why, after we have played the Fool with throwing Whig and Tory at one another, as Boys do Snow-Balls, do we grow angry at a new Name, which by its true signification might do as much to put us into our Wits, as the other hath done to put us out of them?

This innocent word Trimmer signifieth no more than this, That if Men are together in a Boat, and one part of the Company would weigh it down on one side, another would make it lean as much to the contrary; it happeneth there is a third Opinion of those, who conceive it would do as well, if the Boat went even, without endangering the Passengers; now 'tis hard to imagin by what Figure in Language, or by what Rule in Sense this cometh to be a fault, and it is much more a wonder it should be thought a Heresy.

But so it happeneth, that the poor Trimmer hath now all the Powder spent upon him alone, while the Whig is a forgotten, or at least a neglected Enemy; there is no danger now to the State (if some Men may be believed) but from the Beast called a Trimmer, take heed of him, he is the Instrument that must destroy Church and State; a strange kind of Monster, whose deformity is so expos'd, that, were it a true Picture that is made of him, it would be enough to fright Children, and make Women miscarry at the sight of it.

But it may be worth the examining, whether he is such a Beast as he is Painted. I am not of that Opinion, and am so far
from

from thinking him an Infidel either in Church or State, that I am neither afraid to expose the Articles of his Faith in Relation to Government, nor to say that I prefer them before any other Political Creed, that either our angry Divines, or our refined States-men would impose upon us.

I have therefore in the following Discourse endeavour'd to explain the Trimmer's *Principles and Opinions, and then leave it to all discerning and impartial Judges, whether he can with Justice be so Arraign'd, and whether those who deliberately pervert a good Name, do not very justly deserve the worst that can be put upon themselves.*

THE

THE
Trimmer's Opinion
OF THE
LAWS
AND
GOVERNMENT.

OUr Trimmer, as he hath a great Veneration for Laws in general, so he hath a more particular for our own, he looketh upon them as the Chains that tye up our unruly Passions, which else, like wild Beasts let loose, would reduce the world into its first State of Barbarism and Hostility; the good things we injoy, we owe to them; and all the ill things we are freed from is by their Protection.

God himself thought it not enough to be a Creator, without being a Lawgiver, and his goodness had been defective towards mankind in making them, if he had not prescribed Rules to make them happy too.

All Laws flow from that of Nature, and where that is not the Foundation, they may be legally impos'd, but they will be lamely obeyed: By this Nature is not meant that which Fools and Madmen misquote to justify their Excesses; it is innocent and uncorrupted Nature, that which disposeth Men to chuse Vertue, without its being prescribed, and which is so far from inspiring ill thoughts into us, that we take pains to suppress the good ones it infuseth.

The Civilized World hath ever paid a willing subjection to Laws, even Conquerors have done homage to them; as the
Romans,

Romans, who took Patterns of good Laws, even from those they had subdued ; and at the same time that they Triumph'd over an enslav'd People, the very Laws of that place did not only remain safe, but became Victorious ; their new Masters, instead of suppressing them, paid them more respect than they had from those who first made them : and by this wise method they arrived to such an admirable Constitution of Laws, that to this day they Reign by them ; this Excellency of them Triumpheth still, and the World payeth now an acknowledgment of their obedience to that Mighty Empire, though so many Ages after it is dissolved ; and by a later instance, the Kings of *France,* who in practice use their Laws pretty familiarly, yet think their Picture is drawn with most advantage upon their Seals, when they are placed in the Seat of Justice : and tho' the Hierogly-phick is not there of so much use to the People as they would wish, yet it sheweth that no Prince is so Great, as not to think fit, for his own Credit at least, to give an outward, when he re-fuseth a real worship to the Laws.

They are to mankind that which the Sun is to Plants, whilst it cherisheth and preserveth them. Where they have their force and are not clouded or supprest, every thing smileth and flourisheth ; but where they are darkened, and not suffered to shine out, it maketh every thing to wither and decay.

They secure Men not only against one another, but against themselves too ; they are a Sanctuary to which the Crown hath occasion to resort as often as the People, so that it is an Interest as well as a Duty to preserve them.

There would be no end of making a Panegyrick of Laws ; let it be enough to add, that without Laws the World would be-come a Wilderness, and Men little less than Beasts ; but with all this, the best things may come to be the worst, if they are not in good hands ; and if it be true that the wisest Men generally make the Laws, it is as true, that the strongest do often Interpret them : and as Rivers belong as much to the Channel where they run, as to the Spring from whence they first rise, so the Laws depend as much upon the Pipes thro' which they are to pass, as upon the Fountain from whence they flow.

E 2

The

The Authority of a King who is Head of the Law, as well as the Dignity of Publick Justice, is debased, when the clear stream of the Law is puddled and disturbed by Bunglers, or convey'd by unclean Instruments to the People.

Our *Trimmer* would have them appear in their full lustre, and would be grieved to see the day, when, instead of speaking with Authority from the Seats of Justice, they should speak out of a Grate, with a lamenting voice like Prisoners that desire to be rescu'd.

He wisheth that the Bench may have a Natural as well as a Legal Superiority to the Bar; he thinketh Mens abilities very much misplac'd, when the Reason of him that pleadeth is visibly too strong for those who Judge and give Sentence.

When those from the Bar seem to dictate to their Superiours upon the Bench, their Furrs will look scurvily about them, and the respect of the World will leave the bare Character of a Judge, to follow the Essential knowledge of a Lawyer, who may be greater in himself, than the other can be with all his Trappings.

An uncontested Superiority in any Calling, will have the better of any discountenance that Authority can put upon it, and therefore if ever such an unnatural Method should be introduc'd, it is then that *Westminster Hall* might be said to stand upon its Head, and though Justice it self can never be so, yet the Administration of it would be rendred Ridiculous.

A Judge hath such power lodg'd in him, that the King will never be thought to have chosen well, where the voice of Mankind hath not before-hand recommended the Man to his Station; when Men are made Judges of what they do not understand, the World censureth such a Choice, not out of ill will to the Men, but fear to themselves.

If the King had the sole power of chusing Physicians, Men would tremble to see Bunglers preferred, yet the necessity of taking Physick from a Doctor, is generally not so great as that of receiving Justice from a Judge; and yet the Inferences will be very severe in such cases, for either it will be thought that such Men bought what they were not able to deserve, or which

is

is as bad, that Obedience shall be look'd upon as a better Qualification in a Judge, than Skill or Integrity, when such sacred things as the Laws are not only touch'd, but guided by prophane hands; Men will fear that out of the Tree of the Law, from whence we expect Shade and Shelter, such Workmen will make Cudgels to beat us with, or rather that they will turn the Canon upon our Properties, that were intrusted with them for their Defence.

To see the Laws Mangled, Disguised, Speak quite another Language than their own, to see them thrown from the Dignity of protecting Mankind, to the disgraceful Office of destroying them; and notwithstanding their Innocence in themselves, to be made the worst Instruments that the most refined Villany can make use of, will raise Mens Anger above the power of laying it down again, and tempt them to follow the Evil Examples given them of Judging without Hearing, when so provoked by their desire of Revenge. Our *Trimmer* therefore, as he thinketh the Laws are Jewels, so he believeth they are nowhere better set, than in the constitution of our *English* Government, if rightly understood, and carefully preserved.

It would be too great Partiality to say they are perfect or liable to no Objection; such things are not of this world; but if they have more Excellencies and fewer Faults than any other we know, it is enough to recommend them to our Esteem.

The Dispute, which is a greater Beauty, a Monarchy or a Common-wealth, hath lasted long between their contending Lovers, and they have behav'd themselves so like Lovers, (who in good Manners must be out of their Wits,) who used such Figures to exalt their own Idols on either side, and such angry Aggravations, to reproach one another in the Contest, that moderate men have in all times smil'd upon this eagerness, and thought it differ'd very little from a downright Frenzy: we in *England,* by a happy use of the Controversie, conclude them both in the wrong, and reject them from being our Pattern, not taking the words in the utmost extent, which is Monarchy, a thing that leaveth men no Liberty, and a Common-wealth, such a one as alloweth them no Quiet.

We

We think that a wise Mean, between these barbarous Extreams, is that which self-Preservation ought to dictate to our Wishes; and we may say we have attained to this Mean in a greater measure, than any Nation now in being, or perhaps any we have read of, tho never so much Celebrated for the Wisdom or Felicity of their Constitutions: We take from one the too great power of doing hurt, and yet leave enough to govern and protect us; we take from the other, the Confusion, the Parity, the Animosities, and the License, and yet reserve a due care of such a Liberty, as may consist with Mens Allegiance; but it being hard, if not impossible, to be exactly even, our Government hath much the stronger Biass towards Monarchy, which by the general Consent and Practise of Mankind, seemeth to have the Advantage in dispute against a Common-wealth; The Rules of a Common-wealth are too hard for the Bulk of Mankind to come up to; that Form of Government requireth such a spirit to carry it on, as doth not dwell in great Numbers, but is restrained to so very few, especially in this Age, that let the Methods appear never so reasonable in Paper, they must fail in Practice, which will ever be suited more to Mens Nature as it is, than as it should be.

Monarchy is lik'd by the People, for the Bells and the Tinsel, the outward Pomp and Gilding, and there must be milk for Babes, since the greatest part of Mankind are, and ever will be included in that List; and it is approv'd by wise and thinking Men, (all Circumstances and Objections impartially consider'd) that it hath so great an advantage above all other Forms, when the Administration of that Power falleth in good hands, that all other Governments look out of Countenance, when they are set in Competition with it. *Lycurgus* might have sav'd himself the trouble of making Laws, if either he had been Immortal, or that he could have secur'd to Posterity, a succeeding Race of Princes like himself; his own Example was a better Law, than he could with all his skill tell how to make; such a Prince is a Living Law, that dictateth to his Subjects, whose thoughts in that case never rise above their Obedience, the Confidence they have in the Vertue and Knowledge of the master, preventing

the

the Scruples and Apprehensions to which Men are naturally inclin'd, in relation to those that govern them; such a Magistrate is the Life and Soul of Justice, whereas the Law is but a Body and a dead one too, without his Influence to give it warmth and vigour, and by the irresistible Power of his Vertue, he doth so reconcile Dominion and Allegiance, that all disputes between them are silenced and subdued, and indeed no Monarchy can be Perfect and Absolute without exception, but where the Prince is Superior by his Vertue, as well as by his Character and his Power; so that to screw out Precedents of unlimited Power, is a plain diminution to a Prince that Nature hath made Great, and who had better make himself a glorious Example to Posterity, than borrow an Authority from Dark Records, raised out of the Grave, which besides their Non-usage, have always in them matter of Controversie and Debate, and it may be affirmed, that the instances are very rare of Princes having the worst in the dispute with their People, if they were Eminent for Justice in time of Peace, or Conduct in time of War, such advantage the Crown giveth to those who adorn it by their own Personal Vertues.

But since for the greater Honour of Good and wise Princes, and the better to set off their Character by the Comparison, Heaven hath decreed there must be a mixture, and that such as are perverse or insufficient, or perhaps both, are at least to have their equal turns in the Government of the World, and besides, that the Will of Man is so various, and so unbounded a thing, and so fatal too when joined with Power misapply'd; it is no wonder if those who are to be govern'd, are unwilling to have so dangerous as well as so uncertain a Standard of their Obedience.

There must be therefore Rules and Laws : for want of which, or at least the Observation of them, it was as Capital for a Man to say that *Nero* did not play well upon the Lute, as to commit Treason, or Blaspheme the Gods. And even *Vespasian* himself had like to have lost his Life, for sleeping whilst he should have attended and admir'd that Emperours Impertinence upon the Stage. There is a wantonness in great Power that

Men

Men are generally too apt to be corrupted with, and for that Reason, a wise Prince, to prevent the temptation arising from common frailty, would choose to Govern by Rules for his own Sake, as well as for his Peoples, since it only secureth him from Errors, and doth not lessen the real Authority, that a good Magistrate would care to be possess'd of; for if the Will of a Prince is contrary either to Reason it self, or to the universal Opinion of his Subjects, the Law by a kind restraint rescueth him from a disease that would undo him; if his will on the other side is reasonable or well directed, that Will immediately becometh a Law, and he is arbitrary by an easie and natural Consequence, without taking pains, or overturning the World for it.

If Princes consider Laws as things impos'd on them, they have the appearance of Fetters of Iron, but to such as would make them their choice as well as their practice, they are Chains of Gold; and in that respect are Ornaments, as in others they are a defence to them; and by a Comparison, not improper for God's Vicegerents upon Earth, as our Maker never Commandeth our obedience to any thing, that as reasonable Creatures we ought not to make our own Election, so a good and wise Governour, tho' all Laws were abolish'd, would by the voluntary direction of his own Reason, do without restraint the very same things that they would have enjoyed.

Our *Trimmer* thinketh that the King and Kingdom ought to be one Creature, not to be separated in their Political Capacity; and when either of them undertake to act a part, it is like the crawling of Worms after they are cut in pieces, which cannot be a lasting motion, the whole Creature not stirring at a time. If the Body have a dead Palsie, the Head cannot make it move; and God hath not yet delegated such a healing power to Princes, as that they can in a moment say to a Languishing People oppress'd and in despair, Take up your Beds and walk.

The Figure of a King, is so comprehensive and exalted a thing, that it is a kind of degrading him to lodge that power separately in his own Natural Person, which can never be safely or naturally great, but where the People are so united to him
as

as to be Flesh of his Flesh, and Bone of his Bone; for when he is reduc'd to the single definition of a man, he sinketh into so low a Character, that it is a temptation upon Mens Allegiance, and an impairing that veneration which is necessary to preserve their Duty to him; whereas a Prince who is so joined to his people that they seem to be his Limbs, rather than his Subjects, Cloathed with Mercy and Justice rightly apply'd in their several places, his Throne supported by Love as well as by Power, and the warm wishes of his devoted Subjects, like never-failing Incense, still ascending towards him, looketh so like the best Image we can frame to our selves of God Almighty, that men would have much ado not to fall down and worship him, and would be much more tempted to the Sin of Idolatry, than to that of Disobedience.

Our *Trimmer* is of Opinion, that there must be so much Dignity inseparably annexed to the Royal Function, as may be sufficient to secure it from insolence and contempt; and there must be Condescensions from the Throne, like kind showers from Heaven, that the Prince may look so much the more like God Almighty's Deputy upon Earth; for power without love hath a terrifying aspect, and the Worship which is paid to it is like that which the *Indians* give out of fear to Wild Beasts and Devils: he that feareth God only because there is an Hell, must wish there were no God; and he who feareth the King, only because he can punish, must wish there were no King; so that without a principle of Love, there can be no true Allegiance, and there must remain perpetual Seeds of Resistance against a power that is built upon such an unnatural Foundation, as that of fear and terrour. All force is a kind of foul-Play, and whosoever aimeth at it himself, doth by implication allow it to those he playeth with; so that there will be ever Matter prepared in the minds of People when they are provoked, and the Prince, to secure himself must live in the midst of his own Subjects, as if he were in a Conquer'd Country, raise Arms as if he were immediately to meet or resist an Invasion, and all this while sleep as unquietly from the fear of the Remedies, as he did before from that of the Disease; it being hard for him

to

to forget, that more Princes have been destroyed by their Guards than by their People; and that even at the time when the Rule was *Quod Principi placuit Lex esto*, the Armies and *Prætorian* Bands which were the Instruments of that unruly Power, were frequently the means made use of to destroy them who had it. There will ever be this difference between God and his Vicegerents, that God is still above the Instruments he useth, and out of the danger of receiving hurt from them; but Princes can never lodge Power in any hands, which may not at some time turn it back upon them; for tho' it is possible enough for a King to have power to satisfy his Ambition; yet no Kingdom hath Money enough to satisfie the avarice of under-Workmen, who learn from that Prince who will exact more than belongeth to him, to expect from him much more than they deserve, and growing angry upon the first disappointment, they are the Devils which grow terrible to the Conjurers themselves who brought them up, and can't send them down again. And besides that there can be no lasting Radical Security, but where the Governed are satisfied with the Governours, it must be a Dominion very unpleasant to a Prince of an elevated Mind, to impose an abject and sordid servility, instead of receiving the willing Sacrifice of Duty and Obedience. The bravest Princes in all times, who were uncapable of any other kind of fear, have fear'd to grieve their own People; such a fear is a glory, and in this sense 'tis an infamy not to be a Coward: So that the mistaken Heroes who are void of this generous kind of fear, need no other aggravation to compleat their ill Characters.

When a Despotick Prince hath bruised all his Subjects with a slavish Obedience, all the force he can use cannot subdue his own fears; Enemies of his own Creation, to which he can never be reconciled, it being impossible to do injustice and not to fear Revenge: there is no cure for this fear, but the not deserving to be hurt, and therefore a Prince who doth not allow his thoughts to stray beyond the Rules of Justice, hath always the blessing of an inward quiet and assurance, as a natural effect of his good Meaning to his People, and tho he will not neglect due

precautions

precautions to secure himself in all Events, yet he is uncapable of entertaining vain and remote suspicions of those, of whom he resolveth never to deserve ill.

It is very hard for a Prince to fear Rebellion, who neither doth, nor intendeth to do any thing to provoke it; therefore too great a diligence in the Governours, to raise and improve dangers and fears from the People, is no very good Symptom, and naturally begetteth an inference that they have thoughts of putting their Subjects Allegiance to a Tryal; and therefore not without some Reason fear beforehand, that the Irregularities they intend, may raise Men to a Resistance.

Our *Trimmer* thinketh it no advantage to a Government, to endeavour the suppressing all kind of Right which may remain in the Body of the People, or to employ small Authors in it, whose Officiousness or want of Money may encourage them to write, tho' it is not very easie to have Abilities equal to such a Subject; they forget that in their too high strained Arguments for the Rights of Princes, they very often plead against humane Nature, which will always give a Biass to those Reasons which seem of her side; it is the People that Readeth those Books, and it is the People that must judge of them; and therefore no Maxims should be laid down for the Right of Government, to which there can be any Reasonable Objection; for the World hath an Interest, and for that Reason is more than ordinary discerning to find out the weak sides of such Arguments as are intended to do them hurt; and it is a diminution to a Government, to Promote or Countenance such well affected mistakes which are turned upon it with disadvantage whenever they are detected and expos'd; and Naturally the too earnest Endeavours to take from Men the Right they have, tempt them, by the Example, to Claim that which they have not.

In Power, as in most other things, the way for Princes to keep it, is not to grasp more than their Arms can well hold; the nice and unnecessary enquiring into these things, or the Licensing some Books, and suppressing some others without sufficient Reason to Justifie the doing either, is so far from being an Advantage to a Government, that it exposeth it to the

Censure

Censure of being Partial, and to the suspicion of having some hidden designs to be carried on by these unusual methods.

When all is said, there is a Natural Reason of State, an undefinable thing, grounded upon the Common Good of Mankind, which is immortal, and in all Changes and Revolutions, still preserveth its Original Right of saving a Nation, when the Letter of the Law perhaps would destroy it; and by whatsoever means it moveth, carrieth a Power with it, that admitteth of no opposition, being supported by Nature, which inspireth an immediate consent at some Critical times into every individual Member, to that which visibly tendeth to preservation of the whole; and this being so, a Wise Prince instead of Controverting the right of this Reason of State, will by all means endeavour it may be of his side, and then he will be secure.

Our *Trimmer* cannot conceive that the Power of any Prince can be lasting, but where 'tis built upon the foundation of his own unborrowed vertue, he must not only be the first Mover and the Fountain, from whence the great Acts of State originally flow, but he must be thought so to his People that they may preserve their veneration for him; he must be jealous of his Power, and not impart so much of it to any about him, as that he may suffer an Eclipse by it.

He cannot take too much care to keep himself up, for when a Prince is thought to be led by those, with whom he should onely advise, and that the Commands he giveth are transmitted through him, and are not of his own growth; the World will look upon him as a Bird adorned with Feathers that are not his own, or consider him rather as an Engine than a living Creature; besides, 'twould be a Contradiction for a Prince to fear a Common-wealth, and at the same time create one himself, by delegating such a Power to any Number of Men near him, as is inconsistent with the Figure of a Monarch: it is the worst kind of Co-ordination the Crown can submit to; for it is the exercise of Power that draweth the respect along with it, and when that is parted with, the bare Character of a King is not sufficient to keep it up; but tho' it is a diminution to a Prince,

to

to parcel out so liberally his Power amongst his Favourites, it is worse to divide with any other Man, and to bring himself in Competition with a single Rival; a Partner in Government is so unnatural a thing, that it is a squint-ey'd Allegiance that must be paid to such a double bottom'd Monarchy. The two Czars of *Muscovy* are an Example that the more civiliz'd part of the World will not be prone to follow. Whatsoever Gloss may be put upon this method, by those to whom it may be of some use, the Prince will do well to remember, and reflect upon the Story of certain Men who had set up a Statue in Honour of the Sun, yet in a very little time they turned their backs to the Sun, and their Faces to the Statue.

These Mystical Unions are better plac'd in the other World, than they are in this, and we shall have much ado to find, that in a Monarchy Gods Vicegerency is delegated to more Heads than that which is anointed.

Princes may lend some of their Light to make another shine, but they must still preserve the superiority of being the brighter Planet, and when it happeneth that the Reversion is in Mens Eyes, there is more care necessary to keep up the Dignity of Possessions, that Men may not forget who is King, either out of their hopes or fears who shall be. If the Sun shou'd part with all his Light to any of the Stars, the *Indians* would not know where to find their God, after he had so deposed himself, and would make the Light (where-ever it went) the Object of their Worship.

All Usurpation is alike upon Soveraignty, it is no matter from what hand it cometh, and Crowned Heads are to be the more Circumspect, in respect Mens thoughts are naturally apt to ramble beyond what is present; they love to work at a distance, and in their greedy Expectations which their minds may be fill'd with of a new Master, the old one may be left to look a little out of Countenance.

Our *Trimmer* owneth a Passion for liberty, yet so restrained, that it doth not in the least impair or taint his Allegiance; he thinketh it hard for a Soul that doth not love Liberty ever to raise it self to another World; he taketh it to be the foundation of all vertue, and the only seasoning that giveth a relish to life,

and

and tho' the laziness of a slavish subjection, hath its Charms for the more gross and earthly part of Mankind, yet to men made of a better sort of Clay, all that the World can give without Liberty hath no taste; it is true, nothing is sold so cheap by unthinking men, but that doth no more lessen the real value of it, than a Country Fellows Ignorance doth that of a Diamond, in selling it for a Pot of Ale. Liberty is the Mistress of Mankind, she hath powerful Charms which do so dazzle us, that we find Beauties in her which perhaps are not there, as we do in other Mistresses; yet if she was not a Beauty, the World would not run mad for her; therefore since the reasonable desire of it ought not to be restrain'd, and that even the unreasonable desire of it cannot be entirely suppress'd, those who would take it away from a People possessed of it, are likely to fail in the attempting, or be very unquiet in the keeping of it.

Our *Trimmer* admireth our blessed Constitution, in which Dominion and Liberty are so well reconciled; it giveth to the Prince the glorious Power of commanding Freemen, and to the Subject, the satisfaction of seeing the Power so lodged, as that their Liberties are secure; it doth not allow the Crown such a Ruining Power, as that no grass can grow where e'er it treadeth, but a Cherishing and Protecting Power; such a one as hath a grim Aspect only to the offending Subjects, but is the joy and the Pride of all the good ones; their own interest being so bound up in it, as to engage them to defend and support it; and tho in some instances the King is restrain'd, yet nothing in the Government can move without him: our Laws make a distinction between Vassalage and Obedience; between a devouring Prerogative, and a licentious ungovernable Freedom: and as of all the Orders of Building, the Composite is the best, so ours by a happy mixture and a wise choice of what is best in others, is brought into a Form that is our Felicity who live under it, and the envy of our Neighbour that cannot imitate it.

The Crown hath power sufficient to protect our Liberties. The People have so much Liberty as is necessary to make them useful to the Crown.

Our Government is in a just proportion, no Tympany, no unnatural

natural swelling either of Power or Liberty; and whereas in all overgrown Monarchies, Reason, Learning, and Enquiry are hang'd in Effigy for Mutineers; here they are encouraged and cherished as the surest Friends to a Government establish'd upon the Foundation of Law and Justice. When all is done, those who look for Perfection in this World, may look as the *Jews* have for their *Messias*, and therefore our *Trimmer* is not so unreasonably Partial as to free our Government from all objections; no doubt there have been fatal Instances of its Sickness, and more than that, of its Mortality, for sometime, tho' by a Miracle, it hath been reviv'd again: but till we have another race of Mankind, in all Constitutions that are bounded there will ever be some matter of Strife and Contention, and rather than want pretensions, Mens Passions and Interests will raise them from the most inconsiderable Causes.

Our Government is like our Climate, there are Winds which are sometimes loud and unquiet, and yet with all the Trouble they give us, we owe great part of our Health unto them, they clear the Air, which else would be like a standing Pool and in stead of Refreshment would be a Disease unto us.

There may be fresh Gales of asserting Liberty, without turning into such storms of Hurricane, as that the State should run any hazard of being Cast away by them; these struglings which are natural to all mixed Governments, while they are kept from growing into Convulsions, do by a mutual agitation from the several parts, rather support and strengthen, than weaken or maim the Constitution; and the whole frame, instead of being torn or disjointed, cometh to be the better and closer knit by being thus exercised; but what ever faults our Government may have, or a discerning Critick may find in it, when he looketh upon it alone, let any other be set against it, and then it sheweth its Comparative Beauty; let us look upon the most glittering outside of unbounded Authority, and upon a nearer enquiry, we shall find nothing but poor and miserable deformity within; let us imagine a Prince living in his Kingdom, as if in a great Gally, his Subjects tugging at the Oar, laden with Chains, and reduced to real Rags, that they may gain him
imaginary

imaginary Lawrels; let us Represent him gazing among his Flatterers, and receiving their false Worship, like a Child never Contradicted, and therefore always Cozen'd: or like a Lady complemented only to be abused, condemned never to hear Truth, and Consequently never to do Justice, wallowing in the soft Bed of wanton and unbridled Greatness, not less odious to the Instruments themselves, than to the Objects of his Tyranny; blown up into an Ambitious Dropsy, never to be satisfied by the Conquest of other People, or by the Oppression of his own; by aiming to be more than a Man, he falleth lower than the meanest of 'em, a mistaken Creature, swelled with Panegyricks, and flattered out of his Senses, and not only an Incumbrance, but a Nuisance to Mankind, a hardened and unrelenting Soul, and like some Creatures that grow fat with Poisons, he groweth great by other Mens Miseries; an Ambitious Ape of the Divine Greatness, an unruly Gyant that would storm even Heaven it self, but that his scaling Ladders are not long enough; in short, a Wild and devouring Creature in rich Trappings, and with all his Pride, no more than a Whip in God Almighty's hand, to be thrown into the Fire when the World hath been sufficiently scourged with it: This Picture laid in right Colours would not incite Men to wish for such a Government, but rather to acknowledge the happiness of our own, under which we enjoy all the Privilege Reasonable Men can desire, and avoid all the Miseries many others are subject to; so that our *Trimmer* would keep it with all its faults, and doth as little forgive those who give the occasion of breaking it, as he doth those that take it.

Our *Trimmer* is a Friend to Parliaments, notwithstanding all their faults, and excesses, which of late have given such matter of Objection to them; he thinketh that tho' they may at some times be troublesome to Authority, yet they add the greatest strength to it under a wise Administration; he believeth no Government is perfect except a kind of Omnipotence reside in it, to exercise upon great Occasions: Now this cannot be obtained by force alone upon People, let it be never so great, there must be their consent too, or else a Nation moveth only by being driven, a sluggish and constrained Motion, void of that
Life

Life and Vigour which is necessary to produce great things, whereas the virtual Consent of the whole being included in their Representatives, and the King giving the sanction to the united sense of the People, every Act done by such an Authority, seemeth to be an effect of their choice as well as a part of their Duty; and they do, with an eagerness of which Men are uncapable whilst under a force, execute whatsoever is so enjoyned as their own Wills, better explained by Parliament, rather than from the terrour of incurring the Penalty of the Law for omiting it, and by means of this Political Omnipotence, what ever Sap or Juice there is in a Nation, may be to the last drop produc'd, whilst it riseth naturally from the Root; whereas all power exercis'd without consent, is like the giving Wounds and Gashes, and tapping a Tree at unseasonable Times, for the present occasion, which in a very little time must needs destroy it.

Our *Trimmer* believeth, that by the advantage of our Situation, there can hardly any such sudden Disease come upon us, but that the King may have time enough left to consult with his Physicians in Parliament; pretences indeed may be made, but a real necessity so pressing, that no delay is to be admitted, is hardly to be imagin'd, and it will be neither easie to give an instance of any such thing for the time past, or reasonable to Presume it will ever happen for the time to come: but if that strange thing should fall out, our *Trimmer* is not so streight-lac'd, as to let a Nation die, or to be stifled, rather than it should be help'd by any but the proper Officers. The Cases themselves will bring the Remedies along with them; and he is not afraid to allow that in order to its preservation, there is a hidden Power in Government, which would be lost if it was defined, a certain Mystery, by virtue of which a Nation may at some Critical times be secur'd from Ruine; but then it must be kept as a Mystery; it is rendred useless when touch'd by unskilfull hands, and no Government ever had, or deserv'd to have that Power, which was so unwary as to anticipate their claim to it: Our *Trimmer* cannot help thinking it had been better, if the Triennial Act had been observ'd; because 'tis the

Law, and he would not have the Crown, by such an Example, teach the Nation to break it; all irregularity is catching, it hath a Contagion in it, especially in an Age so much more enclin'd to follow ill Patterns than good ones.

He would have had a Parliament, because 'tis an Essential part of the Constitution, even without the Law, it being the only Provision in extraordinary Cases, in which there would be otherwise no Remedy, and there can be no greater Solecism in Government, than a failure of Justice.

He would have had one, because nothing else can unite and heal us, all other Means are meer Shifts and Projects, Houses of Cards, to be blown down with the least Breath, and cannot resist the Difficulties which are ever presum'd in things of this kind; and he would have had one, because it might have done the King good, and could not possibly have done him hurt, without his consent, which in that Case is not to be supposed, and therefore for him to fear it, is so strange and so little to be comprehended, that the Reasons can never be presum'd to grow in our Soyl, or to thrive in it when Transplanted from any other Country; and no doubt there are such irresistible Arguments for calling a Parliament, that tho it might be deny'd to the unmannerly mutinous Petitions of men, that are malicious and disaffected, it will be granted to the soft and obsequious Murmurs of his Majesty's best Subjects, and there will be such Rhetorick in their silent Grief, that it will at last prevail against the Artifices of those, who either out of Guilt or Interest, are afraid to throw themselves upon their Country, knowing how scurvily they have used it; that day of Judgment will come, tho we know neither the day nor the hour. And our *Trimmer* would live so as to be prepared for it, with full assurance in the mean time, that the lamenting Voice of a Nation cannot long be resisted, and that a Prince who could so easily forgive his People when they had been in the wrong, cannot fail to hear them when they are in the right.

The

The Trimmer's *Opinion concerning the Protestant Religion.*

REligion hath such a Superiority above other things, and that indispensable Influence upon all Mankind, that it is as necessary to our Living Happy in this World, as it is to our being Sav'd in the next, without it man is an abandon'd Creature, one of the worst Beasts Nature hath produc'd, and fit only for the Society of Wolves and Bears; therefore in all Ages it hath been the Foundation of Government: and tho' false Gods have been impos'd upon the Credulous part of the World, yet they were Gods still in their Opinion, and the Awe and Reverence Men had to them and their Oracles, kept them within bounds towards one another, which the Laws with all their Authority could never have effected without the help of Religion; the Laws would not be able to subdue the perverseness of Mens Wills, which are Wild Beasts, and require a double Chain to keep them down; for this Reason 'tis said, That it is not a sufficient ground to make War upon a Neighbouring State, because they are of another Religion, let it be never so differing; yet if they Worship nor Acknowledge no Deity at all, they may be Invaded as Publick Enemies of Mankind, because they reject the only thing that can bind them to live well with one another; the consideration of Religion is so twisted with that of Government, that it is never to be separated, and tho the Foundations of it ought to be Eternal and Unchangeable, yet the Terms and Circumstances of Discipline, are to be suited to the several Climates and Constitutions, so that they may keep men in a willing Acquiescence unto them, without discomposing the World by nice disputes, which can never be of equal moment with the publick Peace.

Our Religion here in *England* seemeth to be distinguished by a peculiar effect of God Almighty's goodness, in permiting it to be introduc'd, or rather restored, by a more regular Method than the Circumstances of most other Reformed Churches would allow them to do, in relation to the Government; and the

Dignity

Dignity with which it hath supported it self since, and the great Men our Church hath produced, ought to recommend it to the esteem of all Protestants at least : Our *Trimmer* is very partial to it, for these Reasons, and many more, and desireth that it may preserve its due Jurisdiction and Authority ; so far he is from wishing it oppressed by the unreasonable and malicious Cavils of those who take pains to raise Objections against it.

The Questions will then be, how and by what Methods this Church shall best support it self (the present Circumstances consider'd) in relation to Dissenters of all sorts : I will first lay this for a ground, That as there can be no true Religion without Charity, so there can be no true humane prudence without bearing and condescension : This Principle doth not extend to oblige the Church always to yield to those who are disposed to Contest with her, the expediency of doing it is to be considered and determined according to the occasion, and this leads me to lay open the thoughts of our *Trimmer*, in reference first, to the Protestants, and then to the Popish Recusants.

What hath lately hapned among us, maketh an Apology necessary for saying any thing that looketh like favour towards a sort of Men who have brought themselves under such a disadvantage.

The late Conspiracy hath such broad Symptoms of the disaffection of the whole Party, that upon the first reflections, while our thoughts are warm, it would almost perswade us to put them out of the protection of our good Nature, and to think that the Christian Indulgence which our compassion for other Mens Sufferings cannot easily deny, seemeth not only to be forfeited by the ill appearances that are against them, but even becometh a Crime when it is so misapplied ; yet for all this, upon second and cooler thoughts, moderate Men will not be so ready to involve a whole Party in the guilt of a few, and to admit inferences and Presumptions to be Evidence in a Case, where the Sentence must be so heavy, as it ought to be against all those who have a fixed resolution against the Government established : besides, Men who act by a Principle grounded upon Moral Vertue, can never let it be clearly extinguished, by the

the most repeated Provocations; if a right thing agreeable to Nature and good Sense taketh root in the heart of a Man that is impartial and unbyass'd, no outward Circumstances can ever destroy it; it is true, the degrees of a Mans Zeal for the Prosecution of it may be differing; the faults of other Men, the consideration of the publick, and the seasonable Prudence by which Wise Men will ever be directed, may give great Allays; they may lessen and for a time perhaps suppress the exercise of that, which in general Proposition may be reasonable, but still whatever is so will inevitably grow and spring up again, having a Foundation in Nature, which is never to be destroy'd.

Our *Trimmer* therefore endeavoureth to separate the detestation of those who had either a hand or a thought in the late Plot, from the Principle of Prudential as well as Christian Charity towards Mankind, and for that reason would fain use the means of reclaiming such of the Dissenters as are not incurable, and even of bearing to a degree those that are, as far as may consist with the Publick Interest and Security; he is far from justifying an affected separation from the Communion of the Church, and even in those that mean well and are mistaken, he looketh upon it as a Disease that hath seized upon their Minds, very troublesome as well as dangerous, by the Consequence it may produce: he doth not go about to excuse their making it an indispensable duty, to meet in numbers to say their Prayers; such meetings may prove mischievous to the State; at least the Laws, which are the best Judges, have determined that there is danger in them: he hath good nature enough to lament that the perversness of a Part should have drawn Rigorous Laws upon the whole Body of the Dissenters, but when they are once made no private Opinion must stand in Opposition to them; if they are in themselves reasonable, they are in that respect to be regarded, even without being enjoyned; if by the Change of Time and Circumstances they should become less reasonable than when they were first made, even then they are to be obey'd too, because they are Laws, till they are mended or repealed by the same Authority that Enacted them.

He hath too much deference to the Constitution of our
Government,

Government, to wish for more Prerogative Declarations in favour of scrupulous Men, or to dispence with Penal Laws in such manner, or to such an end, that suspecting Men might with some reason pretend, that so hated a thing as Persecution could never make way for it self with any hopes of Success, otherwise than by preparing the deluded World by a false prospect of Liberty and Indulgence. The inward Springs and Wheels whereby the Engine moved, are now so fully laid open and expos'd that it is not supposable that such a baffled Experiment should ever be tryed again ; the effect it had at the time, and the Spirit it raised, will not easily be forgotten, and it may be presum'd the remembrance of it may secure us from any more attempts of that Nature for the future ; we must no more break a Law to give Men ease, than we are to Rifle an House with a devout intention of giving the plunder to the Poor ; in this case, our Compassion would be as ill directed, as our Charity in the other.

In short, the veneration due to the Laws is never to be thrown off, let the pretences be never so specious ; yet with all this he cannot bring himself to think, that an extraordinary diligence to take the uttermost penalty of Laws, upon the poor offending Neighbour, is of it self such an all sufficient vertue, that without any thing else to recommend Men, it should Entitle them to all kind of Preferments and Rewards ; he would not detract from the merits of those who execute the Laws, yet he cannot think such a piece of service as this, can entirely change the Man, and either make him a better Divine, or a more knowing Magistrate than he was before, especially if it be done with a partial and unequal hand in Reverence to greater and more dangerous Offenders.

Our *Trimmer* would have those mistaken Men ready to throw themselves into the arms of the Church, and he would have those arms as ready to receive them that shall come to us ; he would have no supercilious look to fright those strayed Sheep from coming into the Fold again ; no ill-natur'd maxims of an Eternal suspicion, or a belief that those who have once been in the wrong can never be in the right again ; but a visible preparation
tion

tion of mind to receive with joy all the Proselytes that come amongst us, and much greater earnestness to reclaim than punish them : It is to be confessed, there is a great deal to forgive, a hard task enough for the Charity of a Church so provoked ; but that must not cut off all hopes of being reconciled, yet if there must be some anger left still, let it break out into a Christian Revenge, and by being kinder to the Children of Disobedience than they deserve, let the injur'd Church Triumph, by throwing shame and confusion of face upon them ; there should not always be Storms and Thunder, a clear Sky would sometime make the Church look more like Heaven, and would do more towards the reclaiming those wanderers, than a perpetual terrour, which seemeth to have no intermission ; for there is in many, and particularly in *English Men,* a mistaken pleasure, in resisting the dictates of Rigorous Authority ; a Stomach that riseth against a hard imposition, nay, in some, even a lust in suffering from a wrong point of Honour, which doth not want the applause, from the greater part of Mankind, who have not learnt to distinguish ; constancy will be thought a virtue even where it is a mistake ; and the ill Judging World will be apt to think that Opinion most right, which produceth the greatest number of those who are willing to suffer for it ; all this is prevented, and falleth to the ground, by using well-timed Indulgence ; and the stubborn Adversary who valueth himself upon his Resistance whilst he is oppress'd, yieldeth insensibly to kind Methods, when they are apply'd to him, and the same Man naturally melteth into Conformity, who perhaps would never have been beaten into it. We may be taught by the Compassion that attendeth the most Criminal Men when they are Condemned, that Faults are much more natural things than Punishments, and that even the most necessary acts of severity do some kind of violence to our Nature, whose Indulgence will not be confined within the strait bounds of inexorable Justice ; so that this should be an Argument for gentleness, besides that it is the likeliest way to make these Men asham'd of their Separation, whilst the pressing them too hard, tendeth rather to make them proud of it.

Our

Our *Trimmer* would have the Clergy supported in their Lawful Rights, and in all the Power and Dignity that belongeth to them, and yet he thinketh that possibly there may be in some of them a too great eagerness to extend the Ecclesiastical Jurisdiction; which tho it may be well intended, yet the straining of it too high hath an appearance of Ambition that raiseth mens Objections to it, and is so far unlike the Apostolick Zeal, which was quite otherwise employ'd, that the World draweth inferences from it, which do the Church no service.

He is troubled to see Men of all sides sick of a Calenture of a mistaken Devotion, and it seemeth to him that the devout Fire of mistaken Charity with which the Primitive Christians were inflam'd, is long since extinguish'd, and instead of it a devouring Fire of Anger and Persecution breaketh out in the World; we wrangle now one with another about Religion till the Blood cometh, whilst the Ten Commandments have no more authority with us, than if they were so many obsolete Laws or Proclamations out of date; he thinketh that a Nation will hardly be mended by Principles of Religion, where Morality is made a Heresy; and therefore as he believeth Devotion misplaced when it gets into a Conventicle, he concludeth that Loyalty is so too, when lodg'd in a Drunken Club; those Vertues deserve a better Seat of Empire, and they are degraded, when such Men undertake their defence, as have too great need of an Apology themselves.

Our *Trimmer* wisheth that some knowledge may go along with the Zeal on the right side, and that those who are in possession of the Pulpit, would quote at least so often the Authority of the Scriptures as they do that of the State; there are many who borrow too often Arguments from the Government, to use against their Adversaries, and neglect those that are more proper, and would be more powerful; a Divine groweth less, and putteth a diminution on his own Character, when he quoteth any Law but that of God Almighty, to get the better of those who contest with him; and as it is a sign of a decay'd Constitution, when Nature with good diet cannot expel noxious Humours without calling Foreign Drugs to her Assistance;

So

So it looketh like want of health in a Church, when instead of depending upon the power of that Truth which it holdeth, and the good Examples of them that teach it, to support it self, and to suppress Errors, it should have a perpetual recourse to the secular Authority, and even upon the slightest occasions.

Our *Trimmer* hath his Objections to the too busy diligence, and to the overdoing of some of the dissenting Clergy, and he doth as little approve of those of our Church, who wear God Almighty's Liveries, as some old Warders in the *Tower* do the King's, who do nothing in their place but receive their Wages for it; he thinketh that the Liberty of the late times gave men so much Light, and diffused it so universally amongst the people, that they are not now to be dealt with, as they might have been in Ages of less enquiry; and therefore tho in some well chosen and dearly beloved Auditories, good resolute Nonsense back'd with Authority may prevail, yet generally Men are become so good Judges of what they hear, that the Clergy ought to be very wary how they go about to impose upon their Understandings, which are grown less humble than they were in former times, when the Men in black had made Learning such a sin in the Laity, that for fear of offending, they made a Conscience of being able to read; but now the World is grown sawcy, and expecteth Reasons, and good ones too, before they give up their own Opinions to other Mens Dictates, tho never so Magisterially deliver'd to them.

Our *Trimmer* is far from approving the Hypocrisie, which seemeth to be the reigning Vice amongst some of the Dissenting Clergy, he thinketh it the most provoking sin Men can be guilty of, in Relation to Heaven, and yet (which may seem strange) that very sin which shall destroy the Soul of the Man who preacheth, may help to save those of the Company that hear him, and even those who are cheated by the false Ostentation of his strictness of life, may by that Pattern be encouraged to the real Practice of those Christian Vertues which he doth so deceitfully profess; so that the detestation of this fault may possibly be carry'd on too far by our own Orthodox Divines, if they think it cannot be enough express'd without bending the

Stick

Stick another way ; a dangerous Method, and a worse Extream for Men of that Character, who by going to the outmost line of Christian Liberty, will certainly encourage others to go beyond it ; No Man doth less approve the ill-bred Methods of some of the Dissenters, in rebuking Authority, who behave themselves as if they thought ill manners necessary to Salvation ; yet he cannot but distinguish and desire a Mean between the sawcyness of some of the *Scotch Apostles*, and the undecent Courtship of some of the Silken Divines, who, one would think, do practice to bow at the Altar, only to learn to make the better Legs at Court.

Our *Trimmer* approveth the Principles of our Church, that Dominion is not founded in Grace, and that our Obedience is to be given to a Popish King in other things, at the same time that our Compliance with him in his Religion is to be deny'd ; yet he cannot but think it a very extraordinary thing if a Protestant Church should by a voluntary Election, chuse a Papist for their Guardian, and receive Directions for support- ing their Religion, from one who must believe it a Mortal Sin not to endeavour to destroy it ; such a refined piece of Breeding would not seem to be very well plac'd in the Clergy, who will hardly find Precedents to justify such an extravagant piece of Courtship, and which is so unlike the Primitive Methods, which ought to be our Pattern ; he hath no such unreasonable tenderness for any sorts of Men, as to expect their faults should not be impartially laid open as often as they give occasion for it ; and yet he cannot but smile to see that the same Man, who setteth up all the Sails of his Rhetorick, to fall upon the Dis- senters, when Popery is to be handled, he doth it so gingerly, that he looketh like an Ass mumbling of Thistles, so afraid he is of letting himself loose where he may be in danger of letting his Duty get the better of his Discretion.

Our *Trimmer* is far from relishing the impertinent wandrings of those who pour out long Prayers upon the Congregation, and all from their own Stock, which God knoweth, for the most part is a barren Soil, which produceth weeds instead of Flowers, and by this means they expose Religion it self, rather than promote

promote Mens Devotions: On the other side, there may be too great Restraint put upon Men, whom God and Nature hath distinguished from their Fellow Labourers, by blessing them with a happier Talent, and, by giving them not only good Sense, but a powerful Utterance too, hath enabled them to gush out upon the attentive Auditory, with a mighty stream of Devout and unaffected Eloquence; when a Man so qualified, endued with Learning too, and above all, adorn'd with a good Life, breaketh out into a warm and well deliver'd Prayer before his Sermon, it hath the appearance of a Divine Rapture; he raiseth and leadeth the Hearts of the Assembly in another manner, than the most Compos'd or best Studied Form of set Words can ever do; and the Pray-wees, who serve up all their Sermons with the same Garnishing, would look like so many Statues, or Men of Straw in the Pulpit, compar'd with those who speak with such a powerful Zeal, that men are tempted at the moment to believe Heaven it self hath dictated their words to 'em.

Our *Trimmer* is not so unreasonably indulgent to the Dissenters, as to excuse the Irregularities of their Complaints, and to approve their threatning Stiles, which are so ill-suited to their Circumstances as well as to their Duty; he would have them to shew their Grief, and not their Anger to the Government, and by such a Submission to Authority, as becometh them, if they cannot acquiesce in what is imposed, let them deserve a Legislative Remedy to their Sufferings, there being no other way to give them perfect redress; and either to seek it, or pretend to give it by any other Method, would not only be vain, but Criminal too in those that go about it; yet with all this, there may in the mean time be a prudential Latitude left, as to the manner of prosecuting the Laws now in force against them: The Government is in some degree answerable for such an Administration of them, as may be free from the Censure of Impartial Judges; and in order to that, it would be necessary that one of these methods be pursued, either to let loose the Laws to their utmost extent, without any Moderation or Restraint, in which at least the Equality of the Government

ment would be without Objection, the Penalties being exacted
without Remission from the Dissenters of all kinds; or if that
will not be done (and indeed there is no Reason it should) there
is a necessity of some Connivance to the Protestant Dissenters
to excuse that which in Humanity must be allowed to the
Papists, even without any leaning towards them, which must
not be supposed in those who are or shall be in the administration of publick Business; and it will follow that, according to
our Circumstances, the distribution of such connivance must
be made in such a manner, that the greatest part of it may fall
on the Protestant side, or else the Objections will be so strong,
and the Inferences so clear, that the Friends, as well as the
Enemies of the Crown, will be sure to take hold of them.

It will not be sufficient to say that the Papists may be
conniv'd at, because they are good Subjects and that the
Protestant Dissenters must suffer because they are ill ones;
these general Maxims will not convince discerning Men, neither
will any late Instances make them forget what passed at other
times in the World; both sides have had their Turns in being
good and ill Subjects. And therefore 'tis easie to imagine what
suspicions would arise in the present conjuncture, if such a
partial Argument as this should be impos'd upon us; the truth
is, this Matter speaks so much of it self, that it is not only
unnecessary, but it may be unmannerly to say any more
of it.

Our *Trimmer* therefore could wish, that since notwithstanding
the Laws which deny Churches to say Mass in, not only the
Exercise, but also the Ostentation of Popery is as well or better
performed in the Chappels of so many Foreign Ministers, where
the *English* openly resort in spight of Proclamations and Orders
of Council, which are grown to be as harmless things to them,
as the Popes Bulls and Excommunications are to Hereticks
who are out of his reach; I say he could wish that by a
seasonable as well as an equal piece of Justice, there might
be so much consideration had of the Protestant Dissenters, as
that there might be at some times, and at some places, a Veil
thrown over an Innocent and retired Conventicle; and that
                                                        such

such an Indulgence might be practis'd with less prejudice to the Church, or diminution to the Laws, it might be done so as to look rather like a kind Omission to enquire more strictly, than an allow'd Toleration of that which is against the Rule established.

Such a skilful hand as this is very Necessary in our Circumstances, and the Government by making no sort of Men entirely desperate, doth not only secure it self from Villainous attempts, but lay such a Foundation for healing and uniting Laws, when ever a Parliament shall meet, that the Seeds of Differences and Animosities between the several contending sides may (Heaven consenting) be for ever destroy'd.

The Trimmer's *Opinion concerning the Papists.*

TO speak of Popery leadeth me into such a Sea of Matter, that it is not easie to forbear launching into it, being invited by such a fruitful Theme, and by a variety never to be exhausted; but to confine it to the present Subject, I will only say a short word of the Religion it self; of its influences here at this time; and of our *Trimmer*'s Opinion in Relation to our manner of living with them.

If a Man would speak Maliciously of this Religion, one may say it is like those Diseases, where as long as one drop of the infection remaineth, there is still danger of having the whole Mass of Blood corrupted by it. In *Swedeland* there was an absolute cure, and nothing of Popery heard of, till Queen *Christina,* (whether mov'd by Arguments of this or the other World may not be good Manners to enquire) thought fit to change her Religion and Country, and to live at *Rome,* where she might find better judges of her Virtues, and less ungentle Censures of those Princely Liberties to which she was sometimes disposed, than she left at *Stockholme,* where the good breeding is as much inferior to that of *Rome* in general, as the Civility of the Religion, the Cardinals having rescued the Church

from

from those Clownish Methods the Fishermen had first introduc'd, and mended that Pattern so effectually, that a Man of that Age, if he should now come into the World, would not possibly know it.

In *Denmark* the Reformation was entire; in some States of *Germany*, as well as *Geneva*, the Cure was universal; but in the rest of the World where the Protestant Religion took place, the Popish humour was too tough to be totally expell'd, and so it was in *England*, tho' the Change was made with all the advantage imaginable to the Reformation, it being Countenanc'd and introduc'd by Legal Authority, and by that means, might have been perhaps as perfect as in any other Place, if the short Reign of *Edward* the 6th, and the succession of a Popish Queen had not given such advantage to that Religion, that it hath subsisted ever since under all the hardships that have been put upon it; it hath been a strong Compact Body, and made the more so by these Sufferings; it was not strong enough to prevail, but it was able, with the help of foreign support, to carry on an Interest which gave the Crown trouble, and to make a considerable (not to say dangerous) Figure in the Nation; so much as this could not have been done without some hopes, nor these hopes kept up without some reasonable grounds : In Queen *Elizabeth*'s time, the *Spanish* Zeal for their Religion, and the Revenge for 88, gave warmth to the Papists here, and above all the Right of the Queen of *Scots* to succeed, was while she lived sufficient to give them a better prospect of their Affairs : In King *James*'s time their hopes were supported by the Treaty of the *Spanish* Match, and his gentleness towards them, which they were ready to interpret more in their own Favour, than was either reasonable or became them, so little tenderness they have, even where it is most due, if the Interest of their Religion cometh in competition with it.

As for the late King, tho he gave the most glorious Evidence that ever Man did of his being a Protestant, yet, by the more than ordinary Influence the Queen was thought to have over him, and it so happening that the greatest part of his Anger was directed against the *Puritans*, there was such an advantage

to

to Men dispos'd to suspect, that they were ready to interpret it a leaning towards Popery, without which handle it was Morally impossible, that the ill-affected part of the Nation could ever have seduc'd the rest into a Rebellion.

That which help'd to confirm many well meaning Men in their Misapprehensions of the King, was the long and unusual intermission of Parliaments; so that every year that passed without one, made up a new Argument to increase their Suspicion, and made them presume that the Papists had a principal hand in keeping them off; This raised such Heats in Mens Minds, to think that Men who were obnoxious to the Laws, instead of being punished, should have Credit enough to secure themselves, even at the price of destroying the Fundamental Constitution, that it broke out into a Flame, which before it could be quenched, had almost reduc'd the Nation to Ashes.

Amongst the miserable Effects of that unnatural War, none hath been more fatal to us, than the forcing our Princes to breathe in another Air, and to receive the early impressions of a Foreign Education; the Barbarity of the *English,* towards the King and the Royal Family, might very well tempt him to think the better of every thing he found abroad, and might naturally produce more gentleness, at least, towards a Religion by which he was hospitably received, at the same time that he was thrown off and Persecuted by the Protestants, (tho' his own Subjects, to aggravate the Offence). The Queen Mother, (as generally Ladies do with Age) grew most devout and earnest in her Religion; and besides the temporal Rewards of getting larger Subsidies from the *French* Clergy, she had Motives of another kind, to perswade her to shew her Zeal; and since by the *Roman* Dispensatory, a Soul converted to the Church is a Soveraign Remedy, and layeth up a mighty stock of merit, she was solicitous to secure her self in all Events, and therefore first set upon the Duke of *Glocester,* who depended so much upon her good will, that she might for that reason have been induc'd to believe, the Conquest would not be difficult; but it so fell out, that he either from his own Constancy, or

that

that he had those near him by whom he was otherways advis'd,
chose rather to run away from her importunity, than by staying
to bear the continual weight of it : It is believ'd she had better
success with another of her Sons, who, if he was not quite
brought off from our Religion, at least such beginnings were
made, as made them very easie to be finish'd; his being of
a generous and aspiring Nature, and in that respect, less patient
in the drudgery of Arguing, might probably help to recommend
a Church to him that exempts the Laity from the vexation
of enquiring; perhaps he might (tho by mistake) look upon
that Religion as more favourable to the enlarged Power of
Kings, a consideration which might have its weight with a
young Prince in his warm blood, and that was brought up
in Arms.

I cannot hinder my self from a small digression, to consider
with admiration, that the old Lady of *Rome*, with all her
wrinkles, should yet have Charms, able to subdue great Princes;
so far from handsome, and yet so imperious; so painted, and
yet so pretending; after having abus'd, depos'd, and murther'd
so many of her Lovers, she still findeth others glad and proud
of their new Chains; a thing so strange to indifferent Judges,
that those who will allow no other Miracles in the Church of
Rome, must needs grant that this is one not to be contested;
she sitteth in her Shop, and selleth at dear Rates her Rattles
and her Hobby-Horses, whilst the deluded World still continueth to furnish her with Customers.

But whither am I carried with this Contemplation ? it is
high time to return to my Text, and to consider the wonderful
manner of the Kings coming home again, led by the hand of
Heaven, and called by the Voice of his own People, who
receiv'd him, if possible, with Joys equal to the Blessing of
Peace and Union which his Restauration brought along with
it ; by this there was an end put to the hopes some might have
abroad, of making use of his less happy Circumstances, to
throw him into Foreign Interests and Opinions, which had
been wholly inconsistent with our Religion, our Laws, and all
other things that are dear to us; yet for all this some of those

Tinctures

Tinctures and impressions might so far remain as, tho' they were very innocent in him, yet they might have ill effects here, by softning the Animosity which seemeth necessary to the Defender of the Protestant Faith, in opposition to such a powerful and irreconcilable an Enemy.

You may be sure, that among all the sorts of Men who apply'd themselves to the King at his first coming home, for his Protection, the Papists were not the last, nor as they fain would have flatter'd themselves, the least welcome, having their past Sufferings, as well as their present Professions to recommend them ; and there was something that look'd like a particular Consideration of them, since it so happened, that the Indulgence promised to Dissenters at *Breda*, was carried on in such a manner, that the Papists were to divide with them ; and tho' the Parliament, notwithstanding its Resignation to the Crown in all things, rejected with scorn and anger a Declaration fram'd for this purpose, yet the Birth and steps of it gave such an alarm, that Mens suspicions once raised, were not easily laid asleep again.

To omit other things, the breach of the Tripple League, and the *Dutch* War with its appurtenances, carried Jealousies to the highest pitch imaginable, and fed the hopes of one Party and the fears of the Other to such a degree, that some Critical Revolutions were generally expected, when the ill success of that War, and the Sacrifice *France* thought fit to make of the Papists here to their own interest abroad, gave them another Check; and the Act of enjoyning the Test to all in Offices, was thought to be no ill Bargain to the Nation, tho' bought at the Price of 1200000 pound, and the Money apply'd to continue the War against the *Dutch*, than which nothing could be more unpopular or less approved. Notwithstanding these discouragements, Popery is a Plant that may be mowed down, but the Root will still remain, and in spite of the Laws, it will sprout up and grow again ; especially if it should happen that there should be Men in Power, who in weeding it out of our Garden, will take care to Cherish and keep it alive ; and tho' the Law for excluding them from Places of

Trust was tolerably kept as to their outward Form, yet there were many Circumstances, which being improved by the quick-sighted Malice of ill affected Men, did help to keep up the World in their suspicions, and to blow up Jealousies to such a height both in and out of Parliament, that the remembrance of them is very unpleasant, and the Example so extravagant, that it is to be hop'd nothing in our Age like it will be re-attempted; but to come closer to the Case in question: in this Condition we stand with the Papists, what shall now be done, according to our *Trimmer*'s Opinion, in order to the better Bearing this grievance, since as I have said before, there is no hopes of being entirely free from it; Papists we must have among us, and if their Religion keep them from bringing honey to the Hive, let the Government try at least by gentle means to take away the Sting from them. The first Founda-tion to be laid is, that a distinct Consideration is to be had of the Popish Clergy, who have such an eternal Interest against all accommodation, that it is a hopeless thing to propose any thing to them less than all; their Stomachs have been set for it ever since the Reformation, they have pinned themselves to a Principal that admits no mean: they believe Protestants will be damn'd, and therefore by an extraordinary Effect of Christian Charity, they would destroy one half of *England* that the other might be saved; then for this World, they must be in possession for God Almighty, to receive his Rents for him, not to accompt till the Day of Judgment, which is a good kind of Tenure, and ye cannot well blame the good Men, that will stir up the Laity to run any hazard in order to the getting them restor'd. What is it to the Priest, if the deluded Zealot undoeth himself in the Attempt? he singeth Masses as jollily, and with as good a Voice at *Rome* or *St. Omers* as ever he did; is a single Man, and can have no wants but such as may be easily supply'd, yet that he may not seem altogether insensible, or ungrateful to those that are his Martyrs, he is ready to assure their Executors, and if they please, will procure a Grant *sub Annulo Piscatoris*, that the good Man by being hanged, hath got a good Bargain, and sav'd the singeing of

some

some hundred of years, which he would else have had in
Purgatory. There's no Cure for this Order of Men, no Expedient to be propos'd, so that tho the utmost severity of
the Laws against them may in some sort be mitigated, yet no
Treaty can be made with Men who in this Case have left themselves no free Will, but are so muffled by Zeal, tyed by Vows,
and kept up by such unchangeable Maxims of the Priesthood,
that they are to be left as desperate Patients, and look'd upon
as Men that will continue in an Eternal State of Hostility, till
the Nation is entirely subdued to them. It is then only the
Lay Papists that are capable of being treated with, and we are
to examine of what temper they are, and what Arguments are
the most likely to prevail upon them, and how far 'tis adviseable for the Government to be Indulgent to them ; the Lay
Papists generally keep their Religion, rather because they will
not break Company with those of their Party, than out of any
settled Zeal that hath Root in them ; most of them do by the
Mediation of the Priests Marry amongst one another, to keep
up an Ignorant Position by hearing only one side ; others by
a mistake look upon it as they do upon Escutcheons, the more
Antient Religion of the two ; and as some Men of a good
Pedigree will despise meaner Men, tho' never so much superior
to them by Nature, so these undervalue Reformation as an
Upstart, and think there is more Honour in supporting an old
Errour, than in embracing what seemeth to them to be a new
Truth ; the Laws have made them Men of Pleasure, by excluding them from Publick Business, and it happeneth well
they are so, since they will the more easily be perswaded by
Arguments of Ease and Conveniency to them ; they have not
put off the Man in general, nor the *Englishman* in particular,
those who in the late storm against them went into other
Countries, tho they had all the Advantage that might recommend them to a good Reception, yet in a little time they chose
to steal over again, and live here with hazard, rather than
abroad with security. There is a Smell in our Native Earth,
better than all the Perfumes in the East ; there is something
in a Mother, tho never so Angry, that the Children will more

naturally

naturally trust Her, than the Studied Civilities of Strangers, let them be never so Hospitable; therefore 'tis not adviseable nor agreeing with the Rules of Governing Prudence, to provoke Men by hardships to forget that Nature, which else is sure to be of our side.

When these Men by fair Usage are put again into their right Senses, they will have quite differing Reflections from those which Rigour and Persecution had raised in them: A Lay Papist will first consider his Abby-Lands, which notwithstanding whatever hath or can be alledged, must sink considerably in the Value, the moment that Popery prevails; and it being a disputable Matter, whether Zeal might not in a little time get the better of the Law in that case, a considering Man will admit that as an Argument to perswade him to be content with things as they are, rather than run this or any other hazard by Change, in which perhaps he may have no other Advantage, than that his now humble Confessor may be rais'd to a Bishoprick, and from thence look down superciliously upon his Patron, or which is worse, run to take Possession for God Almighty of his Abby, in such a manner as the usurping Landlord (as he will then be called) shall hardly be admitted to be so much as a Tenant to his own Lands, lest his Title should prejudge that of the Church, which will then be the Landlord; he will think what disadvantage 'tis to be looked upon as a separate Creature, depending upon a Foreign Interest and Authority, and for that reason, expos'd to the Jealousie and Suspicion of his Country-men; he will reflect what an Incumbrance it is to have his House a Pasture for hungry Priests to graze in, which have such a never-failing Influence upon the Foolish, which is the greatest part of every Man's Family, that a Man's Dominion, even over his own Children, is mangled, and divided, if not totally undermin'd by them; then to be subject to what Arbitrary Taxes the Popish Convocation shall impose upon him for the carrying on the Common Interest of that Religion, under Penalty of being mark'd out for half an Heretick by the rest of the Party; to have no share in Business, no opportunity of shewing his own Value to the World; to live

at

at the best an useless, and by others to be thought a dangerous Member of the Nation where he is born, is a burthen to a generous Mind that cannot be taken off by all the Pleasure of a lazy unmanly life, or by the nauseous enjoyment of a dull Plenty, that produceth no food for the Mind, which will be considered in the first place by a Man that hath a Soul ; when he shall think, that if his Religion, after his wading through a Sea of Blood, come at last to prevail, it would infinitely lessen, if not entirely destroy the Glory, Riches, Strength and Liberty of his own Country, and what a Sacrifice is this to make to *Rome,* where they are wise enough to wonder there should be such Fools in the World, as to venture, struggle, and contend, nay even die Martyrs for that which, should it succeed, would prove a Judgment instead of a Blessing to them ; he will conclude that the advantages of throwing some of their Children back again to God Almighty when they have too many of them, are not equal to the Inconveniencies they may either feel or fear, by continuing their separation from the Religion established.

Temporal things will have their weight in the World, and tho Zeal may prevail for a time, and get the better in a Skirmish, yet the War endeth generally on the side of Flesh and Blood, and will do so till Mankind is another thing than it is at present : And therefore a wise Papist in cold Blood, considering these and many other Circumstances, which 'twill be worth his pains to see if he can unmuffle himself from the Mask of Infallibility, will think it reasonable to set his Imprison'd Senses at Liberty, and that he hath a right to see with his own Eyes, hear with his own Ears, and judge by his own Reason ; the consequence of which might probably be, that weighing things in a right Scale, and seeing them in their true Colours, he would distinguish between the merit of suffering for a good Cause, and the foolish ostentation of drawing inconveniences upon himself ; and therefore will not be unwilling to be convinc'd that our Protestant Creed may make him happy in the other World, and the easier in this. A few of such wise Proselytes would by their Example draw so many after them, that the Party would insensibly melt away, and in a little time, without

any

any angry word, we should come to an Union that all Good
Men would have Reason to rejoyce at ; but we are not to presume upon these Conversions, without preparing Men for them
by kind and reconciling Arguments ; nothing is so against our
Nature, as to believe those can be in the right who are too hard
upon us ; there is a deformity in every thing that doth us hurt,
it will look scurvily in our Eye while the smart continueth, and
a Man must have an extraordinary Measure of Grace, to think
well of a Religion that reduceth him and his Family to Misery ;
in this respect our *Trimmer* would consent to the mitigation
of such Laws as were made (as it is said King *Henry* VIII. got
Queen *Elizabeth*) in a heat against *Rome* : It may be said that
even States as well as private Men are subject to Passion ; a just
indignation of a villainous Attempt produceth at the same time
such Remedies, as perhaps are not without some mixture of
Revenge, and therefore tho time cannot Repeal a Law, it may
by a Natural Effect soften the Execution of it ; there is less
danger to Rouse a Lyon when at Rest, than to awake Laws that
were intended to have their times of Sleeping, nay more than
that, in some Cases their Natural periods of Life, dying of themselves without the Solemnity of being revok'd any otherwise
than by the common consent of Mankind, who do cease to
Execute when the Reasons in great Measure fail that first
Created and Justify'd the Rigour of such unusual Penalties.

Our *Trimmer* is not eager to pick out some places in History against this or any other Party ; quite contrary, is very
sollicitous to find out any thing that may be healing, and tend
to an Agreement ; but to prescribe the means of this Gentleness
so as to make it effectual, must come from the only place that
can furnish Remedies for this Cure, *viz.* a Parliament ; in the
mean time, it is to be wished there may be such a mutual calm-
ness of Mind, as that the Protestants might not be so jealous,
as still to smell the Match that was to blow up the King and
both Houses in the Gunpowder Treason, or to start at every
appearance of Popery, as if it were just taking Possession. On
the other side, let not the Papists suffer themselves to be led
by any hopes, tho never so flattering, to a Confidence or Ostentation

tation which must provoke Men to be less kind to them ; let them use Modesty on their sides, and the Protestants Indulgence on theirs ; and by this means there would be an overlooking of all Venial Faults, a tacit connivence at all things that do not carry Scandal with them, and would amount to a kind of Natural Dispensation with the severe Laws, since there would be no more Accusers to be found, when the occasions of Anger and Animosity are once remov'd ; let the Papists in the mean time remember, that there is a respect due from all lesser numbers to greater, a deference to be paid by an Opinion that is Exploded, to one that is Established ; such a Thought well digested will have an influence upon their Behaviour, and produce such a Temper as must win the most eager Adversaries out of their ill Humour to them, and give them a Title to all the Favour that may be consistent with the Publick Peace and Security.

The Trimmer's *Opinion in Relation to things abroad.*

THE World is so compos'd, that it is hard, if not impossible, for a Nation not to be a great deal involv'd in the fate of their Neighbours, and tho by the felicity of our Situation, we are more Independant than any other People, yet we have in all Ages been concern'd for our own sakes in the Revolutions abroad. There was a time when *England* was the over balancing Power of Christendom, and that either by Inheritance or Conquest, the better part of *France* receiv'd Laws from us ; after that we being reduc'd into our own Limits, *France* and *Spain* became the Rivals for the Universal Monarchy, and our third Power, tho in it self less than either of the other, hapned to be Superiour to any of them, by that choice we had of throwing the Scales on that side to which we gave our Friendship. I do not know whether this Figure did not make us as great as our former Conquest ; to be a perpetual Umpire of two great

contending

contending Powers, who gave us all their Courtship, and offer'd all their Incense at our Altar, whilst the Fate of either Prince seemed to depend upon the Oracles we delivered ; for the King of *England* to sit on his Throne, as in the Supream Court of Justice, to which the two great Monarchs appeal, pleading their Cause, and expecting their Sentence declaring which side was in the right, or at least if we pleas'd which side should have the better of it, was a piece of Greatness which was peculiar to us, and no wonder if we endeavoured to preserve it, as we did for a considerable time, it being our Safety, as well as Glory, to maintain it ; but by a Fatality upon our Councils, or by the re-fin'd Policy of this latter Age, we have thought fit to use industry to destroy this mighty Power, which we have so long enjoyed ; and that equality between the Two Monarchs, which we might for ever have preserved, hath been chiefly broken by us, whose Interest it was above all others to maintain it ; when one of them, like the overflowing of the Sea, had gained more upon the other than our convenience, or indeed our safety, would allow, instead of mending the Banks, or making new ones, we our selves with our own hands helpt to cut them, to invite and make way for a farther Inundation. *France* and *Spain* have had their several turns in making use of our Mistakes, and we have been formerly as deaf to the Instances of the then weaker part of the World to help them against the House of *Austria*, as we can now be to the Earnestness of *Spain*, that we would assist them against the Power of *France*. *Gondamar* was as sawcy, and as powerful too in King *James* his Court, as any French Ambassadour can have been at any time since ; Men talked as wrong then on the *Spanish* side, and made their Court by it as well as any can have done since by talking as much for the *French* ; so that from that time, instead of weighing in a wise Balance the power of either Crown, it looketh as if we had learnt only to weigh the Pensions, and take the heaviest.

It would be tedious, as well as unwelcome, to recapitulate all our wrong steps, so that I will go no farther than the King's Restauration, at which time the Balance was on the side of *France*, and that by the means of *Cromwell*, who for a separate
Interest

Interest of his own had sacrificed that of the Nation, by joining with the stronger side, to suppress the Power of *Spain*, which he ought to have supported. Such a Method was natural enough to an Usurper, and shew'd he was not the Lawful Father of the People, by his having so little care of them; and the Example coming from that hand, one would think should, for that Reason, be less likely to be follow'd. But to go on, home cometh the King, followed with Courtships from all Nations abroad, of which some did it not only to make them forget how familiarly they had us'd him when he was in other Circumstances, but to bespeak the Friendship of a Prince, who besides his other Greatness, was yet more considerable by being re-established by the love of his people. *France* had an Interest either to dispose us to so much good will, or at least to put us into such a Condition, that we might give no Opposition to their Designs; and *Flanders* being a perpetual Object in their Eye, a lasting Beauty for which they have an incurable passion, and not being kind enough to consent to them, they meditated to commit a Rape upon her, which they thought would not be easie to do, while *England* and *Holland* were agreed to rescue her, when-ever they should hear her cry out for help to them; to this end they put in practice Seasonable and Artificial Whispers, to widen things between us and the States. *Amboyna* and the Fishery must be talk'd of here; the freedom of the Seas, and the preservation of Trade must be insinuated there; and there being combustible matter on both sides, in a little time it took Fire, which gave those that kindled it, sufficient cause to smile and hug themselves, to see us both fall into the Net they had laid for us. And it is observable and of good example to us, if we will take it, That their Design being to set us together at Cuffs to weaken us, they kept themselves Lookers-on till our Victories began to break the Balance; then the King of *France*, like a wise Prince, was resolved to support the beaten side, and would no more let the Power of the Sea, than we ought to suffer the Monarchy of *Europe*, to fall into one hand: In pursuance to this, he took part with the *Dutch*, and in a little time made himself Umpire of the Peace between us; some time after, upon pretence of his

Queen's

Queen's Title to part of *Flanders*, by Right of Devolution, he
falleth into it with a mighty Force, for which the *Spaniard* was
so little prepared, that he made a very swift Progress, and
had such a Torrent of undisputed Victory, that *England* and
Holland, tho the Wounds they had given one another were yet
green, being struck with the apprehension of so near a danger
to them, thought it necessary, for their own defence, to make
up a sudden League, into which *Sweden* was taken to interpose
for a Peace between the two Crowns.

This had so good an effect, that *France* was stopt in its Career,
and the Peace of *Aix le Chapelle* was a little after concluded.
'Twas a forc'd put; and tho *France* wisely dissembled their
inward dissatisfaction, yet from that very moment they resolv'd
to unty the Triple knot, whatever it cost them; for his
Christian Majesty, after his Conquering Meals, ever riseth
with a stomach, and he lik'd the Pattern so well, that it gave
him a longing desire to have the whole Piece. Amongst the
other means used for the attaining this end, the sending over
the Dutchess of *Orleans*, was not the least powerful; she was
a very welcome Guest here, and her own Charms and Dexterity
joined with other Advantages that might help her perswasions,
gave her such an Ascendant, that she should hardly fail of
success. One of the Preliminaries of her Treaty, tho a trivial
thing in it self, yet was considerable in the Consequence, as
very small circumstances often are in relation to the Government
of the World. About this time a general Humour, in opposition
to *France*, had made us throw off their Fashion, and put on
Vests, that we might look more like a distinct People, and not
be under the servility of imitation, which ever payeth a greater
deference to the Original, than is consistent with the Equality
all Independent Nations should pretend to; *France* did not
like this small beginning of ill Humours, at least of Emulation,
and wisely considering that it is a natural Introduction first to
make the World their Apes, that they may be afterwards their
Slaves, it was thought that one of the Instructions Madam
brought along with her, was to laugh us out of these Vests;
which she performed so effectually, that in a moment, like so
many

many Footmen who had quitted their Masters Livery, we all took it again, and returned to our old Service ; so that the very time of doing it gave a very critical Advantage to *France*, since it lookt like an Evidence of our returning to their Interest, as well as to their Fashion, and would give such a distrust of us to our new Allies, that it might facilitate the dissolution of the knot, which tied them so within their bounds, that they were very impatient till they were freed from the restraint.

But the Lady had a more extended Commission than this and without doubt laid the Foundation of a new strict Alliance, quite contrary to the other in which we had been so lately engag'd. And of this there were such early appearances, that the World began to look upon us as falling into Apostacy from the common Interest. Notwithstanding all this, *France* did not neglect at the same time to give good words to the *Dutch*, and even to feed them with hopes of supporting them against us, when on a sudden, that never to be forgotten Declaration of War against them cometh out, only to vindicate his own Glory, and to revenge the Injuries done to his Brother in *England*, by which he became our Second in this Duel; so humble can this Prince be, when at the same time he doth us more Honour than we deserve, he layeth a greater share of the blame upon our Shoulders, than did naturally belong to us ; the particulars of that War, our part in it while we staid in it, and when we were out of breath, our leaving the *French* to make an end of it, are things too well known to make it necessary, and too unwelcome in themselves to incite me to repeat them ; only the wisdom of *France* is in this to be observ'd, That when we had made a separate Peace, which left them single to oppose the united Force of the Confederates, they were so far from being angry, that they would not shew so much as the least coldness, hoping to get as much by our Mediation for a Peace, as they would have expected from our Assistance in the War, our Circumstances at that time considered ; This seasonable piece of Indulgence in not reproaching us, but rather allowing those Necessities of State which we gave for our Excuse, was such an engaging Method, that it went a great way to keep us still

in

in their Chains, when, to the Eye of the World, we had absolutely broke loose from them : And by what pass'd afterwards
at *Nimeguen,* tho the King's Neutrality gave him the outward
Figure of a Mediator, it appear'd that his Interposition was
extremely suspected of Partiality by the Confederates, who upon
that Ground did both at and before the Conclusion of that
Treaty, treat his Ministers there with a great deal of neglect.
In this Peace as well as in that of the *Pyreneans* and *Aix le
Chapelle,* the King of *France,* at the Moment of making it, had
the thought of breaking it ; for a very little time after he
broach'd his Pretensions upon *Alost*; which were things that
if they had been offer'd by a less formidable hand, would have
been smiled at; but ill Arguments being seconded by good
Armies, carry such a power with them, that naked sense is
a very unequal Adversary.   It was thought that these airy
Claims were chiefly rais'd with the prospect of getting *Luxenburg* for the Equivalent ; and this Opinion was confirm'd by the
blocking it up afterwards, pretending to the Country of *Chimay,*
that it might be entirely surrounded by the French Dominions,
and it was so pressed that it might have fallen in a little time,
if the King of *France* had not sent Orders to his Troops to
retire, and his Christian Generosity which was assign'd for the
reason of it, made the World smile, since it is seen how differently
his devout Zeal worketh in *Hungary* : that specious Reason
was in many respects ill-tim'd, and *France* it self gave it so
faintly, that at the very time it look'd out of Countenance ;
the true ground of his Retiring is worth our observation ; for
at the instance of the Confederates, Offices were done, and
Memorials given, but all ineffectual till the word *Parliament*
was put into them ; that powerful word had such an effect, that
even at that distance it rais'd the Seige, which may convince us of
what efficacy the King of *England*'s words are, when he will give
them their full weight, and threaten with his *Parliament*; it is
then that he appeareth that great Figure we ought to represent
him in our Minds, the Nation his Body, he the Head, and joined
with that Harmony, that every word he pronounceth is the
Word of a Kingdom : Such words, as appeareth by this
                                                          Example,

Example, are as effectual as Fleets and Armies, because they can create them, and without this his words sound abroad like a faint Whisper, that is either not heard, or (which is worse) not minded. But tho *France* had made this step of forced Compliance, it did not mean to leave off the pursuit of their pretensions; and therefore immediately proposed the Arbitration to the King; but it appear'd, that notwithstanding his *Merit* towards the Confederates, in saving *Luxenburg*, the remembrances of what had passed before, had left such an ill taste in their *Mouths*, that they could not Relish our being put into a Condition to dispose of their Interests, and therefore declin'd it by insisting upon a general Treaty, to which *France* hath ever since continued to be averse; our great earnestness also to perswade the Confederates to consent to it, was so unusual, and so suspicious a method, that it might naturally make them believe, that *France* spake to them by our *Mouth*, and for that Reason, if there had been no other, might hinder the accepting it; and so little care hath been taken to cure this or other Jealousies the Confederates may have entertain'd, that quite contrary, their *Ministers* here every day take fresh Alarms, from what they observe in small, as well as in greater Circumstances; and they being apt both to take and improve apprehensions of this kind, draw such Inferences from them, as make them entirely despair of us.

Thus we now stand, far from being Innocent Spectators of our Neighbours Ruine, and by a fatal mistake forgetting what a Certain Fore-runner it is to our own; and now it is time our *Trimmer* should tell something of his Opinion, upon this present State of things abroad; he first professeth to have no Biass, either for or against *France*, and that his thoughts are wholly directed by the Interest of his own Country; he alloweth, and hath read that *Spain* used the same Methods, when it was in its heighth, as *France* doth now, and therefore it is not Partiality that moveth him, but the just fear which all reasonable Men must be possess'd with, of an over-growing Power; *Ambition* is a devouring Beast, when it hath swallow'd one Province, instead of being cloyed, it hath so much the greater *Stomach*
to

to another, and being fed, becometh still the more hungry; so
that for the Confederates to expect a security from any thing
but their own united strength, is a most miserable fallacy; and
if they cannot resist the *Incroachments* of *France* by their Arms,
it is in vain for them to dream of any other means of preservation; it would have the better grace, besides the saving so much
Blood and Ruin, to give up all at once; make a Present of
themselves, to appease this haughty Monarch, rather than be
whisper'd, flatter'd, or cozened out of their liberty. Nothing is
so soft as the first applications of a greater Prince, to engage
a weaker, but that smiling Countenance is but a Vizard, it is
not the true Face; for as soon as their turn is serv'd, the Courtship flies to some other Prince or State, where the same part
is to be acted over again; leaveth the old mistaken Friend to
Neglect and Contempt, and like an insolent Lover to a Cast off
Mistress, Reproaches her with that Infamy, of which he himself was the Author. *Sweden, Bavaria, Palatine, &c.* may by
their Fresh Examples, teach other Princes what they are
reasonably to expect, and what Snakes are hid under the
Flowers the Court of *France* so liberally throweth upon them
whilst they can be useful. The various Methods and deep
Intrigues, with the differing Notes in several Countries, do not
only give suspicion, but assurance that every thing is put in
Practice, by which universal Monarchy may be obtain'd. Who
can reconcile the withdrawing of his Troops from *Luxenburg*, in
consideration of the War in *Hungary*, which was not then declared,
and presently after encouraging the *Turk* to take *Vienna*, and
consequently to destroy the Empire? Or who can think that
the Persecution of the Poor Protestants of *France*, will be
accepted of God, as an Atonement for hazarding the loss of
the whole Christian Faith? Can he be thought in earnest, when
he seem'd to be afraid of the *Spaniards*, and for that reason
must have *Luxenburg*, and that he cannot be safe from *Germany*,
unless he is in possession of *Strasburg?* All Injustice and
Violence must in it self be grievous, but the aggravations of
supporting 'em by false Arguments, and insulting Reasons, has
something in it yet more provoking than the Injuries themselves;

selves; and the World hath ground enough to apprehend, from such a Method of arguing, that even their Senses are to be subdu'd as well as their Liberties. Then the variety of Arguments used by *France* in several Countries is very observable: In *England* and *Denmark,* nothing insisted on but the Greatness and Authority of the Crown; on the other side, the Great Men in *Poland* are commended, who differ in Opinion with the King, and they argue like Friends to the Privilege of the Dyet, against the separate Power of the Crown: In *Sweden* they are troubled that the King should have chang'd something there of late, by his single Authority, from the antient and settled Authority and Constitutions: At *Ratisbone,* the most Christian Majesty taketh the Liberties of all the Electors and free States into his Protection, and telleth them the Emperour is a dangerous Man, an aspiring Hero, that would infallibly devour them, if he was not at hand to resist him on their behalf; but above all in *Holland,* he hath the most obliging tenderness for the *Commonwealth,* and is in such disquiets, lest it should be invaded by the Prince of *Orange,* that they can do no less in gratitude, than undo themselves when he bids them, to show how sensible they are of his excessive good Nature; yet in spight of all these Contradictions, there are in the World such refin'd *States-men,* as will upon their Credit affirm the following Paradoxes to be real truth; first that *France* alone is sincere and keepeth its Faith, and consequently that it is the only Friend we can rely upon; that the King of *France,* of all Men living, hath the least mind to be a Conqueror; that he is a sleepy, tame Creature, void of all Ambition, a poor kind of a Man, that hath no farther thoughts than to be quiet; that he is charm'd by his Friendship to us; that it is impossible he should ever do us hurt, and therefore tho *Flanders* was lost, it would not in the least concern us; that he would fain help the Crown of *England* to be absolute, which would be to take pains to put it into a condition to oppose him, as it is, and must be our Interest, as long as he continueth in such an overballancing Power and Greatness.

Such a Creed as this, if once receiv'd, might prepare our
belief

belief for greater things, and as he that taught Men to eat a Dagger, began first with a Pen knife; so if we can be prevail'd with to digest the smaller Mistakes, we may at last make our stomachs strong enough for that of Transubstantiation. Our *Trimmer* cannot easily be converted out of his senses by these State Sophisters, and yet he hath no such peevish Obstinacy as to reject all Correspondence with *France* because we ought to be apprehensive of the too great power of it; he would not have the kings Friendship to the Confederates extended to the involving him in any unreasonable or dangerous Engagements, neither would he have him lay aside the consideration of his better establishment at home, out of his excessive Zeal to secure his Allies abroad; but sure there might be a Mean between these two opposite Extreams, and it may be wish'd that our Friendship with *France* should at least be so bounded, that it may consist with the humour as well as the Interest of *England*. There is no Woman but hath her fears of contracting too near an intimacy with a much greater Beauty, because it exposeth her too often to a Comparison that is not advantageous to her; and sure it may become a Prince to be as jealous of his Dignity, as a Lady can be of her good looks, and to be as much out of Countenance, to be thought an humble Companion to so much a greater Power. To be always seen in an ill Light, to be so darkned by the brightness of a greater Star, is somewhat mortifying; and when *England* might ride Admiral at the head of the Confederates, to look like the Kitching-Yacht to the Grand *Louis*, is but a scurvy Figure for us to make in the Map of *Christendom*; it would rise upon our *Trimmer*'s stomach, if ever (which God forbid) the power of calling and intermitting Parliaments here should be transferred to the Crown of *France*, and that all the opportunities of our own settlements at home should give way to their Projects abroad, and that our Interests should be so far sacrific'd to our Compliance, that all the Omnipotence of *France* can never make us full amends for it. In the mean time, he shrinketh at the dismal prospect he can by no means drive away from his thoughts, that when *France* hath gather'd all the fruit arising from our Mistakes, and that we

can

can bear no more with them, they will cut down the Tree and throw it into the fire. All this while, some Superfine States-Men, to comfort us, would fain perswade the World that this or that accident may save us, and for all that is or ought to be dear to us, would have us to rely wholly upon Chance, not considering that Fortune is Wisdoms Creature, and that God Almighty loves to be on the Wisest as well as the Strongest side; therefore this is such a miserable shift, such a shameful Evasion, that they would be laught to death for it, if the ruining Consequence of this Mistake did not more dispose Men to rage, and a detestation of it.

Our *Trimmer* is far from Idolatry in other things, in one thing only he cometh near it, his Country is in some degree his Idol; he doth not Worship the Sun, because 'tis not peculiar to us, it rambles about the World, and is less kind to us than others; but for the Earth of *England*, tho perhaps inferior to that of many places abroad, to him there is Divinity in it, and he would rather dye, than see a spire of *English* Grass trampled down by a Foreign Trespasser: He thinketh there are a great many of his mind, for all plants are apt to taste of the Soyl in which they grow, and we that grow here, have a Root that produceth in us a Stalk of English Juice, which is not to be changed by grafting or foreign infusion; and I do not know whether any thing less will prevail, than the Modern Experiment, by which the Blood of one Creature is transmitted into another; according to which, before the *French* blood can be let into our Bodies, every drop of our own must be drawn out of them.

Our *Trimmer* cannot but lament, that by a Sacrifice too great for one Nation to make to another, we should be like a rich Mine, made useless only for want of being wrought, and that the Life and Vigour which should move us against our Enemies is miserably apply'd to tear our own Bowels; that being made by our happy situation, not only safer, but if we please greater too, than other Countries which far exceed us in extent; that having Courage by Nature, Learning by Industry, and Riches by Trade, we should corrupt all these Advantages, so as to make them insignificant, and by a fatality which seemeth peculiar to

us, misplace our active rage one against another, whilst we are
turn'd into Statues on that side where lieth our greatest danger ;
to be unconcern'd not only at our Neighbours ruine but our
own, and let our Island lie like a great Hulk in the Sea, without
Rudder or Sail, all the Men cast away in her, or as if we were all
Children in a great Cradle, and rockt asleep to a foreign Tune.

I say when our *Trimmer* representeth to his Mind, our
Roses blasted and discolour'd, whilst the Lilies Triumph and
grow Insolent upon the Comparison ; when he considereth our
own once flourishing Lawrel, now withered and dying, and
nothing left us but a remembrance of a better part in History
than we shall make in the next Age, which will be no more to
us than an Escutcheon hung upon our Door when we are dead ;
when he foreseeth from hence growing Infamy from abroad,
confusion at home, and all this without the possibility of a Cure,
in respect of the voluntary fetters good Men put upon
themselves by their Allegiance ; without a good measure of
preventing Grace, he would be tempted to go out of the World
like a *Roman* Philosopher, rather than endure the burthen of
Life under such a discouraging Prospect. But Mistakes, as all
other things, have their Periods, and many times the nearest way
to Cure, is not to oppose them, but stay till they are crusht with
their own weight : for Nature will not allow any thing to
continue long that is violent ; violence is a wound, and as a
wound must be curable in a little time, or else 'tis Mortal, but
a Nation comes near to be Immortal, therefore the wound will
one time or another be cured, tho perhaps by such rough
Methods, if too long forborn, as may even make the best
Remedies we can prepare, to be at the same time a Melancholy
Contemplation to us ; there is but one thing (God Almighties
Providence excepted) to support a Man from sinking under
these afflicting thoughts, and that is the hopes we draw singly
from the King himself, without the mixture of any other
consideration.

Tho the Nation was lavish of their Kindness to him at his first
coming, yet there remaineth still a stock of Warmth in Mens
Hearts for him. Besides, the good Influences of his happy
                                                    Planet

Planet are not yet all spent, and tho the Stars of Men past their youth are generally declining, and have less Force, like the Eyes of decaying Beauties, yet by a Blessing peculiar to himself, we may yet hope to be sav'd by his Autumnal Fortune ; He hath something about him that will draw down a healing Miracle for his and our Deliverance ; a Prince which seemeth fitted for such an offending Age, in which Mens Crimes have been so general, that the not forgiving his People had been the destroying of them ; whose Gentleness giveth him a natural Dominion that hath no bounds, with such a noble mixture of Greatness and Condescention, an engaging Look, that disarmeth Men of their ill Humours, and their Resentments ; something in him that wanteth a Name, and can be no more defined than it can be resisted ; a Gift of Heaven, of its last finishing, where it will be peculiarly kind ; the only Prince in the World that dares be familiar, or that hath right to triumph over those forms which were first invented to give awe to those who could not judge, and to hide Defects from those that could ; a Prince that hath exhausted himself by his Liberality, and endanger'd himself by his Mercy ; who out-shineth by his own Light and natural Virtues all the varnish of studied Acquisitions ; his Faults are like Shades to a good Picture, or like Allay to Gold, to make it the more useful ; he may have some, but for any Man to see them through so many reconciling Virtues, is a Sacrilegious piece of ill nature, of which no generous Mind can be guilty ; a Prince that deserveth to be lov'd for his own sake, even without the help of a Comparison ; our Love, our Duty, and our Danger all join to cement our Obedience to him ; in short, whatever he can do, it is no more possible for us to be angry with him, than with the Bank that secureth us from the raging Sea, the kind Shade that hideth us from the scorching Sun, the welcome Hand that reacheth us a Reprieve, or with the Guardian Angel, that rescueth our Souls from the devouring Jaws of wretched Eternity.

CONCLUSION.

TO Conclude, our *Trimmer* is so fully satisfy'd of the Truth of those Principles by which he is directed in reference to the Publick, that he will neither be Bawled, Threatned, Laught, nor Drunk out of them; and instead of being converted by the Arguments of his Adversaries to their Opinions, he is very much confirmed in his own by them; he professeth solemnly that were it in his Power to chuse, he would rather have his Ambition bounded by the Commands of a Great and Wise Master, than let it range with a Popular Licence, tho' crown'd with success; yet he cannot commit such a Sin against the glorious thing call'd Liberty, nor let his Soul stoop so much below it self, as to be content without repining to have his Reason wholly subdu'd, or the Privilege of Acting like a sensible Creature torn from him by the imperious Dictates of unlimited Authority, in what hand soever it happens to be plac'd. What is there in this that is so Criminal, as to deserve the Penalty of that most singular Apophthegm, *A* Trimmer *is worse than a Rebel*? What do angry men ail to rail so against Moderation; doth it not look as if they were going to some very scurvy Extreme, that is too strong to be digested by the more considering part of Mankind? These Arbitrary Methods, besides the injustice of them, are (God be thanked) very unskilful too, for they fright the Birds, by talking so loud, from coming into the Nets that are laid for them; and when Men agree to rifle a House, they seldom give warning, or blow a Trumpet; but there are some small States-Men, who are so full charg'd with their own Expectations, that they cannot contain. And kind Heaven by sending such a seasonable Curse upon their undertakings, hath made their ignorance an Antidote against their Malice; some of these cannot treat peaceably; yielding will not satisfy them, they will have men by storm; there are others, that must have Plots, to make their Service more necessary, and have an Interest to keep them alive, since

they

they are to live upon them ; and perswade the King to retrench
his own Greatness, so as to shrink into the head of a
Party, which is the betraying him into such an Unprincely
mistake, and to such a wilful diminution of himself, that they
are the last Enemies he ought to allow himself to forgive ; such
Men, if they could, would prevail with the Sun to shine only
upon them and their Friends, and to leave all the rest of the
World in the dark ; this is a very unusual Monopoly, and may
come within the Equity of the Law, which maketh it Treason
to Imprison the King, when such unfitting bounds are put to his
Favour, and he confin'd to the narrow limits of a particular set
of Men, that would inclose him ; these Honest and only Loyal
Gentlemen, if they may be allow'd to bear Witness for
themselves, make a King their Engine, and degrade him into a
property at the very time that their Flattery would make him
believe they paid Divine Worship to him ; besides these there is
a flying Squadron on both sides, that are afraid the World
should agree, small dabblers in Conjuring, that raise angry
Apparitions to keep Men from being reconcil'd, like Wasps that
fly up and down, buz and sting to keep Men unquiet ; but
these Insects are commonly short-liv'd Creatures, and no doubt
in a little time Mankind will be rid of them ; they were Gyants
at least who fought once against Heaven, but for such Pigmies
as these to contend against it, is such a provoking Folly, that
the insolent Bunglers ought to be laught and hist out of the
World for it ; they should consider there is a Soul in that great
body of the People, which may for a time be drowzy and
unactive, but when the Leviathan is rouz'd, it moveth like an
angry Creature, and will neither be convinc'd nor resisted : the
People can never agree to shew their united Powers, till they
are extremely tempted and provoked to it, so that to apply
Cupping-Glasses to a great Beast naturally dispos'd to sleep,
and to force the Tame thing whether it will or no to be Valiant,
must be learnt out of some other Book than *Machiavil*, who
would never have prescrib'd such a preposterous Method.   It is
to be remembred, that if Princes have Law and Authority on
their sides, the People on theirs may have Nature, which is a
                                                    formidable

formidable Adversary; Duty, Justice, Religion, nay, even
Humane Prudence too, biddeth the People suffer any thing
rather than resist; but uncorrected Nature, where e're it feels
the smart will run to the nearest Remedy. Mens Passions in
this Case are to be consider'd as well as their Duty, let it be
never so strongly enforc'd, for if their Passions are provok'd,
they being as much a part of us as our Limbs, they lead Men
into a short way of Arguing, that admitteth no distinction,
and from the foundation of Self-Defence they will draw
Inferences that will have miserable effects upon the quiet of a
Government.

Our *Trimmer* therefore dreads a general discontent, because
he thinketh it differeth from a Rebellion, only as a Spotted
Fever doth from the Plague, the same Species under a lower
degree of Malignity; it worketh several ways; sometimes like
a slow Poyson that hath its Effects at a great distance from the
time it was given, sometimes like dry Flax prepared to catch at
the first Fire, or like Seed in the ground ready to sprout upon
the first Shower; in every shape 'tis fatal, and our *Trimmer*
thinketh no pains or precaution can be so great as to prevent it.

In short he thinketh himself in the right, grounding his
Opinion upon that Truth, which equally hateth to be under the
Oppressions of wrangling Sophistry of the one hand, or the
short dictates of mistaken Authority on the other.

Our *Trimmer* adoreth the Goddess Truth, tho' in all Ages she
hath been scurvily used, as well as those that Worshipped her;
'tis of late become such a ruining Virtue, that Mankind seemeth
to be agreed to commend and avoid it; yet the want of Practice
which Repealeth the other Laws, hath no influence upon the
Law of Truth, because it hath root in Heaven, and an Intrinsick
value in it self, that can never be impaired; she sheweth her
Greatness in this, that her Enemies even when they are
successful are asham'd to own it; nothing but powerful Truth
hath the prerogative of Triumphing, not only after Victories,
but in spite of them, and to put Conquest her self out of
Countenance; she may be kept under and supprest, but her
Dignity still remaineth with her, even when she is in Chains;
Falshood

Falshood with all her Impudence hath not enough to speak ill of her before her Face, such Majesty she carrieth about her, that her most prosperous Enemies are fain to whisper their Treason; all the Power upon Earth can never extinguish her; she hath liv'd in all Ages; and let the Mistaken Zeal of prevailing Authority christen any opposition to it with what Name they please, she maketh it not only an ugly and unmannerly, but a dangerous thing to persist; she hath lived very retired indeed, nay sometime so buried, that only some few of the discerning part of Mankind could have a Glimpse of her; with all that she hath Eternity in her, she knoweth not how to die, and from the darkest Clouds that shade and cover her, she breaketh from time to time with Triumph for her Friends, and Terrour to her Enemies.

Our *Trimmer* therefore inspired by this Divine Virtue, thinketh fit to conclude with these Assertions, That our Climate is a *Trimmer*, between that part of the World where men are Roasted, and the other where they are Frozen; That our Church is a *Trimmer* between the Phrenzy of Platonick Visions, and the Lethargick Ignorance of Popish Dreams; That our Laws are *Trimmers*, between the Excess of unbounded Power, and the Extravagance of Liberty not enough restrained; That true Virtue hath ever been thought a *Trimmer*, and to have its dwelling in the middle between the two Extreams; That even God Almighty himself is divided between his two great Attributes, his Mercy and his Justice.

In such Company, our *Trimmer* is not asham'd of his Name, and willingly leaveth to the bold Champions of either Extream, the Honour of contending with no less Adversaries, than Nature, Religion, Liberty, Prudence, Humanity and Common Sense.

T H E

THE
ANATOMY
OF AN
EQUIVALENT.

I. THE World hath of late years never been without some extraordinary *Word* to furnish the Coffee-Houses and fill the Pamphlets. Sometimes it is a *new* one invented, and sometimes an *old* one revived. They are usually fitted to some present purpose, with intentions as differing as the various designs several parties may have, either to delude the People, or to expose their Adversaries : They are not of long continuance, but after they have passed a little while, and that they are grown nauseous by being so often repeated, they give place to something that is newer. Thus after *Whig, Tory,* and *Trimmer* have had their time, now they are dead and forgotten, being supplanted by the word 𝔈𝔮𝔲𝔦𝔟𝔞𝔩𝔢𝔫𝔱, which reigneth in their stead.

The Birth of it is in short this : After many repeated Essayes to dispose Men to the Repeal of Oaths and Tests, made for the security of the Protestant Religion, the general aversion to comply in it was found to be so great, that it was thought adviseable to try another manner of attempting it, and to see whether by putting the *same thing* into *another Mould,* and softning an *harsh Proposition* by a *plausible Term,* they might not have better success.

To this end, instead of an *absolute quitting* of these Laws, without any Condition ; which was the *first* Proposal ; now it is put into gentler Language, and runneth thus ; *If you will take away the* Oaths *and* Tests, *you shall have as good a thing for them.* This put into the fashionable Word, is now called an 𝔈𝔮𝔲𝔦𝔟𝔞𝔩𝔢𝔫𝔱.

II. So

II. So much to the Word it self. I will now endeavour in short to examine and explain, in order to the having it fully understood,

First, What *is* the nature of a true *Equivalent*; and

In the next place, What things *are not* to be admitted under that denomination.

I shall treat these as general Propositions, and though I cannot undertake how far they may be *convincing*, I may safely do it that they are *impartial*; of which there can be no greater evidence than that I make neither Inference nor Application, but leave that part entirely to the Reader, according as his own Thoughts shall direct and dispose him.

III. I will first take notice, that this Word, by the application which hath been made of it in some modern instances lieth under some *Disadvantage*, not to say some *Scandal*. It is transmitted hither from *France*; and if as in most other things that we take from them, we carry them beyond the Pattern, it should prove so in this, we should get into a more *partial* stile than the principles of English Justice will I hope ever allow us to be guilty of.

The French King's *Equivalents* in *Flanders* are very *extra-ordinary Bargains*; his manner of proposing and obtaining them is very differing from the usual methods of *equal* dealing. In a later instance, *Denmark*, by the encouragement as well as by the example of *France*, hath propos'd things to the Duke of *Holstein*, which are called *Equivalents*, but that they are so, the World is not yet sufficiently convinc'd, and probably the Parties concern'd do not think them to be so, and consequently do not appear to be at all disposed to accept them. Princes enjoyn and prescribe such things when they have *Strength* and *Power* to supply the want of *Arguments*; and according to practice in these Cases, the weaker are never thought to have an *ill Bargain*, if they have *any thing* left them. So that the first Qualification of an *Equivalent*, must be, that the Appraisers be *indifferent*, else it is only a *Sound*, there can be nothing *real* in it: For, where the same party that *proposeth* a Bargain, claimeth a Right to set the *Value*; or which is worse, hath *power* too to

make

make it good, the other may be forced to *submit* to the Conditions, but he can by no means ever be perswaded to *treat* upon them.

IV. The next thing to be consider'd is, that to make an *Equivalent* in reality an equal thing in the Proposer, it must be a *better* thing than that which is required by him; *just as good* is subject to the hazard of not being *quite so good*: It is not easie to have such an even hand as to make the Value exactly equal; besides, according to the Maxim in Law, *Melior conditio possidentis*, the Offer is not fair, except the thing offered is better in value than the thing demanded. There must be allowance for removing what is fixed, and there must be something that may be a justification for *changing*. The value of things very often dependeth more upon other circumstances, than upon what is meerly intrinsick to them; therefore the calculation must be made upon that foot, perhaps in most cases; and particularly the *want* which one of the parties may have of the thing he requireth, maketh it more valuable to *him* than it is in *it self*. If the party *proposing* doth not want the thing he would have in Exchange, his requiring it is *Impertinent*: If he doth, his want of it must go *into* the appraisement, and by consequence every Proposer of an *Equivalent* must offer a *better* thing, or else he must not take it unkindly to be refused, except the other party hath an *equal want* of the *same* thing, which is very improbable, since naturally he that wanteth most will speak first.

V. Another thing necessary to the making a fair Bargain is, that let the parties who treat be never so unequal in themselves, yet as to the particular thing proposed, there must be an *exact equality*, as far as it relateth to the full Liberty of *taking* or *refusing, concurring* or *objecting*, without any consequence of Revenge, or so much as Dissatisfaction; for it is impossible to *treat* where it is an Affront to *differ*; in that case there is no mean between the two extreams, either an open Quarrel or an intire Submission; the *way* of *Bargaining* must be equal, else the Bargain *it self* cannot be so: For example, the Proposer is not only to use *equal* terms as to the *matter*, but *fair* ones in the

the *manner* too. There must be no intimations of *Anger* in case of *refusal*, much less any open *Threatning*. Such a Stile is so ill suited to the usual way of Treating, that it looketh more like a Breach of the Peace, than the making a Bargain. It would be yet more improper and less agreeing with the nature of an *Equivalent*, if whilst two Men are chaffering about the *Price*, one of them should actually *take* the thing in question at his *own rate*, and afterwards desire to have his possession *confirmed* by a formal Agreement ; such a proceeding would not only *destroy* that *particular* contract, but make it impossible to have any *other* with the party that could be guilty of such a practice.

VI. *Violence* preceding destroyeth all Contract, and even tho the party that offereth it should have a right to the thing he so taketh, yet it is to be obtained by *legal* means, else it may be *forfeited* by his *irregularity* in the pursuit of it : The *Law* is such an Enemy to *Violence*, and so little to be reconciled to it, that in the Case of a *Rape*, the Punishment is not taken off though the party injured afterwards *consenteth*. The Justice of the Law hath its eye upon the first act, and the Maxim of *Volenti non fit injuria*, doth not in this case help the Offender, it being a plea *subsequent* to the Crime, which maketh it to be rejected as a thing wrong dated and out of time.

In taking away Goods or Money it is the same thing. The party robbed, by *giving* them afterwards to the taker, doth not exempt him from the Punishment of the *Violence* : Quite contrary, the Man from whom they were taken is punishable, if he doth not *prosecute*. If the case should be, that a Man thus taking away a thing without price, claimeth a *right* to take it, then whether it is well or ill founded is not the Question ; but sure, the party from whom it is so taken, whilst he is treating to *Sell* or *Exchange* it, can never make a Bargain with so *arbitrary* a Chapman, there being no room left after that to talk of the Value.

VII. To make an equal Bargain there must be a liberty of *differing*, not only in every thing that is *really essential*, but in every thing that is *thought so* by *either* party, and most
especially

especially by him who is in *possession* of the thing demanded : His *Opinion* must be a *Rule* to him, and even his *Mistake* in the Value, though it may not convince the Man he hath to deal with, yet he will be justified for *not accepting* what is offered, till that *Mistake* is fairly rectified and over-ruled.

When a *Security* is desired to be *changed*, that side which *desireth* it must not pretend to *impose* upon the other, so as to dictate to them, and tell them without debate, that they are *safe* in what is proposed, since of that the Counsel on the *other side* must certainly be the most *competent Judges*. The *hand* it cometh *from* is a great Circumstance, either to invite or discourage in all matters of Contract ; the Qualifications of the *Party offering* must sute with the *Proposition* it self, else let it be never so fair, there is ground for *Suspicion*.

VIII. When Men are of a temper, that they think they have *wrong* done them, if they have not always the *better* side of a *Bargain* : If they happen to be such as by experience have been found to have an *ill Memory* for their *Word* : If the Character they bear, doth not recommend their *Justice*, whereever their *Interest* is concern'd : In these cases, thinking Men will avoid dealing, not only to prevent *surprize*, but to cut off the occasions of *difficulty* or *dispute*.

It is yet *more discouraging*, when there are, either a *precedent* Practice, or *standing* Maxims of *gross Partiality*, in assuming a privilege of *exemption* from the usual methods of *equal* dealing.

To illustrate this by an Instance. Suppose that in any case, the Church of *Rome* should have an *Interest* to promote a Bargain ; let her *way of dealing* be a little examin'd, which will direct those with whom she treateth, how far they are to rely upon what *she proposeth* to them. We may begin with the Quality in the World the least consisting with equal dealing, *viz.* An incurable *Partiality* to *herself*; which, that it may arrive to its full perfection, is crowned with *Infallibility*. At the first setting out, she maketh her self uncapable of dealing upon terms of *Equality*, by the Power she claimeth of *binding* and *loosing*, which hath been so often applyed to *Treaties*, as well as to *Sins*.

If

If the definition of *Justice* is to deal *equally*, she cannot be guilty of it without *betraying her Prerogative*, and according to her Principles, she giveth up the Superiority derived to her by *Apostolical Succession*, if she degradeth her self so as to be judged by the Rules of *common Right*, especially if the Bargain should be with *Hereticks*, who in her Opinion have *forfeited* the claim they might otherwise have had to it.

IX. Besides, her Taste hath been so spoiled by *unreasonable Bargains*, that she can never bring down her Palate to any thing that is *fair* or *equal*. She hath not only judg'd it an *Equivalent*, but a *great Bargain* for the other side, to give them *Absolutions* and *Indulgence* for the *real Payment* of great Sums, for which she hath drawn Bills to have them repayed with Interest in *Purgatory*.

This *Spiritual Bank* hath carried on such a Trade upon these *advantageous Terms*, that it can never submit to the small Profits an *ordinary Bargain* would produce.

The several Popes have in exchange for the *Peter-Pence*, and all their other *Rents* and *Fines* out of *England*, sent *sanctified Roses, Reliques*, and other such Wonder-working *Trifles*. And by virtue of their Character of *Holy Fathers*, have used Princes like *Children*, by sending them such *Rattles* to play with, which they made them buy at extravagant Rates; besides which, they were to be *thankful* too, in to the bargain.

A Chip of the Cross, a piece of St. *Laurence's* Grid-iron, a Hair of St. *Peter*, have been thought *Equivalents*, for much more *substantial* things. The Popes being Masters of the Jewel-House, have set the *Rates* upon them, and they have passed; though the whole Shop would not take up the value of a Bodkin in *Lombard street* upon the credit of them.

They are *unconscionable Purchasers*, for they get all the Money from the *living* by praying for them when they are *dead*. And it is observable, that the Northern part of Christendom, which best understandeth *Trade*, were the first that *refused* to make any more Bargains with them; so that it looketh as if the chief quarrel to the *Hereticks* was not as they were *ill Christians*, but

but as they were *unkind Merchants,* in so discourteously rejecting the Commodities of the growth of *Rome.*

To conclude this Head, There is no bartering with *Infallibility,*
it being so much *above Equality,* that it cannot bear the Indig-
nity of a *true Equivalent.*

X. In all Bargains there is a necessity of looking back, and
reflecting how far a *present proposal* is reconcilable with
a *former practice* ; For Example, if at any time a thing is
offered, quite *differing* from the *Arguments* used by the Proposer, and *inconsistent* with the *Maxims* held out by him at
other times.   Or in a Publick case, if the *same* men who promote
and press a thing with the *utmost violence,* do in a little time
after with *as much violence* press the *contrary,* and profess
a *detestation* of the *very thing,* for which they had before
imployed *all* their *Interest* and *Authority.*   Or if in the case of
a Law *already* made, there should be a privilege claimed to
exempt those from the obligation of observing it, who yet should
afterwards desire and *press* to have a *new Law* made in exchange
for the *old* one, by which they would not be bound ; and that
they should propose a *security* by a thing of the very *same*
nature as that which they did *not* allow to be any *before.*   These
Incoherences must naturally have the effect of raising *suspicion,*
or rather they are a *certain proof,* that in such circumstances it
is *irrational* for men to expect an *effectual Equivalent.*

XI. If whatsoever is more than *ordinary* is *suspicious,* every
thing that is *unnatural* is *more* so ; It is not only *unnecessary*
but *unnatural* too to *perswade* with *violence* what it is *folly* to
refuse ; to *push* men with eagerness into a *good* bargain for
themselves, is a stile very much unsuitable to the *nature* of the
thing.   But it goeth further and is yet more absurd, to grow
angry with men for *not* receiving a proposal that is for their
advantage ; Men ought to be content with the Generosity of
offering good bargains, and should give their *compassion* to
those who do *not understand* them : but by carrying their good
nature so far as to be *Cholerick* in such a case, they would
follow the example of the *Church of Rome,* where the definition
of *Charity* is very extraordinary.   In her Language, the Writ

                                                            de

de Hæretico Comburendo is a *Love letter,* and *burning* men for differing with them in Opinion, howsoever miscalled *Cruelty,* is as they understand it, the *perfection* of *flaming Charity.*

When *Anger* in these cases lasteth *long,* it is most probable that it is for our *own sakes*; Good nature for *others* is one of those Diseases that is *cured* by *time,* and especially where it is *offered* and *rejected*; but for *our selves* it *never faileth,* and cannot be extinguished but with our life. It is fair if men can believe that their friends love them *next* to themselves, to love them *better* is too much; the Expression is so *unnatural* that it is *cloying,* and men must have no *sense,* who in this case have no *suspicion.*

XII. Another Circumstance necessary to a *fair* bargain is, That there must be *openness* and *freedom* allowed, as the effect of that *Equality* which is the foundation of Contracting. There must be full liberty of *objecting,* and making *doubts* and *scruples* : If they are such as can be *answered,* the party convinced is so much the more *confirmed* and *incouraged* to deal, instead of being hindred by them; but if instead of an *answer* to satisfy, there is nothing but *anger* for a reply, it is impossible not to conclude that there is never a good one to give; so that the objection *remaining* without being fully *confuted,* there is an absolute *bar* put to any further Treaty.

There can be no dealing where one side assumeth a privilege to *impose,* so as to make an *offer* and not bear the *examination* of it, this is giving *judgment* not making a *bargain.* Where it is called *unmannerly* to *object,* or *criminal* to *refuse,* the surest way is for men to stay where they are, rather than treat upon such disadvantage.

If it should happen to be in any Country where the governing power should allow men *Liberty of Conscience* in the choice of their *Religion,* it would be strange to deny them *liberty of speech* in making a *bargain.* Such a contradiction would be so discouraging, that they must be *unreasonably sanguine,* who in that case can entertain the hopes of a *fair Equivalent.*

XIII. An *equal* Bargain must not be a *Mystery* nor a *Secret,* The purchaser or proposer is to tell *directly* and *plainly,* what
it

it is he intendeth to give in Exchange for that which he requireth. It must be *viewed* and *considered* by the *other* party, that he may judge of the value; for without *knowing* what it is, he cannot determine whether he shall *take* or *leave* it. An assertion in *general*, that it shall be *as good* or a *better* thing, is not in this a *sufficient* excuse for the mistake of dealing upon such *uncertain* terms. In all things that are dark and not enough explained, *suspicion* naturally followeth: A *secret* generally implieth a *defect* or a *deceit*; and if a *false light* is an objection, *no light* at all is yet a greater. To pretend to give a *better* thing, and to refuse to *shew* it, is very near saying it is *not so good* a one; at least so it will be taken in common construction. A *Mystery* is yet a more discouraging thing to a *Protestant*; especially if the Proposition should come from a *Papist*; it being one of his great Objections to that Church, that there are so many of them *Invisible* and *Impossible*, which are so violently thrust upon their understandings, that they are overlaid with them. They think that *rational creatures* are to be convinced only by *reason*, and that *reason* must be *visible* and *freely exposed*; else they will think themselves used with *contempt* instead of *equality*, and will never allow such a *suspected secrecy* to be a fit preface to a *real Equivalent*.

XIV. In matters of Contract not only the *present* value, but the *contingences* and *consequences*, as far as they can be fairly supposed, are to be considered. For Example, if there should be a *possibility*, that one of the Parties may be *ruined* by *accepting*, and the other only *disappointed* by his *refusing*; the consequences are so extreamly *unequal*, that it is not imaginable, a man should take that for an *Equivalent*, which hath such a *fatal possibility* at the heels of it.

If it should happen in a *publick* case, that such a proposal should come from the *minor* part of an Assembly or Nation, to the *greater*; It is very just, that the *hazard* of such a *possibility* should more or less likely fall upon the *lesser* part, rather than upon the *greater*; for *whose sake* and *advantage* things are and must be calculated in all *publick Constitutions*. Suppose in any mixed Government, the *chief Magistrate* should propose

propose upon a condition, in the *Senate, Diet,* or other *Supreme Assembly,* either to Enact or Abrogate one or more Laws, by which a *possibility* might be let in of *destroying* their *Religion* and *Property,* which in other language signifieth no less than *Soul* and *Body* ; where could be the *Equivalent* in the case, not only for the *real loss,* but even for the *fear of losing* them ? Men can fall no lower than to *lose* all, and if *losing all* destroyeth them, the *venturing all* must *fright* them.

In an instance when Men are secure, that how far soever they may be over-run by *Violence,* yet they can never be undone by *Law,* except they give their assistance to make it possible, though it should neither be likely nor intended, still the *consequence* which *may* happen is too big for any present thing to make amends for it. Whilst the word 𝔓𝔬𝔰𝔰𝔦𝔟𝔩𝔢 remaineth, it must *forbid* the bargain. Where-ever it falleth out therefore, that in an Example of a publick nature, the Changing, Enacting, or Repealing a Law, *may naturally* tend to the *misplacing* the Legislative power in the hands of those who have a *separate interest* from the body of a People, there can be no treating, till it is demonstrably made out, that *such* a consequence shall be *absolutely impossible* ; for if that shall be *denied* by those who make the proposal, if it is because they *cannot* do it, the motion at first was very *unfair.* If they *can* and *will not,* it would be yet less reasonable to expect that such *partial* dealers would ever give an *Equivalent* fit to be *accepted.*

XV. It is necessary in all dealing to be *assured* in the first place, that the *party proposing* is in a condition to *make good* his Offer; that he is neither under any *former Obligations* or *pretended Claims,* which may render him uncapable of performing it ; else he is so far in the condition of a *Minor,* that whatever he disposeth by sale or exchange may be afterwards resumed, and the Contract becometh void, being *originally defective,* for want of a *sufficient* legal *power* in him that made it.

In the case of a strict Settlement, where the party is only *Tenant* for *life,* there is no possibility of treating with one under such fetters ; no purchase or exchange of Lands or any thing else can be good, where there is such an *incapacity* of making out a Title; the interest vested in him being so *limited,* that he can do little more than pronounce the *words* of a Contract, he can by no means perform the *effect* of it.

In more *publick* instances, the *impossibility* is yet more express; as suppose in any Kingdom, where the *people* have so much liberty left them, as that they may make Contracts with the *Crown,* there should be some *peculiar rights* claimed to be so *fixed* to the Royal Function, that no King for the time being could have power to *part* with them, being so *fundamentally* tied to the Office, that they can *never* be *separated.* Such *Rights* can upon no occasion be received in *exchange* for any thing the Crown may desire from the People : That can never be *taken* in payment, which cannot lawfully be *given,* so that if they should part with that which is required upon those terms, it must be a *gift,* it cannot be a *bargain.*

There is not in the whole *Dictionary* a more untractable word than *Inherent,* and less to be reconciled to the word *Equivalent.*

The party that will Contract in spight of such a Claim, is content to *take* what is *impossible* to *grant,* and if he complaineth of his Disappointment, he neither *can have* Remedy, nor *deserveth* it.

If a Right so claimed hapneth to be of so *comprehensive* a *nature,* as that by a clear inference it may extend to *every thing else,* as well as to the *particular* matter in question, as often as the Supream Magistrate shall be so disposed, there can in that case be *no treating* with a Prerogative that swalloweth all the Right the People can pretend to; and if they have no right to any thing of which they are possessed, it is a *Jest* and not a *Bargain,* to observe any Formality in parting with it.

A Claim may be so stated, that by the *power* and *advantage* of *interpreting,* it shall have such a murthering eye, that if it looketh upon a Law, like a *Basilisk,* it shall strike it dead : Where is the possibility of Treating, where *such a Right is assumed*? Nay, let it be supposed, that such a Claim is *not well founded* in *Law,* and that upon a free disquisition it could *not be made out*; yet even in this case, none that are well advised will

will conclude a Bargain, till it is *fully stated* and *cleared*, or indeed, so much as *engage* in a *treaty*, till by way of preliminary all *possibility* shall be *remov'd* of any trouble or dispute.

XVI. There is a *collateral* circumstance in making a Contract, which yet deserveth to be considered, as much as any thing that belongeth to it ; and that is the *character* and *figure* of the *parties* contracting ; if they treat only by *themselves*, and if by *others*, the *Qualifications* of the *Instruments* they employ.

The *Proposer* especially, must not be so *low* as to want *credit*, nor so *raised* as to carry him *above* the reach of *ordinary dealing*. In the first, There is *scandal*, in the other *danger*. There is no Rule without some Exception, but generally speaking the *means* should be suited to the *end*, and since all Men who treat, pretend an *equal bargain*, it is desirable that there may be *equality* in the *persons* as well as in the *thing*.

The *manner* of doing things hath such an influence upon the *matter*, that Men may guess at the *end* by the *instruments* that are used to obtain it, who are a very *good direction* how far to rely upon or suspect the *sincerity* of that which is proposed. An Absurdity in the way of *carrying on* a Treaty, in any *one* Circumstance, if it is very gross, is enough to perswade a thinking Man to break off, and take warning from such an *ill appearance*. Some things are so glaring that it is impossible not to *see*, and consequently not to *suspect* them ; as suppose in a private case, there should be a Treaty of *Marriage* between two Honourable Families, and the proposing side should think fit to send a *Woman* that had been *Carted*, to perswade the *young Lady* to an approbation and consent ; the *unfitness* of the *Messenger* must naturally dispose the other party to *distrust* the *Message*, and to resist the temptation of the *best Match* that could be offered, when conveyed by *that hand*, and ushered in by such a *discouraging preliminary*.

In a *publick* instance the suspicion arising from *unfit Mediators*, still groweth more reasonable in proportion, as the *consequence* is much *greater* of being deceived. If a *Jew* should be employed to sollicite all sorts of *Christians* to *unite* and *agree* ; the *contrariety* of his *profession*, would not allow Men

I 2

to

to stay till they heard his Arguments, they would conclude from his *Religion,* that either the Man *himself* was *mad,* or that he thought *those* to be *so,* whom he had the Impudence to endeavour to perswade.

Or suppose an *Adamite* should be very sollicitous and active, in all places, and with all sorts of Persons, to settle the *Church of England* in particular, and a fair *Liberty of Conscience* for all Dissenters; though nothing in the World has more to be said for it than *Naked Truth,* yet if such a Man should run up and down without Cloaths, let his Arguments be never so good, or his Commission never so Authentick, his *Figure* would be such a *contradiction* to his *business,* that how serious soever that might be in it self, *his interposition* would make a Jest of it.

Though it should not go so far as this, yet if Men have *contrarieties* in their *way of living* not to be reconciled; as if they should pretend infinite *zeal for liberty,* and at that time be in great *favour* and *imployed* by those who will *not endure* it.

If they are affectedly *singular,* and conform to the generality of the World in *no one* thing, but in playing the *knave.*

If *demonstration* is a familiar word with them, most especially where the thing is *impossible.*

If they quote *Authority* to supply their want of *sense,* and justifie the value of their Arguments, not by *reason,* but by their being *paid* for them, (in which, by the way, those who pay them have probably a very *melancholy Equivalent.*) If they brandish a *Prince's Word* like a Sword in a Crowd, to make way for their own *impertinence*; and in dispute, as Criminals formerly fled to the *Statue* of the Prince for Sanctuary; if they should now, when baffled, creep under the protection of a Kings *Name,* where out of respect they are no farther to be pursued.

In these cases, Though the propositions should be *really* good, they will be corrupted by passing through such *Conduits,* and it would be a sufficient *Mistake* to enter into a *Treaty*; but it would be little less than *Madness* from such hands to expect an *Equivalent.*

XVII. Having touched upon these particulars as necessary in order

order to the stating the nature of an *equal Bargain*, and the Circumstances belonging to it, let it now be examined in two or three instances, what things are *not* to be admitted by way of Contract, to pass under the Name of an *Equivalent*.

First, Though it will be allowed, that in the general corruption of mankind, which will not admit *Justice* alone to be a sufficient tie to make good a Contract, that a *Punishment* added for the breach of it, is a *fitting* or rather a *necessary* Circumstance; yet it does not follow, that in *all* cases, a *great Penalty* upon the party offending is an *absolute* and an *entire Security*. It must be considered in every particular case, how far the *Circumstances* may rationally lead a Man to *rely more* or *less* upon it.

In a private instance, the *Penalty* inflicted upon the breach of Contract must be first, such a one as the party injured *can enforce*, and Secondly, such a one as he *will enforce*, when it is in his power.

If the *Offending party* is in a capacity of *hindring* the other from bringing the Vengeance of the Law upon him; if he hath *strength* or *privilege* sufficient to *over rule* the Letter of the Contract; in that case, a *Penalty* is but a *Word*, there is no consequence belonging to it. Secondly, The *forfeiture* or *punishment* must be such as the Man aggrieved will *take*; for Example, if upon a Bargain, one of the Parties shall stipulate to subject himself, in case of his *failure*, to have his *Ears cut*, or his *Nose slit* by the other, with *security* given, that he shall not be prosecuted for *executing* this part of the Agreement; the *Penalty* is no doubt *heavy enough* to discourage a Man from breaking his Contract; but on the other side it is of *such a kind*, that the other how much soever he may be provoked, will not in cold Blood care to inflict it. Such an extravagant Clause would seem to be made only for *shew* and *sound*, and no Man would think himself safer by a thing which one way or other is sure to prove *ineffectual*.

In a *publick* Case, Suppose in a Government so constituted that a *Law* may be made in the nature of a *Bargain*, it is in *it self* no more than a *dead letter*, the *life* is given to it by the

execution

execution of what it containeth; so that let it in it self be never so perfect, it *dependeth* upon those who are intrusted with seeing it *observed*.

If it is in any Country, where the *chief Magistrate* chuseth the *Judges*, and the *Judges* interpret the *Laws*; a *Penalty* in any one particular Law can have no effect but what is *precarious*. It may have a *loud voice* to threaten, but it has not an *hand* to give a blow; for as long as the Governing Power is in possession of this Prerogative, let who will chuse the *Meat*, if they chuse the *Cooks*, it is they that will give the *tast* to it. So that it is clear that the *rigour* of a *Penalty* will not in all cases *fix* a *Bargain*, neither is it Universally a true Position, that the increase of *punishment* for the breach of a *new Law*, is an *Equivalent* for the consent to part with an *old* one.

XVIII. In most Bargains there is a reference to the *time to come*, which is therefore to be considered as well as that which cometh within the compass of the *present* valuation.

Where the *party Contracting*, hath not a *full power* to dispose what belongeth to him or them in *Reversion*, who shall succeed after him in his Right; he cannot make any part of what is so *limited* to be the *condition* of the Contract. Further, he cannot enjoyn the *Heir* or *Successor* to forbear the exercise of any Right that is *inherent* to him, as he is a Man: neither can he *restrain* him without his own consent, from doing any act which in it self is *lawful*, and liable to *no objection*. For Example, A *Father* cannot stipulate with any other Man, that in Consideration of such a thing done, or to be done, his *Son* shall *never Marry*; because Marriage is an Institution *Established* by the Laws of God, and Man, and therefore no body can be so restrained by any power from doing *such* an act, when he thinketh fit, being *warranted* by an Authority that is not to be controuled.

XIX. Now as there are *Rights inherent* in Mens persons in their *single capacities*, there are *Rights* as much *fixed* to the *Body Politick*, which is a Creature that never dieth. For instance, There can be no Government without a *Supreme Power*; that Power is not always in the *same* hands, it is in
different

different shapes and dresses, but still where-ever it is lodged, it must be *unlimited* : It hath a jurisdiction over every thing *else*, but it cannot have it above *it self*. *Supreme Power* can no more be *limited* than *Infinity* can be *measured*; because it ceaseth to be the thing; its very being is dissolved, when any bounds can be put to it.

Where this Supreme Power is *mixed*, or *divided*, the *shape* only *differeth*, the *Argument* is still the *same*.

The present State of *Venice* cannot restrain those who succeed them in the same power, from having an entire and unlimited Sovereignty; they may indeed make *present Laws* which shall retrench their *present Power*, if they are so disposed, and those *Laws* if not *repealed* by the *same authority* that enacted them, are to be *observed* by the succeeding Senate till they think fit to Abrogate them, and no longer ; for if the Supreme Power shall still reside in the Senate, perhaps composed of *other* Men, or of *other* minds (which will be sufficient) the necessary consequence is, that *one* Senate must have as much right to *alter* such a Law, as *another* could have to *make* it.

XX. Suppose the *Supreme Power* in any State should make a *Law*, to enjoin all subsequent Law-makers to take an *Oath* never to *alter it*, it would produce these following Absurdities.

First, All *Supreme Power* being instituted to promote the *safety* and *benefit*, and to prevent the *prejudice* and *danger* which may fall upon those who live under the *protection* of it ; the *consequence* of such an *Oath* would be, that all Men who are so trusted, shall take God to witness, that such a Law once made, being judged *at the time* to be *advantageous* for the publick, though *afterwards* by the vicissitude of times, or the variety of accidents or interests, it should plainly appear to them to be *destructive*, they will suffer it to have its course, and will never repeal it.

Secondly, If there could in any Nation be found a *set of Men*, who having a *part* in the *Supreme* legislative *Power*, should as much as in them lieth, betray their Country by such a criminal engagement, so *directly opposite* to the *nature* of their *Power*,

and

and to the *Trust* reposed in them; If these Men have their power only for *life,* when they are dead such an Oath can operate *no farther*; and tho that would be *too long* a Lease for the life of such a *Monster* as an *Oath so composed,* yet it must *then* certainly give up the Ghost. It could bind none but the *first* makers of it, *another* generation would never be tied up by it.

Thirdly, In those Countries where the *Supreme Assemblies* are not constant *standing* Courts, but called together upon *occasions,* and Composed of such as the People chuse for *that time* only, with a Trust and Character that remaineth no longer with them than till that Assembly is *regularly dissolved*; such an Oath taken by the Members of a Senate, Diet, or other Assembly so chosen, can have very little effect, because at the *next meeting* there may be quite *another set of Men* who will be under *no Obligation* of that kind. The eternity intended to that Law by those that made it, will be cut off by *new Men* who shall succeed them in their power, if they have a *differing Taste,* or another *Interest.*

XXI. To put it yet farther, Suppose a Clause in such a Law, that it shall be *criminal* in the last degree for any Man chosen in a subsequent Assembly, to *propose* the *repealing* of it; and since nothing can be *Enacted* which is not first *proposed,* by this means it seemeth as if a Law might be Created which should *never die.* But let this be Examined.

First, such a clause would be so *destructive* to the *being* of such a Constitution, as that it would be as reasonable to say, that a King had right to *give* or *sell* his Kingdom to a *foreign Prince,* as that any number of Men who are *entrusted* with the Supreme Power, or any part of it, should have a right to *impose* such Shackles upon the Liberty of those who are to *succeed* them in the *same Trust.* The ground of that *Trust* is, that every Man who is chosen into such an Assembly, is to do all that in him lieth for the *good* of those who *chose* him: The English of such a Clause would be, that he is *not* to do his *best* for those that *chose* him, because though he should be *convinc'd* that it might be very *fatal* to *continue* that *Law,*
and

and therefore very *necessary* to *repeal* it, yet he must not repeal it, because it is made a *Crime*, and attended with a *Penalty*.

But secondly, to shew the *emptiness* as well as *injustice* of such a Clause, it is clear, that although such an Invasion of Right should be imposed, it will never be obeyed : There will only be *Deformity* in the *Monster*, it will neither *sting* nor *bite*. Such *Law-givers* would only have the honour of attempting a *contradiction* which can never have any success ; for as such a *Law* in it self would be a *Madness*, so the *Penalty* would be a *Jest* ; which may be thus made out.

XXII. A Law that carrieth in it self *Reason* enough to *support* it, is so far from wanting the *protection* of such a Clause, or from *needing* to take such an *extraordinary receipt* for long Life, that the *admitting* it must certainly be the *likeliest* and the *shortest* way to *destroy* it ; such a Clause in a Law must imply an opinion that the *greatest* part of mankind is *against* it, since it is impossible such an exorbitance should be done for its *own sake* ; the end of it must be to *force* Men by a *Penalty*, to that which they could *not* be *perswaded* to, whilst their Reason is left at *liberty*. This Position being granted, which I think can hardly be denied, put the case that a Law should be made with this *imaginary* Clause of *Immortality*, after which another *Assembly* is chosen, and if the majority of the *Electors* shall be *against* this Law, the greater part of the *Elected* must be *so* too, if the choice is fair and regular ; which must be presumed, since the supposition of the contrary is not to come within this Argument. When these Men shall meet, the *Majority* will be visible beforehand of those who are *against* such a Law, so that there will be no *hazard* to any single Man in proposing the *Repeal* of it, when he cannot be *punished* but by the *Majority*, and he hath such a kind of assurance as cometh near a Demonstration, that the *greater Number* will be of his mind, and consequently, that for their own sakes they will *secure* him from any danger.

For these Reasons, where-ever in order to the making a Bargain, a Proposition is advanc'd to make a *new Law*, which is

to

to tye up those who neither *can* nor *will be bound* by it, it may be a good *Jest,* but it will never be a good *Equivalent.*

XXIII. In the last place, let it be examined how far a *Promise* ought to be taken for a *Security* in a Bargain.

There is great Variety of Methods for the *Security* of those that deal, according to their *Dispositions* and *Interests*; some are *binding,* others inducing circumstances, and are to be so distinguished.

First, *Ready Payment* is without exception, so of that there can be no dispute; in default of that, the *good Opinion* Men may have of one another is a great ingredient to supply the want of *immediate* Performances. Where the Trust is grounded upon *Inclination* only, the Generosity is not always *return'd*; but where it springeth from a *long Experience* it is a better foundation, and yet that is not always *secure.* In ordinary dealing, *one Promise* may be an *Equivalent* to *another*, but it is not so for a thing *actually* granted or conveyed; especially if the thing required in exchange for it, is of great *value,* either in *it self* or in its *consequences.* A *bare* Promise as a *single Security* in such a case is not an *equal* proposal; if it is offered by way of *addition,* it generally giveth cause to doubt the Title is crazy, where so *slender* a thing is brought in to be a *supplement.*

XXIV. The *Earnest* of making good a Promise, must be such a behaviour *preceding,* as may encourage the party to whom it is made to depend upon it: Where instead of that, there hath been *want of Kindness,* and which is worse an *Invasion* of *Right,* a Promise hath no perswading force; and till the *Objection* to such a Proceeding is *forgotten,* (which can only be the work of time) and the Skin is a little grown over the tender part, the Wound must not be touch'd. There must be some *Intermission* at least to abate the smart of *unkind usage,* or else a Promise in the Eye of the party injur'd is so far from *strengthening* a Security, that it raiseth more *doubts,* and giveth more justifiable cause to *suspect* it.

A *Word* is not like a Bone, that being broken and well set again, is said to be sometimes stronger in that very part: It is

far

far from being so in a *Word* given and *not made good*. Every single Act either *weakeneth* or *improveth* our Credit with other Men ; and as an habit of being *just* to our Word will *confirm*, so an habit of too freely *dispensing* with it must necessarily *destroy* it. A *Promise* hath its effect to perswade a Man to lay some weight upon it, where the *Promiser* hath not only the *power*, but may reasonably be supposed to have the *will* of performing it ; and further, that there be no *visible interest* of the party promising to excuse himself from it, or to evade it.

All Obligations are *comparative*, and where they seem to be opposite, or between the greater and the lesser, which of them ought to have precedence in all respects every man is apt to be his *own Judge*.

XXV. If it should fall out that the *Promiser* with full *intent* at the *time* to perform, might by the interposition of *new Arguments*, or *differing Advice* think himself oblig'd to turn the matter of Conscience on the *other* side, and should look upon it to be much a *greater* fault to *keep* his word than to *break* it ; such a Belief will *untye* the *strictest Promise* that can be made, and though the Party thus absolving himself should do it *without* the mixture or temptation of *private interest*, being moved to it meerly by his *Conscience*, as then informed ; yet how far soever that might diminish the *Fault* in *him*, it would in no degree lessen the *inconveniences* to the *party* who is *disappointed*, by the breach of an engagement upon which he relyed.

XXVI. A *Promise* is to be understood in the *plain* and *natural* sense of the words, and to be sure not in his who *made* it, if it was given as part of a Bargain. That would be like giving a Man power to *raise* the *value* of his Money in the payment of his *Debt*, by which, tho he paid but half or less, he might pretend according to the letter to have made good the Contract.

The *power* of *interpreting* a Promise intirely taketh away the *virtue* of it. A Merchant who should once assume that privilege, would save himself the trouble of making any more Bargains.

It

It is still worse if this *Jurisdiction* over a Man's *Promise*, should be *lodg'd* in hands that have Power to support such an *extraordinary Claim*; and if in *other* Cases, forbearing to deal upon those terms is *advisable*, in this it becometh absolutely *necessary*.

XXVII. There must in all respects be a full liberty to *claim* a Promise, to make it reasonable to *take* it in any part of payment; else it would be like agreeing for a *Rent*, and at the same time making it *criminal* to *demand it*.

A *superiority* of *Dignity* or *Power* in the party promising maketh it a more *tender* thing for the other party to treat upon that security. The first maketh it a *nice* thing to *claim*, the latter maketh it a *difficult* thing to *obtain*.

In some cases, a *Promise* is in the nature of a *Covenant*, and then between *equal* parties the breach of it will bear a *Suit*; but where the *greatness* of the Promiser is very much raised above the level of *equality*, there is no Forfeiture to be taken. It is so far from the party grieved his being able to *sue* or *recover Damages*, that he will not be allowed to *explain* or *expostulate*, and instead of his being *relieved* against the breach of Promise, he will run the hazard of being *punished* for breach of Good Manners. Such a difficulty is putting all or part of the Payment in the Fire, where Men must burn their Fingers before they can come at it.

That cannot properly be called *good payment*, which the party to whom it is due may not receive with *ease* and *safety*. It was a Kings Brother of *England* who refused to lend the Pope money, for this reason, *That he would never take the Bond of one, upon whom he could not distrain.*

The Argument is still *stronger* against the Validity of a Promise, when the Contract is made between a *Prince* and a *Subject*. The very offering a Kings Word in Mortgage is rather a *threatning* in case of refusal, than an *inducing* Argument to accept it; it is *unfair* at *first*, and by that giveth greater cause to be cautious, especially if a thing of that *value* and *dignity* as a Kings Word ought to be, should be put into the hands of *State-Brokers* to strike up a Bargain with it.

XXVIII.

XXVIII. When God Almighty maketh Covenants with Mankind, *His Promise* is a *sufficient Security*, notwithstanding his *Superiority* and his *Power*; because first, he can neither *err* nor do *injustice*. It is the *only* Exception to his Omnipotence, that by the Perfection of his *being* he is incapacitated to do *wrong*. Secondly, at the *instant* of his *Promise*, by the extent of his Foresight, which cannot fail, there is no room left for the possibility of any thing to *intervene*, which might *change* his mind. Lastly, he is above the receiving either *Benefit* or *Inconvenience*, and therefore can have no *Interest* or *Temptation* to vary from his Word, when once he hath granted it.

Now though Princes are God's Vicegerents, yet their Commission not being so *large*, as that *these Qualifications* are devolved to them, it is quite another case, and since the *offering* a Security implyeth it to be *examined* by the party to whom it is proposed, it must not be taken ill that Objections are made to it, even though the Prince himself should be the *immediate Proposer*.

Let a familiar Case be put; Suppose a Prince, tempted by a Passion too strong for him to resist, should descend so as to promise Marriage to one of his Subjects, and as Men are naturally in great haste upon such occasions, should press to take possession before the *necessary Forms* could be complyed with; would the poor Ladies *Scruples* be called *criminal* for not taking the Security of the Royal Word? Or would her *Allegiance* be tainted by her *resisting* the sacred Person of her Sovereign, because he was impatient of delay? *Courtesie* in this case might perswade her to *accept* it, if she was so disposed, but sure the *just exercise* of Power can never *claim* it.

XXIX. There is one Case where it is more particularly a *Duty* to use very *great caution* in accepting the security of a Promise, and that is, when Men are *authorized* and *trusted* by *others* to act for them. This putteth them under much *greater restraints*, than those who are at liberty to treat for *themselves*. It is *lawful*, though it is not *prudent* for any man to make an *ill Bargain* for *himself*, but it is neither the one nor the other, where the party contracting treateth on behalf of

another,

another, by whom he is *intrusted*. Men who will unwarily accept an *ill security*, if it is for *themselves*, forfeit their own discretion, and undergo the Penalty, but they are not responsible to any body else. They lie under the Mortification and the loss of committing the error, by which though they may expose their *Judgment* to some *censure*, yet their *Morality* suffers no *reproach* by it.

But those who are *deputed* by *others* to treat for them, upon terms of *best advantage*, though the *Confidence* placed in them should prevent the putting any *limits* to their Power in their Commission, yet the *Condition implied* if not *expressed*, is that the Persons so Trusted shall neither make an *ill Bargain*, nor accept a *slight Security*.

The Obligation is yet *more* binding when the Trust is of a *Publick* Nature. The aggravation of disappointing a *Body* of Men that *rely* upon them, carrieth the Fault as *high* as it can go, and perhaps no Crime of any kind can outdo such a *deliberate breach* of *Trust*, or would more justly make Men *forfeit* the protection of *humane Society*.

XXX. I will add one thing more upon this Head, which is, that it is not *always* a *true Proposition*, that 'tis safe to rely upon a Promise if, at the *time* of making it, it is the *Interest* of the *Promiser* to make it good. This, though many times it is a good *Inducement*, yet it hath these Exceptions to it. First, if the Proposer hath at *other* times gone plainly *against* his *visible Interest*, the Argument will turn the other way, and his *former Mistakes* are so many *Warnings* to others, not to come within the danger of any more: let the *Inducements* to those Mistakes be never so *great* and *generous*, that does not alter the Nature, they are *Mistakes* still.

Interest is an *uncertain* thing, It goeth and cometh, and varieth according to times and circumstances; as good build upon a *Quicksand*, as upon a presumption that *Interest* shall not *alter*. Where are the Men so distinguished from the rest of Mankind, that it is impossible for them to *mistake their Interest*? Who are they that have such an exemption from humane Frailty, as that it can never happen to them not to *see their*

their Interest for want of Understanding, or not to *leap over it* by excess of Zeal.

Above all, *Princes* are the *most* liable to Mistake; not out of any *defect* in their Nature, which might put them under such an unfortunate distinction; quite contrary, the blood they derive from wise and great Ancestors, doth rather distinguish them on the better side; besides that their great Character and Office of Governing giveth a noble Exercise to their Reason, which can very hardly fail to raise and improve it. But there is one Circumstance annexed to their Glorious Calling, which in this respect is sufficient to outweigh all those Advantages; it is that *Mankind,* divided in most things else, agree in this, to *conspire* in their endeavors to *deceive* and *mislead* them; which maketh it above the power of humane understanding, to be so exactly guarded as never to admit a surprise, and the highest applause that could ever yet be given to the greatest Men that ever wore a Crown, is that they *were no oftner deceived.*

Thus I have ventur'd to lay down my thoughts of the *Nature* of a *Bargain,* and the *due Circumstances* belonging to an *Equivalent,* and will now conclude with this short word. " Where " *Distrusting* may be the cause of provoking 𝔄𝔫𝔤𝔢𝔯, and *Trusting* " may be the cause of bringing ℜ𝔲𝔦𝔫, *the Choice is too easie to* " *need the being Explained.*"

A

A
LETTER
TO A
DISSENTER,

Upon Occasion of His Majesties late Gracious Declaration of Indulgence.

SIR,

SINCE Addresses are in fashion, give me leave to make one to you. This is neither the Effect of Fear, Interest, or Resentment; therefore you may be sure it is sincere: and for that reason it may expect to be kindly received. Whether it will have power enough to Convince, dependeth upon the Reasons, of which you are to judge; and upon your Preparation of Mind, to be perswaded by Truth, whenever it appeareth to you. It ought not to be the less welcome, for coming from a friendly Hand, one whose kindness to you is not lessened by difference of Opinion, and who will not let his Thoughts for the Publick be so tied or confined to this or that Sub-division of Protestants, as to stifle the Charity, which, besides all other Arguments, is at this time become necessary to preserve us.

I am neither surprized nor provoked, to see that in the Condition you were put into by the Laws, and the ill Circumstances you lay under by having the Exclusion and Rebellion laid to your Charge, you were desirous to make your selves less uneasy and obnoxious to Authority. Men who are sore, run to the nearest Remedy with too much hast to consider all the

consequences:

consequences : Grains of allowance are to be given, where Nature giveth such strong Influences. When to Men under Sufferings it offereth Ease, the present Pain will hardly allow time to examine the Remedies ; and the strongest Reason can hardly gain a fair Audience from our Mind, whilst so possessed, till the Smart is a little allayed.

I do not know whether the Warmth that naturally belongeth to new Friendships, may not make it a harder Task for me to perswade you. It is like telling Lovers, in the beginning of their Joys, that they will in a little time have an end. Such an unwelcome Stile doth not easily find Credit : but I will suppose you are not so far gone in your new Passion, but that you will *Hear* still ; and therefore I am under the less Discouragement, when I offer to your Consideration two things. The *First* is, The Cause you have to suspect your new Friends. The *Second*, The Duty incumbent upon you, in Christianity and Prudence, not to hazard the Publick Safety, neither by desire of Ease, nor of Revenge.

To the *First* : Consider that notwithstanding the smooth Language which is now put on to engage you, these new Friends did not make you their Choice, but their Refuge : They have ever made their first Courtships to the Church of *England*, and when they were rejected there, they made their Application to you in the second place. The Instances of this might be given in all times. I do not repeat them, because whatsoever is unnecessary, must be tedious, the truth of this Assertion being so plain, as not to admit a Dispute. You cannot therefore reasonably flatter your selves, that there is any Inclination to you. They never pretended to allow you any Quarter, but to usher in Liberty for themselves under that shelter. I refer you to Mr. *Coleman's Letters*, and to the *Journals* of *Parliament*, where you may be convinced, if you can be so mistaken as to doubt ; nay, at this very hour, they can hardly forbear, in the height of their Courtship, to let fall hard Words of you. So little is Nature to be restrained ; it will start out sometimes, disdaining to submit to the Usurpation of Art and Interest.

This Alliance, between *Liberty* and *Infallibility*, is bringing

HALIFAX   K   together

together the Two most contrary things that are in the World. The Church of *Rome* doth not only dislike the allowing Liberty, but by its Principles it cannot do it. Wine is not more expressly forbid to the *Mahometans*, than giving Hereticks Liberty to the *Papists*: They are no more able to make good their Vows to you, than Men married before, and their Wife alive, can confirm their Contract with another. The continuance of their kindness, would be a habit of Sin, of which they are to repent, and their Absolution is to be had upon no other terms, than their promise to destroy you. You are therefore to be hugged now, only that you may be the better squeezed at another time. There must be something extraordinary, when the Church of *Rome* setteth up Bills, and offereth Plaisters, for tender Consciences: By all that hath hitherto appeared, her skill in Chirurgery lieth chiefly in a quick Hand to cut off Limbs; but she is the worst at healing, of any that ever pretended to it.

To come so quick from another Extream, is such an unnatural Motion, that you ought to be upon your Guard; the other day you were *Sons of Belial*: Now, you are *Angels of Light*. This is a violent change, and it will be fit for you to pause upon it, before you believe it: If your Features are not altered, neither is their Opinion of you, what ever may be pretended. Do you believe less than you did, that there is Idolatry in the Church of *Rome*? Sure you do not. See then, how they treat both in Words and Writing, those who entertain that Opinion. Conclude from hence, how inconsistent their Favour is with this single Article, except they give you a Dispensation for this too, and by a *Non Obstante*, secure you that they will not think the worse of you.

Think a little how dangerous it is to build upon a Foundation of Paradoxes. Popery now is the only Friend to Liberty; and the known Enemy to Persecution: The Men of *Taunton* and *Tiverton*, are above all other Eminent for Loyalty. The *Quakers* from being declared by the Papists not to be Christians, are now made Favourites, and taken into their particular Protection; they are on a sudden grown the most accomplished

Men

Men of the Kingdom in good Breeding, and give Thanks with the best Grace, in double refined Language. So that I should not wonder, though a Man of that Perswasion, in spite of his Hat, should be Master of the Ceremonies. Not to say harsher words, these are such very new things, that it is impossible not to suspend our Belief, till by a little more Experience we may be inform'd whether they are Realities or Apparitions: We have been under shameful mistakes if these Opinions are true; but for the present, we are apt to be incredulous, except we could be convinced, that the Priests words in this case too, are able to make such a sudden and effectual change, and that their Power is not limited to the Sacrament, but that it extendeth to alter the nature of all other things, as often as they are so disposed.

Let me now speak of the Instruments of your Friendship, and then leave you to judge, whether they do not afford matter of Suspition. No sharpness is to be mingled where Healing only is intended; so nothing will be said to expose particular men, how strong soever the Temptation may be, or how clear the Proofs to make it out. A word or two in general, for your better caution, shall suffice: Suppose then, for Argument's sake, that the Mediators of this new Alliance, should be such as have been formerly imployed in Treaties of the same kind, and there detected to have Acted by Order, and to have been Impower'd to give Encouragements and Rewards. Would not this be an Argument to suspect them?

If they should plainly be under Engagements to one side, their Arguments to the other ought to be received accordingly; their fair Pretences are to be looked upon as part of their Commission, which may not improbably give them a Dispensation in the case of Truth, when it may bring a prejudice upon the Service of those by whom they are imployed:

If there should be men who having formerly had Means and Authority to perswade by Secular Arguments, have in pursuance of that Power, sprinkled Money amongst the Dissenting Ministers: and if those very men should now have the same Authority, practice the same Methods, and Disburse, where they cannot

otherwise

otherwise perswade : It seemeth to me to be rather an Evidence than a Presumption of the Deceit.

If there should be Ministers amongst you, who by having fallen under Temptations of this kind, are in some sort engaged to continue their Frailty, by the awe they are in lest it should be exposed ; the Perswasions of these unfortunate Men must sure have the less force, and their Arguments, though never so specious, are to be suspected, when they come from Men who have mortgaged themselves to severe Creditors, that expect a rigorous Observation of the Contract, let it be never so unwarrantable.

If these, or any others, should at this time Preach up Anger and Vengeance against the Church of *England*; may it not without Injustice be suspected, that a thing so plainly out of Season, springeth rather from Corruption than Mistake; and that those who act this Cholerick part, do not believe themselves, but only pursue higher Directions, and endeavour to make good that part of their Contract which obligeth them, upon a Forfeiture, to make use of their inflaming Eloquence ? They might apprehend their Wages would be retrenched if they should be Moderate : And therefore whilst Violence is their Interest, those who have not the same Arguments, have no reason to follow such a partial Example.

If there should be Men, who by the load of their Crimes against the Government, have been bowed down to comply with it against their Conscience; who by incurring the want of a Pardon, have drawn upon themselves a necessity of an entire Resignation ; such men are to be lamented, but not to be believed. Nay, they themselves, when they have discharged their Unwelcome Task, will be inwardly glad that their forced Endeavours do not succeed, and are pleased when men resist their Insinuations; which are far from being Voluntary or Sincere, but are squeezed out of them by the weight of their being so Obnoxious.

If in the heighth of this great dearness by comparing things, it should happen, that at this instant, there is much a surer Friendship with those who are so far from allowing Liberty,
that

that they allow no Living to a Protestant under them, let the Scene lie in what part of the World it will, the Argument will come home, and sure it will afford sufficient ground to suspect. Apparent Contradictions must strike us; neither Nature nor Reason can digest them: Self-Flattery, and the desire to Deceive our selves to gratifie present Appetite, with all their Power, which is Great, cannot get the better of such broad Conviction as some things carry along with them. Will you call these vain and empty Suspitions? have you been at all times so void of Fears and Jealousies as to justifie your being so unreasonably Valiant in having none upon this occasion? Such an extraordinary Courage at this unseasonable time, to say no more, is too dangerous a Virtue to be commended.

If then for these and a thousand other Reasons, there is cause to suspect, sure your new Friends are not to dictate to you, or advise you ; for instance, The Addresses that fly abroad every Week, and Murther us with *Another to the same* ; the first Draughts are made by those who are not very proper to be Secretaries to the Protestant Religion : and it is your part only to Write them out fairer again. Strange! that you who have been formerly so much against *Set Forms,* should now be content the Priests should Indite for you. The nature of Thanks is an unavoidable consequence of being pleased or obliged ; they grow in the Heart, and from thence shew themselves either in Looks, Speech, Writing, or Action : No man was ever Thankful because he was bid to be so, but because he had, or thought he had some Reason for it. If then there is cause in this Case to pay such extravagant Acknowledgments, they will flow naturally, without taking such pains to procure them ; and it is unkindly done to Tire all the Post-Horses with carrying Circular Letters to solicite that which would be done without any trouble or constraint : If it is really in it self such a Favour, what needeth so much pressing men to be thankful, and with such eager circumstances, that where Perswasions cannot delude, Threatnings are employed to fright them into a Compliance. Thanks must be voluntary, not only unconstrained, but unsolicited, else they are either Trifles or Snares; they either

signifie

signifie nothing, or a great deal more than is intended by those that give them. If an Inference should be made, That whosoever thanketh the King for his Declaration, is by that ingaged to Justifie it in point of Law; it is a greater Stride than, I presume, all those care to make who are perswaded to Address: If it shall be supposed, that all the Thankers will be Repealers of the TEST, whenever a *Parliament* shall meet, such an Expectation is better prevented before, than disappointed afterwards; and the surest way to avoid the lying under such a Scandal, is not to do any thing that may give a colour to the Mistake: These bespoken Thanks are little less improper than Love Letters that were solicited by the Lady to whom they are to be directed: so, that besides the little ground there is to give them, the manner of getting them doth extreamly lessen their Value. It might be wished that you would have suppressed your impatience, and have been content for the sake of Religion, to enjoy it within your selves without the Liberty of a publick Exercise, till a Parliament had allowed it; but since that could not be, and that the Artifices of some amongst you have made use of the Well-meant Zeal of the generality to draw them into this Mistake, I am so far from blaming you with that sharpness which, perhaps, the Matter in strictness would bear, that I am ready to err on the side of the more gentle construction.

There is a great difference between enjoying quietly the Advantages of an Act irregularly done by others, and the going about to support it against the Laws in being: the Law is so Sacred, that no Trespass against it is to be defended; yet Frailties may in some measure be excused, when they cannot be justified. The Desire of enjoying a Liberty from which Men have been so long restrained, may be a Temptation that their Reason is not at all times able to resist. If in such a case, some Objections are leapt over, indifferent Men will be more inclined to lament the Occasion, than to fall too hard upon the Fault, whilst it is covered with the Apology of a good Intention; but where, to rescue your selves from the Severity of one Law, you give a Blow to all the Laws, by which your Religion and Liberty are to be protected, and instead of silently

receiving

receiving the Benefit of this Indulgence, you set up for Advocates to support it, you become voluntary Aggressors, and look like Counsel retained by the Prerogative against your old Friend *Magna Charta*, who hath done nothing to deserve her falling thus under your Displeasure.

If the Case then should be, that the Price expected from you for this Liberty, is giving up your Right in the Laws, sure you will think twice, before you go any further in such a losing Bargain. After giving Thanks for the Breach of one Law, you lose the Right of Complaining of the Breach of all the rest; you will not very well know how to defend your selves when you are pressed; and having given up the Question when it was for your Advantage, you cannot re-call it when it shall be to your Prejudice. If you will set up at one time a Power to help you, which at another time, by parity of Reason, shall be made use of to destroy you, you will neither be pitied, nor relieved against a Mischief you draw upon your selves, by being so unreasonably thankful. It is like calling in Auxiliaries to help, who are strong enough to subdue you: In such a case your Complaints will come too late to be heard, and your Sufferings will raise Mirth instead of Compassion.

If you think, for your Excuse, to expound your Thanks so as to restrain them to this particular Case, others, for their Ends, will extend them further: And in these differing Interpretations, that which is back'd by Authority will be the most likely to prevail; especially when by the Advantage you have given them, they have in truth the better of the Argument, and that the Inferences from your own Concessions are very strong and express against you. This is so far from being a groundless Supposition, that there was a late Instance of it, the last Session of Parliament, in the House of Lords, where the first Thanks, though things of course, were interpreted to be the Approbation of the Kings whole Speech, and a Restraint from the further Examination of any part of it, though never so much disliked; and it was with difficulty obtained, not to be excluded from the liberty of objecting to this mighty Prerogative of Dispensing, meerly by this innocent and usual piece of

good

good Manners, by which no such thing could possibly be intended.

This sheweth, that some Bounds are to be put to your good Breeding, and that the Constitution of *England* is too valuable a thing to be ventured upon a Compliment. Now that you have for some time enjoyed the Benefit of the End, it is time for you to look into the Danger of the Means : The same Reason that made you desirous to get Liberty, must make you sollicitous to preserve it; so that the next Thought will naturally be, not to engage your self beyond Retreat, and to agree so far with the Principles of all Religion, as not to rely upon a Death-Bed Repentance.

There are certain Periods of Time, which being once past, make all Cautions ineffectual, and all Remedies desperate. Our Understandings are apt to be hurried on by the first Heats, which, if not restrained in time, do not give us leave to look back, till it is too late. Consider this in the Case of your Anger against the Church of *England,* and take warning by their Mistake in the same kind, when after the late King's Restauration, they preserved so long the bitter Taste of your rough Usage to them in other times, that it made them forget their Interest, and sacrifice it to their Revenge.

Either you will blame this Proceeding in them, and for that reason not follow it, or if you allow it, you have no reason to be offended with them; so that you must either dismiss your Anger, or lose your Excuse; except you should argue more partially than will be supposed of Men of your Morality and Understanding.

If you had now to do with those rigid Prelates, who made it a matter of Conscience to give you the least Indulgence, but kept you at an uncharitable Distance, and even to your most reasonable Scruples continued stiff and inexorable, the Argument might be fairer on your side; but since the common Danger hath so laid open that Mistake, that all the former Haughtiness towards you is for ever extinguished, and that it hath turned the Spirit of Persecution into a Spirit of Peace, Charity, and Condescension; shall this happy Change only affect the
Church

Church of *England*? And are you so in love with Separation, as not to be mov'd by this Example? It ought to be followed, were there no other Reason than that it is Vertue; but when besides that, it is become necessary to your Preservation, it is impossible to fail the having its Effect upon you.

If it should be said, that the Church of *England* is never humble but when she is out of power, and therefore loseth the Right of being believed when she pretendeth to it: The Answer is, *First*, it would be an uncharitable Objection, and very much mistimed; an unseasonable Triumph, not only ungenerous, but unsafe: So that in these respects it cannot be urged, without Scandal, even though it could be said with Truth. *Secondly*, This is not so in Fact, and the Argument must fall, being built upon a false Foundation; for whatever may be told you at this very Hour, and in the Heat and Glare of your present Sunshine, the Church of *England* can in a Moment bring Clouds again, and turn the Royal Thunder upon your Heads, blow you off the Stage with a Breath, if she would give but a Smile or a kind Word; the least Glimpse of her Compliance would throw you back into the State of Suffering, and draw upon you all the Arrears of Severity, which have accrued during the time of this Kindness to you, and yet the Church of *England*, with all her Faults, will not allow her self to be rescued by such unjustifiable means, but chuseth to bear the Weight of Power, rather than lie under the Burthen of being criminal.

It cannot be said, that she is unprovoked; Books and Letters come out every Day, to call for Answers, yet she will not be stirred. From the supposed Authors, and the Stile, one would swear they were Undertakers, and had made a Contract to fall out with the Church of *England*. There are Lashes in every Address, Challenges to draw the Pen in every Pamphlet: In short, the fairest Occasions in the World given to quarrel; but she wisely distinguisheth between the Body of Dissenters, whom she will suppose to act as they do with no ill Intent; and these small Skirmishers, pickt and sent out to picqueer, and to begin a Fray amongst the Protestants, for the Entertainment as well as the Advantage of the Church of *Rome*.

This

This Conduct is so good, that it will be scandalous not to applaud it. It is not equal Dealing to blame our Adversaries for doing ill, and not commend them when they do well.

To hate them because they persecuted, and not to be reconciled to them when they are ready to suffer, rather than receive all the Advantages that can be gained by a Criminal Complyance, is a Principle no sort of Christians can own, since it would give an Objection to them never to be answered.

Think a little who they were that promoted your former Persecutions, and then consider how it will look to be angry with the Instruments, and at the same time to make a League with the Authors of your Sufferings.

Have you enough considered what will be expected from you? Are you ready to stand in every Borough by Vertue of a *Congé d'eslire,* and instead of Election, be satisfied if you are Returned?

Will you in *Parliament* justifie the Dispensing Power, with all its Consequences, and Repeal the *Test,* by which you will make way for the Repeal of all the Laws, that were made to preserve your Religion, and to Enact others that shall destroy it?

Are you disposed to change the Liberty of Debate into the Merit of Obedience; and to be made Instruments to repeal or enact Laws, when the *Roman Consistory* are *Lords of the Articles?*

Are you so linked with your new Friends, as to reject any Indulgence a *Parliament* shall offer you, if it shall not be so comprehensive as to include the Papists in it?

Consider, that the implyed Conditions of your new Treaty are no less, than that you are to do every thing you are desired, without examining, and that for this pretended Liberty of Conscience, your real Freedom is to be sacrificed: Your former Faults hang like Chains still about you, you are let loose only upon Bayl; the first Act of Non-compliance, sendeth you to Jayl again.

You may see that the Papists themselves do not relie upon the Legality of this Power, which you are to justifie, since the

being

being so very earnest to get it established by a Law, and the doing such very hard things in order, as they think, to obtain it, is a clear Evidence, that they do not think that the single Power of the Crown is in this Case a good Foundation ; especially when this is done under a Prince, so very tender of all the Rights of Sovereignty, that he would think it a Diminution to his Prerogative, where he conceiveth it strong enough to go alone, to call in the Legislative help to strengthen and support it.

You have formerly blamed the *Church of England,* and not without reason, for going so far as they did in their Compliance ; and yet as soon as they stopped, you see they are not only deserted, but prosecuted : Conclude then from this Example, that you must either break off your Friendship, or resolve to have no Bounds in it. If they do not succeed in their Design, they will leave you first ; if they do, you must either leave them, when it will be too late for your Safety, or else after the queaziness of starting at a Surplice, you must be forced to swallow Transubstantiation.

Remember that the other day those of the *Church of England* were *Trimmers* for enduring you, and now by a sudden Turn, you are become the Favourites ; do not deceive your selves, it is not the nature of lasting Plants thus to shoot up in a Night ; you may look gay and green for a little time, but you want a Root to give you a Continuance. It is not so long since, as to be forgotten, that the *Maxim* was, *It is impossible for a Dissenter not to be a REBEL.* Consider at this time in *France,* even the new Converts are so far from being imployed, that they are disarmed ; their sudden Change maketh them still to be distrusted, notwithstanding that they are reconciled ; What are you to expect then from your dear Friends, to whom, when ever they shall think fit to throw you off again, you have in other times given such Arguments for their excuse ?

Besides all this, you Act very unskilfully against your visible Interest, if you throw away the Advantages, of which you can hardly fail in the next probable Revolution. Things tend naturally to what you would have, if you would let them alone, and not by an unseasonable Activity lose the Influences of

your

your good Star, which promiseth you every thing that is prosperous.

The *Church of England* convinced of its Error in being severe to you; the *Parliament,* when-ever it meeteth, sure to be gentle to you; the next Heir bred in the Country which you have so often quoted for a Pattern of Indulgence; a general Agreement of all thinking Men, that we must no more cut our selves off from the Protestants abroad, but rather inlarge the Foundations upon which we are to build our Defences against the Common Enemy; so that in truth, all things seem to conspire to give you Ease and Satisfaction, if by too much haste to anticipate your good Fortune, you do not destroy it.

The Protestants have but one Article of Humane Strength, to oppose the Power which is now against them, and that is, not to lose the advantage of their Numbers, by being so unwary as to let themselves be divided.

We all agree in our Duty to our Prince; our Objections to his Belief do not hinder us from seeing his Vertues; and our not complying with his Religion, hath no effect upon our Allegiance; we are not to be laughed out of our Passive-Obedience, and the Doctrine of Non-Resistance; though even those who perhaps owe the best part of their Security to that Principle, are apt to make a Jest of it.

So that if we give no advantage by the fatal Mistake of misapplying our Anger, by the natural course of things, this Danger will pass away like a shower of Hail; fair weather will succeed, as lowering as the Sky now looketh, and all this by plain and easie Receipt; *Let us be still, quiet, and undivided, firm at the same time to our Religion, our Loyalty, and our Laws; and so long as we continue this method, it is next to impossible, that the odds of* 200 *to one should lose the Bett; except the Church of* Rome, *which hath been so long barren of Miracles, should now in her declining Age, be brought to Bed of One that would out-do the best she can brag of in her* Legend.

To conclude, the short Question will be, Whether you will join with those who must in the end run the same Fate with you? If Protestants of all sorts, in their Behaviour to one
another,

another, have been to blame, they are upon the more equal terms, and for that very reason it is fitter for them now to be reconciled. Our Dis-union is not only a Reproach, but a Danger to us; those who believe in modern Miracles, have more Right, or at least more Excuse, to neglect all Secular Cautions; but for us, it is as justifiable to have no Religion, as wilfully to throw away the Humane Means of preserving it. I am,

Dear Sir,

Your most Affectionate humble Servant,

T. W.

Some

Some Cautions offered to the Consideration of those who are to chuse Members *to serve for the Ensuing* Parliament.

I Will make no other Introduction, than that it is hoped the Counties and Boroughs will remember in general, That besides other Consequences, they will have the Credit of a good Choice, or the Scandal that belongeth to an ill one.

The Creators will be thought like their Creatures; and therefore an ill Choice will either be a disparagement of their Understanding, or their Morals.

There cannot be a fuller Approbation of a thing, than the Chusing of it; so that the fault of the Members chosen, if known before-hand, will be judged to be of the growth of that County or Borough, after such a solemn Approbation of them.

In short, those who send up their Representatives to *Westminster*, should take care they may be such as will do them Right, and their Countrey Honour.

Now to the particulars.

I. A very extraordinary earnestness to be chosen, is no very good Symptom : A desire to serve the Nation in Parliament, is an *English* Man's Ambition, always to be Encouraged, and never to be disapproved.

A Man may not only be willing to stand, but he may declare that willingness to his Friends, that they may assist him, and by all the means becoming a modest and prudent Man, he may endeavour to succeed, and prevent the being disappointed in it.

But there is a wide difference between this and the raising a kind of petty War in the County or Corporation ; entring the Lists rather for a Combat than an Election ; throwing Fire-balls

to

to put Men into heat, and omitting to spread no Reports, whether true or false, which may give an advantage by laying a Blemish upon a Competitor.

These Methods will ever be suspicious; it will never be thought a Natural thing for Men to take such extravagant pains for the meer sake of doing good to others.

To be content to suffer something for a good end, is that which many would do without any great repugnance: but where a Man can honestly propose nothing to himself, except Troubles, Charge, and Loss, by absence from his own Affairs, to be so violent in the pursuit of so ill a Bargain, is not at all suited to the languishing Virtue of Mankind so corrupted.

Such a self-denying Zeal in such a self-seeking Age, is so little to be imagin'd, that it may without injury be suspected.

Therefore when these blustring Pretenders come upon the Stage, their natural Temper and other Circumstances ought to be very well consider'd, before Men trust them with the disposal of their Money, or their Liberty.

And I am apt to believe, there could hardly be found one single Man whose other Qualifications would over-balance the Objections that lie against such importunate Suitors.

II. Recommending Letters ought to have no effect upon Elections.

In this I must distinguish; for tho in strictness perhaps there should be no Exception; yet in compliance with long practice, and out of an Indulgence that is necessary in a time when Mankind is too much loosened from severe Rules to be kept close up to them, Letters sent only from Equal Men, doing Good Men right by giving Evidence in their behalf, offering them as fitly qualified, when they really are so, and freeing them from unjust Aspersions, may be still allowed.

The Letters I mean, are from Men of Power, where it may be beneficial to comply, and inconvenient to oppose.

Choice must not only be free from Force, but from Influence, which is a degree of Force: There must be no difficulty, no apprehension that a Refusal will be ill taken, or resented.

The Freeholders must be Freemen too; they are to have no
Shackles

Shackles upon their Votes in an Election: and the Men who stand, should carry their own Letters of Recommendation about them, which are their good Character and Behaviour in the World, without borrowing Evidence, especially when it cometh from suspected hands.

Those who make use of these Epistles, ought to have no more advantage from them, than the *Muscovites* have from the Letters put into their hands, when they are buried, to recommend them to St. *Nicholas*.

The first should as little get admittance for Men into the Parliament, as these Letters can introduce the Bearers into Heaven.

The Scandal of such Letters lieth first in the arrogant imposing of those that write them, and next in the wretched Meanness of those that need them.

Men must be fallen very low in their Credit, who upon such an occasion have a recourse to Power to support it: Their Enemies could not give stronger Evidence of their not being fit for that which they pretend to. And if the Electors judge otherwise, they will be pretty sure in a little time to see their Mistake, and to repent it.

III. Non-Attendance in former Parliaments ought to be a Bar against the Choice of Men who have been guilty of it.

It is one of the worst kinds of Non-Residence, and the least to be excused: It is very hard that Men should despise a Duty, which perhaps is the only ground of the respect that is paid to them.

It is such a piece of Sawciness for any one to press for the Honour of serving in Parliament, and then to be careless in Attending it, that in a House where there were so many Officers, the Penalty had not been improper to have Cashier'd them for not appearing at the General Muster.

If men forbear to come out of Laziness, let them be gratified by taking their ease at Home without Interruption; If out of small Cunning to avoid Difficulties, and to escape from the Inconvenience of Voting in Critical Cases, let them enjoy that despicable pitch of Wisdom, and never pretend to make a Figure where the Publick is to be served.

If

If it would not be thought advisable to trust a Man immediately after he hath been drawn out of a Gaol, it may be as reasonable to look upon one who for his Non-attendance in the House hath been sent for in Custody, as a kind of Bankrupt, which putteth him upon unequal terms with those who have been assiduous in the discharge of their Duty.

They who thought fit in one Session to neglect the Publick Business, may be justly suspected, by their standing, in the next to intend their own.

Besides these more deliberate Offenders, there are some who do not Attend even when they are in the House; absent in their Thoughts for want of Comprehending the Business that is doing, and therefore diverted from it by any thing that is Trivial.

Such Men are Nusances to a serious Assembly; and when they are Numerous, it amounteth almost to a Dissolution; it being scarce possible for good sence to be heard, whilst a noise is made by the buzzing of these Horse flies.

The *Roman* Censors who degraded a Senator for yawning whilst there was a Debate, would have much more abundant matter here upon which they might exercise their Jurisdiction.

To conclude this Head, There are so few that ever mended in these Cases, that after the first Experiment it is not at all reasonable to take them upon a new Tryal.

IV. Men who are unquiet and busy in their Natures, are to give more than ordinary proofs of their Integrity, before the Electing them into a Publick Trust can be justified. As a hot Summer breedeth greater swarms of Flies, so an active time breedeth a greater number of these shining Gentlemen.

It is pretty sure, That men who cannot allow themselves to be at rest, will let no body else be at quiet. Such a perpetual Activity is apt by degrees to be applied to the pursuit of their private interest. And their thoughts being in a continual motion, they have not time to dwell long enough upon any thing to entertain a scruple.

So that they are generally at full liberty to do what is most convenient for them, without being fettered by any Restraints.

Nay further; Whenever it hapneth that there is an Impunity

for Cheating, these nimble Gentlemen are apt to think it a disparagement to their Understandings not to go into it.

I doubt it is not a wrong to the present Age, to say, that a Knave is a less unpopular Calling than it hath been in former times. And to say truth, it would be ingratitude in some Men to turn Honest, when they owe all they have to their Knavery.

The People are in this respect unhappy; they are too many to do their own business; their numbers, which make their strength, are at the same time the cause of their weakness; they are too unweildy to move; and for this Reason nothing can ever redeem them from this incurable Impotency: So that they must have Solicitors to pursue and look after their Interests; who are too often disposed to dispense with the Fidelity they owe to those that trust them; especially if the Government will pay their Bills without Abatement.

It is better these Gentlemen's dexterity should be employed any where than in Parliament, where the ill consequence of their being Members is too much diffused, and not restrained to the County or Borough who shall be so unwary as to Chuse them.

V. Great Drinkers are less fit to Serve in Parliament than is apprehended.

Men's Virtue, as well as their Understanding, is apt to be tainted by it.

The appearance of it is Sociable and well-natur'd, but it is by no means to be rely'd upon.

Nothing is more frail than a Man too far engaged in wet Popularity.

The habit of it maketh Men careless of their business, and that naturally leadeth them into Circumstances that make them liable to Temptation.

It is seldom seen, That any Principles have such a root, as that they can be proof against the continual droppings of a Bottle.

As to the Faculties of the Mind, there is not less Objection; the vapours of Wine may sometimes throw out sparks of Wit, but they are like scattered pieces of Ore, there is no Vein to work upon.

Such

Such Wit, even the best of it, is like paying great Fines; in which case there must of necessity be an abatement of the constant Rent.

Nothing sure is a greater Enemy to the Brain, than too much moisture; it can the least of any thing bear the being continually steeped: And it may be said, that Thought may be resembled to some Creatures which can live only in a dry Country.

Yet so arrogant are some men, as to think they are so much Masters of Business, as that they can play with it; they imagine they can drown their Reason once a day, and that it shall not be the worse for it; forgetting, that by too often diving the Understanding at last groweth too weak to rise up again.

I will suppose this fault was less frequent when *Solon* made it one of his Laws, That it was Lawful to Kill a Magistrate if he was found Drunk. Such a Liberty taken in this Age, either in the Parliament or out of it, would do terrible Execution.

I cannot but mention a Petition in the year 1647, from the County of *Devon*, to the House of Commons, against the undue Election of Burgesses who are strong in Wine and weak in Wisdom.

The cause of such Petitions is to be prevented by Chusing such as shall not give handle for them.

VI. Wanting-Men give such cause of suspicion where ever they deal, that surely the Chusers will be upon their guard, as often as such dangerous pretenders make their application to them.

Let the behaviour of such Men be never so plausible and untainted, yet they who are to pitch upon those they are to trust with all they have, may be excused, if they do not only consider what they are but what they may be.

As we Pray our selves we may not be led into Temptation, we ought not by any means to thrust others into it; even though our own Interest was not concerned; And sure when it is, the Argument hath not less force.

If a Man hath a small Estate, and a numerous Family;

where it happeneth that a Man hath as many Children as he hath Tenants, It is not a Recommending Circumstance for his Election.

When it cometh to be the Question with such a Man, Whether he shall be Just to the Publick, or Cruel to his Family? It is very possible the decision may be on the side of Corrupted Nature.

It is a Compliment to this Age, which it doth not deserve, to suppose Men are so ty'd up to Morality, as that they cannot be pinched out of it: especially now when it is called Starving not to be Embroidered, or served in Plate.

The Men Chosen to serve their Country, should not be loaden with Suits that may tempt them to assume Privileges; much less under such Necessities as may more immediately prepare them for Corruption.

Men who need a Parliament for their own particular Interest, have more reason to offer their Service than others have to accept of it. And though I do not doubt, but there may be some whose Virtue would triumph over their Wants, let them be never so pressing; yet to expose the Publick to the hazard of being deceived, is that which can never be justifi'd by those that Chuse. And tho it must be allow'd possible for a wanting-Man to be honest, yet it is impossible for a Man to be wise that will depend upon it.

VII. There is a sort of Men that have a Tinsel-wit, which make them shine among those who cannot judge.

Club and Coffee-house Gentlemen, Petty Merchants of small Conceits, who have an Empty habit of prating without meaning; They always aim at Wit and generally make false Fire.

Their business is less to learn, than to set themselves out; which makes them chuse to be with such as can only be Witnesses of their small Ingenuity, rather than with such as might improve it.

There is a subordinate Wit, as much inferior to a Wit of business, as a Fidler at a Wake is to the lofty Sound of an Organ.

Men of this Size are in no degree suited to the business of redressing Grievances, and making Laws.

There

There is a Parliament Wit to be distinguish'd from all other kinds; those who have it, do not stuff their heads only with Cavils and Objections.

They have a deliberate and an observing Wit, a Head turned to Publick things; Men who place a greater pleasure in mending a Fault than in finding it out.

Their Understanding directeth them to object in the right place, and not like those who go by no other Rule, than to conclude, That must be the best Counsel which was not taken.

These Whole-sale Judges shew such a gross and peevish Ignorance that it appeareth so openly in all they say or do, That they give loud warning to all considering Men, not to chuse them.

VIII. The dislike of slight Airy Men must not go so far, as to recommend heaviness in opposition to it, especially where men are convicted of it by Experience in former Sessions.

As a lively Coxcomb will seldom fail to lay in his claim for Wit; so a Blockhead is apt to pretend, That his heaviness is a proof of his Judgment.

Some have an universal Lethargy spread upon their Understanding without exception; others have an Insufficiency *quoad hoc*, as in some Cases men have *quoad hanc*; These last can never so turn their thoughts to publick Business, as to give the attention that is necessary to Comprehend it.

There are those who have such a thick Shell upon their Brains, that their Ignorance is impenetrable, and maketh such a stout resistance against Common Sense, that it will never be subdued by it: True Heart of Oak Ignorance that will never yield, let Reason beat never so hard upon it; and though their kind Neighbours have at several Elections sent them up to School again, they have still return'd the same incurable Dunces.

There is a false Gravity that is a very ill symptom; and it may be said, That as Rivers, which run very slowly, have always the most Mud at the bottom; so a solid stiffness in the constant course of a man's Life, is a sign of a thick bed of Mud at the bottom of his Brain.

A dull man is so near a dead Man, that he is hardly to be
ranked

ranked in the List of the Living; and as he is not to be buri'd whilst he is half alive, so he is as little to be imploy'd whilst he is half dead.

Parliaments are now grown to be quite other things than they were formerly.

In Ancient Times they were little more than Great Assizes; A Roll of Grievances; *Magna Charta* confirmed; Privileges of Holy Church preserved; so many Sacks of Wool given; and away.

Now there are Traps and Gins laid for the well-meaning Country-Gentleman; he is to grapple with the Cunning of Men in Town, which is not a little improv'd by being rewarded and encourag'd.

So that men whose good Intentions are not seconded and supported by some degree of Ability, are as much the more dangerous, as they are less criminal than Cunning Knaves. Their honest Mistakes, for want of distinguishing, either give a Countenance to, or at least lessen the Scandal of the injurious things that are done to the Publick: and with leave ask'd for so odd an expression, Their Innocent Guilt is as mischievous to the Laws and Liberties, as the most deliberate Malice of those that would destroy them.

IX. There is an Abuse which daily increaseth, of sending such to Parliament, as are scarce old enough to be sent to the University.

I would not in this restrain the Definition of these Boys to the Age of Twenty One: If my Opinion might take place, I should wish that none might be chosen into the House of Commons under Thirty; and to make some Equality, I should from the same Motives think it convenient, That no Lord should have a Vote in Judicature under that Age.

But to leave this Digression; I cannot see why the Chusers should not at least make it a Rule among themselves, Not to send any Man to Represent them under the Age of Twenty five, which is the time of Majority in most other places of the world.

Surely it is not that we are Earlier plants than our Neighbours. Such supposition could neither be justifi'd by our Climate,

nor

nor by the degree of Latitude in which we are placed; I must therefore attribute it to the haste our Ancestors had (and not without reason) to free themselves from the Severity of Wardships.

But whether this, or any thing else, was the cause of our earlier stepping into Man's Estate; so it is now, that according to our Laws, Twenty one is the Age of Discretion; and the Young Man is then vested with a Legal, how defective soever he may be in his Natural Understanding.

With all this, there ought to be a difference made between coming out of Pupilage, and leaping into Legislatorship.

It is perhaps inconvenient enough that a man should be so soon let loose to destroy his own Estate; but it is yet worse, that he should then have a Power of giving away other men's.

The Law must make General Rules, to which there always will be some Objections.

If there were Tryers appointed to judge when Leading-Strings should be left off, many would wear them a very great while, and some perhaps with their Gray Hairs; there being no small number of Old Boys in all times and especially in this.

It is necessary therefore to make Exceptions to this General Rule, where the Case so much requireth it, as it doth in the matter in question.

The ground of sending these *Minors* to Parliament ought not to recommend the Continuance of it to those who are Lovers of Liberty; since it was by the Authority and Influence of Great Men, that their Stripling Sons were first receiv'd by the humble depending Boroughs, or the complying Counties.

They called it, as many do still, the best School for Young Men. Now Experience hath shew'd us, that it is like a School only in this respect, That these Youngsters when they are admitted, deserve to be whipp'd in it.

If the House of Commons is a School, it must be for Men of riper Age; these are too young to learn there, and being elevated by a mistaken smattering in small Politicks, they grow too supercilious to learn any where else; so that instead of improving young promising Plants, they are destroy'd by being misplac'd.

If

If then they do themselves hurt by it, it is surer yet that they do the House no good by coming into it.

They were not Green Geese that are said to have sav'd the Capitol; they were certainly of full Age, or else their Cackling could not have been heard, so as to give warning.

Indeed it look'd of late, when the Fashion was to have long continu'd Parliaments, as if we might plant a Boy in the House with a Prospect that he might continue there till he had Gray Hairs: And that the same Sapling might have such a Root, as that he might grow up to be Timber without being remov'd.

If these Young Men had skill enough to pitch upon somebody in the House, to whom they might resign their Opinion, and upon whose Judgment they might lean without Reserve, there might be less Objection.

But to speak Truth, they know as little how to chuse, as those did who Elected them; so that there is no other Expedient left, than the letting them alone.

One may say, generally speaking, That a young Man being too soon qualifi'd for the serious Business of Parliaments, would really be no good Symptom.

It is a sign of too much Phlegm, and too little Fire in the beginning of Age, if Men have not a little more heat than is convenient; for as they grow older they will run a hazard of not having so much as is necessary.

The Truth is, The vigour of Youth is soften'd and misapply'd, when it is not spent either in War or close Studies; all other Courses have an idle Mixture that cometh to nothing, and maketh them like Trees, which for want of Pruning run up to Wood, and seldom or never bear any Fruit.

To conclude this Head, it must be own'd, That there is no Age of our Life which doth not carry Arguments along with it to humble us: and therefore it would be well for the Business of the World, if young Men would stay longer before they went into it, and old Men not so long before they went out of it.

X. Next to these may be rank'd a sort of superfine Gentlemen, Carpet-Knights, Men whose Heads may be said to be only

only Appurtenances to their Perukes, which intirely ingross all their Care and Application.

Their Understanding is so strictly appropriated to their Dress, that no part of it is upon pain of their utmost Displeasure to be diverted to any other use.

It is not by this intended to recommend an affected Clown, or to make it a necessary Qualification for a Member of Parliament, that he must renounce clean Linen or good Manners; but surely a too earnest Application to make every thing sit Right about them, striketh too deep into their small stock of Thoughts to allow it Furniture for any thing else.

To do Right to these fine-spun Gentlemen, Business is too coarse a thing for them, which maketh it an unreasonable Hardship upon them to oppress them with it; so that in tenderness to them, no less than out of care to the Publick, it is best to leave them to their Taylors with whom they will live in much better Correspondence, when the Danger is prevented of their falling out about Privileges.

XI. Men of Injustice and Violence, in their private Dealings, are not to be trusted by the People with a Commission to treat for them in Parliament.

In the 4*th* of *Edw.* 3. the King Commandeth in his Writs not to chuse any Knights who had been Guilty of Crime, or Maintenance.

These warm Men seldom fail to run into Maintenance, taken in a larger Extent.

It is an unnatural Sound to come from a Man that is arbitrary in his Neighbourhood, to talk of Laws and Liberties at *Westminster*; he is not a proper Vehicle for such Words, which ought never to be prophaned.

An habitual Breaker of the Laws, to be made one of the Law-makers, is as if the Benches in *Westminster-hall* should be filled with Men out of *Newgate*.

Those who are of this Temper cannot change their Nature out of respect to their Countrey.

Quite contrary, they will less scruple to do Wrong to a Nation where no Body taketh it to himself, than to particular

ticular Men to whose Resentments they are more immediately exposed.

In short they lie under such strong Objections, that the overbalance of better Men cannot altogether purify an Assembly where these unclean Beasts are admitted.

XII. Excessive Spenders and unreasonable Savers are to be Excluded, being both greedy from differing Causes.

They are both of them Diseases of Infection, and for that Reason are not to be admitted into Publick Assemblies.

A prodigal Man must be greedy, because he thinketh he can never spend enough.

The Wretch must be so, because he will never think he can hoard enough.

The World first admireth Men's Wisdom for getting Money, and then raileth at them if they do not throw it away; so that the Prodigal Man is only the less unpopular Extreme; he is every jot as well prepared as the Miser to fall out with his Morals, when once a good Temptation is offered him to lay them aside.

On the other side, some Rich Men are as eager to overtake those that are Richer, as a Running horse is to get to the Racepost before the other that contendeth with him.

Men often desire to heap, rather because others have more, than that they know what to do with that which they covet with so much Impatience.

So that it is plain, the Fancy hath as great a share in this imaginary Pleasure of Gathering as it hath in Love, Ambition, or any other Passion.

It is pretty sure, that as no Man was ever the Richer for having a good Estate, if he did not look after it; so neither will he be the Honester if he hath never so much.

Want of care will always create want of Money; so that whether a Man is a begger because he never had any Money, or because he can never keep any, it is all one to those who are to trust him.

Upon this head of Prodigality, it may be no unreasonable Caution to be afraid of those who in former Service have been extravagantly Liberal of the Publick Money.

Trusting

Trusting is so hazardous a thing, that it should never be done but where it is necessary; so that when Trustees are found upon Tryal to be very Lavish, even without examining into the Causes of it, (which are generally very suspicious) it is a reasonable part of preventing Wit to change Hands, or else the Chusers will pay the Penalty that belongeth to good Nature so misplaced, and the Consequences will be attended with the Aggravation of their not being made Wiser by such a severe and costly warning.

XIII. It would be of very great use to take a general Resolution throughout the Kingdom, That none should be chosen for a County but such as have either in Possession, or Reversion, a considerable Estate in it; nor for a Burrough, except he be Resiant, or that he hath some Estate in the County, in present or Expectancy.

There have been Eminent Men of Law who were of opinion, That in the Case of a Burgess of a Town not Resiant, the Court is to give Judgment according to the Statute, notwithstanding Custom to the contrary.

But not to insist now upon that, the prudential part is Argument enough to set up a Rule to abrogate an ill Custom.

There is not, perhaps, a greater Cause of the Corruption of Parliaments, than by adopting Members, who may be said to have no title by their Births.

The Juries are by the Law to be *Ex vicineto*; And shall there be less care that the Representatives of the People be so too?

Sure the Interest of the County is best placed in the hands of such as have some share in it.

The Outliers are not so easily kept within the pale of the Laws.

They are often chosen without being known, which is more like chusing Valentines, than Members of Parliament. The Motive of their standing is more justly to be supposed, that they may redress their own Grievances which they know, than those of the Countrey, to which they are strangers.

They are chosen at *London* to serve in *Cornwall*, &c. and
are

are often Parties, before they come to be Representatives : One would think the Reproach it is for a County not to have Men within their own Circle to serve them in Parliament, should be Argument enough to reject these Trespassers, without urging the ill Consequences in other Respects of their being admitted.

XIV. As in some Cases it is advisable to give a total exclusion to Men not fitly qualified; so in others it is more proper to lay down a general Rule of Caution, with allowance of some Exceptions, where Men have given such proofs of themselves, as create a Right for them to be distinguished.

Of this nature is that which I shall say concerning Lawyers, who, by the same Reason that they may be useful, may be also very dangerous.

The Negligence, and want of Application in Gentlemen, hath made them to be thought more necessary than naturally they are in Parliament.

They have not only ingrossed the Chair of the Speaker, but that of a Committee is hardly thought to be well filled, except it be by a Man of the Robe.

This maketh it worthy of the more serious reflection of all Gentlemen, that it may be an Argument to them to qualify themselves in Parliamentary Learning, in such a manner, as that they may rely upon their own Abilities, in order to the serving their Countrey.

But to come to the point in question; It is not without Precedent, that Practising-Lawyers have been excluded from serving in Parliament; and, without following those Patterns strictly, I cannot but think it reasonable, that whilst a Parliament sitteth, no Member of Parliament should plead at any Bar.

The Reason of it is in many respects strong in it self, and is grown much stronger by the long sitting of Parliaments of late; but I will not dwell upon this : The matter now in question being concerning Lawyers being Elected, which I conceive should be done with so much circumspection, that probably it would not often happen.

If Lawyers have great Practice, that ought to take them up;

if

if not, it is no great sign of their Ability; and at the same time giveth a suspicion, that they may be more liable to be tempted.

If it should be so in Fact, That no King ever wanted Judges to soften the stiffness of the Laws that were made, so as to make them suit better with the Reason of State, and the Convenience of the Government; it is no Injury now to suppose it possible for Lawyers in the House of Commons, so to behave themselves in the making of New Laws, as the better to make way for the having their Robes lined with Fur.

They are Men used to argue on both sides of a Question; And if ordinary Fees can inspire them with very good Reasons in a very ill Cause, that Faculty exercised in Parliaments, where it may be better encouraged, may prove very inconvenient to those that chuse them.

And therefore, without arraigning a Profession, that it would be scandalous for a man not to honour; one may, by a Suspicion which is the more excusable when it is in the behalf of the People, imagine that the habit of taking Money for their Opinion, may create in some such a forgetfulness to distinguish, that they may take it for their Vote.

They are generally Men who by a laborious study hope to be advanced: They have it in their Eye as a Reward for the Toil they undergo.

This maketh them generally very slow, and ill disposed (let the Occasion never so much require it) to wrestle with that Soil where Preferment groweth.

Now if the Supposition be in its self not unreasonable, and that it should happen to be strengthen'd and confirm'd by Experience, it will be very unnecessary to say any more upon this Article, but leave it to the Electors to consider of it.

XV. I cannot forbear to put in a Caveat against Men ty'd to a Party.

There must in every body be a Leaning to that sort of Men who profess some Principles, more than to others who go upon a different Foundation; but when a man is drowned in a Party, plunged in it beyond his depth, he runneth a great hazard of

being

being upon ill terms with good Sense, or Morality, if not with both of them.

Such a man can hardly be called a Free-Agent, and for that reason is very unfit to be trusted with the Peoples Liberty, after he hath given up his own.

It is said, That in some part of the *Indies* they do so affect little Feet, that they keep them squeezed while they are Children, so that they stay at that small size after they are grown Men.

One may say something like this of Men lock'd up in a Party; They put their Thoughts into such a Narrow Mould, that they can never be enlarged nor released from their first Confinements.

Men in a Party have *Liberty* only for their *Motto*; in reality they are greater Slaves than any body else would care to make them.

A Party, even in times of Peace, (tho against the Original Contract, and the Bill of Rights) sets up and continues the exercise of Martial Law: Once inrolled, the Man that quitteth, if they had their will, would be hanged for a Deserter.

They communicate Anger to one another by Contagion: And it may be said, that if too much Light dazzleth the Eyesight, too much Heat doth not less weaken the Judgment.

Heat reigneth in the Fancy; and Reason, which is a colder Faculty of the Brain, taketh more time to be heard, than the other will allow.

The Heat of a Party is like the Burning of a Fever; and not a Natural Warmth, evenly distributed to give Life and Vigor.

There was a time indeed when Anger shew'd a good sign of Honesty; but that Evidence is very much weakned by Instances we have seen since the Days of Yore: And the Publick spirited Choler hath been thrown off within time of Memory, and lost almost all its Credit with some People, since they found what Governments thought fit to make their so doing a step to their preferment.

A strong blustring Wind seldom continues long in one Corner.

                                                            Some

Some men knock loud only to be let in ; the Bustle they make is animated by their private Interest. The outward Blaze only is for Religion and Liberty : The true lasting Fire, like that of the Vestals which never went out, is an eagerness to get somewhat for themselves.

A House of Commons composed of such Men, would be more properly so many Merchants incorporated in a Regular Company, to make their particular Adventures, than Men sent from the People to serve and represent them.

There are some Splenetick Gentlemen who confine their favourable Opinion within so narrow a compass, that they will not allow it to any man that was not hanged in the late Reigns.

Now by that rule one might expect they should rescue themselves from the disadvantage of being now alive ; and by abdicating a World so little worthy of them, get a great Name to themselves, with the general satisfaction of all those they would leave behind them.

Amongst the many other ill consequences of a stated Party, it is none of the least, that it tempteth low and insignificant men to come upon the Stage, to expose themselves, and to spoil Business.

It turneth a Cypher into a Figure, such an one as it is : A man in a Party is able to make a noise, let it be never so empty a sound.

A weak man is easily blown out of his small senses, by being muster'd into a Party ; he is flatter'd till he liketh himself so well, that he taketh it extremely ill if he hath not an Employment.

Nothing is more in fashion, than for men to desire good Places, and I doubt nothing is less so than to deserve them.

From Nobody to somebody is such a violent stride, that Nature, which hath the Negative Voice, will not give its Royal Assent to it : So that when insufficient Men aim at being in business, the worst of their Enemies might out of malice to them pray for their Preferment.

There could be no end, if one did not stop till this Theme had no more matter to furnish. I will only say, Nothing is
more

more evident, than that the Good of the Nation hath been sacrificed to the Animosities of the several Contending Parties; and without entring into the dispute which of them are more or less in the right, it is pretty sure, that whilst these Opposite Sets of Angry Men are playing at Foot-ball, they will break all the Windows, and do more hurt than their pretended Zeal for the Nation will ever make amends for.

In short, a man so engaged is retained before the people take him for their Council; he hath such a Reserve for his Party, that it is not adviseable for those who would chuse him, to depend upon his Professions; all Parties assuming such a Dispensing Power, that by their Sovereign Authority they cancel and dissolve any Act or Promise that they do not afterwards approve.

These things considered, those who will chuse such men deserve whatever followeth.

XVI. Pretenders to Exorbitant Merit in the late Revolution, are not without Objections against them, when they stand to serve in Parliament. It would not only be a low, but a Criminal kind of Envy, to deny a distinguishing Justice to Men who have been instrumental and active, when the Service of their Countrey requir'd it. But there ought to be Moderation in men's Claims, or else it is out of the Power of our poor Island to satisfy them. It is true, Service of all kinds is grown much dearer, like Labourer's Wages, which formerly occasioned several Statutes to regulate them.

But now the men who only carried Mortar to the Building, when it is finished, think they are ill dealt with if they are not made Master-Workmen.

They presently cry out, The Original Contract is broken, if their Merit is not rewarded, at their own Rate too.

Some will think there never ought to be an end of their Rewards; when indifferent Judges would perhaps be puzzled to find out the beginning of their Merit.

They bring in such large Bills, that they must be examin'd: Some bounds must be put to men's Pretensions; else the Nation, which is to pay the Reckoning, will every way think it a scurvy thing to be undone, whether it be by being

over-run

over-run by our Enemies, or by the being exhausted by our Friends.

There ought therefore to be deductions where they are reasonable, the better to justifie the paying what remaineth.

For example, if any of these passionate Lovers of the Protestant Religion should not think fit, in their manner of Living, to give the least evidence of their Morality, their claims upon that Head might sure be struck off without any Injustice to them.

If there are any who set down great Sums as a Reward due to their Zeal for rescuing Property from the Jaws of Arbitrary Power; their pretensions may fairly be rejected, if now they are so far from shewing a care and tenderness of the Laws, that they look rather like Counsel retained on the other side.

It is no less strange, than I doubt it is true, that some Men should be so in Love with their dear Mistress, *Old England,* with all her Wrinkles, as out of an Heroick Passion to Swim over to rescue her from being Ravish'd; and when they have done the Feat, the first thing after Enjoyment is, that they go about to Strangle her.

For the sake of true Love, it is not fit that such ungenteel Gallants should be too much encourag'd; and their Arrogance for having done well at first, will have no right to be excused, if their so doing ill at last doth not make them a little more modest.

True Merit, like a River, the deeper it is the less noise it maketh.

These loud proclaimers of their own Deserts, are not only to be suspected for their truth, but the Electors are to consider that such meritorious Men lay an assessment upon those that Chuse them.

The Publick Taxes are already heavy enough without the addition of these private Reckonings. It is therefore the safer way not to employ Men, who will expect more for their Wages, than the mistaken Borough that sendeth them up to Parliament could be sold for.

XVII. With all due regard to the noblest of Callings,

Military Officers are out of their true Element when they are misplaced in a House of Commons.

Things in this World ought to be well suited. There are some Appearances so unnatural, that men are convinc'd by them without any other Argument.

The very Habit in some Cases, recommendeth or giveth Offence.

If the Judges upon the Bench should, instead of their Furrs, which signifie Gravity, and bespeak Respect, be Cloathed like the Jockeys at *New-Market*, or wear Jack-Boots and *Steenkirks*; they would not in reality have less Law, but Mankind would be so struck with this unusual Object, that it would be a great while before they could think it possible to receive Justice from Men so Accouter'd.

It is to some degree the same thing in this Case; such Martial Habits, Blue-Coats, Red-Stockings, *&c.* make them look very unlike Grave Senators. One would almost swear they were Creatures apart, and of a differing Species from the rest of the Body.

In former times, when only the Resiant Shopkeeper was to Represent his Corporation (which by the way is the Law still at this day) the Military Looks of one of these Sons of *Mars*, would have stared the Quaking Member down again to his Burrough.

Now the number of them is so encreased, that the Peaceable part of the House may lawfully swear they are in fear of their Lives, from such an Awful Appearance of Men of War.

It maketh the Room look like a Guard-house by such an ill-suited mixture. But this is only the out-side, the bark of the Argument; the root goeth yet deeper against Chusing such Men, whose Talents ought to be otherwise applied.

Their Two Capacities are so inconsistent, that Mens undertaking to serve both the Cures, will be the cause in a little time, that we shall neither have Men of War, nor Men of Business, good in their several kinds.

An Officer is to give up his Liberty to obey Orders; and it is necessarily incident to his Calling that he should do so.

A

A Member of Parliament is originally to be tender of his own Liberty, that other Men may the better trust him with theirs.

An Officer is to enable himself by his Courage, improved by Skill and Experience, to support the Laws (if Invaded) when they are made; but he is not supposed to be at leisure enough to understand how they should be made.

A Member of Parliament is to fill his thoughts with what may best conduce to the Civil Administration; which is enough to take up the whole Man, let him be never so much raised above the ordinary Level.

These two opposite Qualifications, being placed in one Man, make him such an ambiguous divided Creature, that he doth not know how to move.

It is best to keep Men within their proper Sphere; few Men have Understanding enough exactly to fill even one narrow Circle, fewer are able to fill two; especially when they are both of so great compass, and that they are so contrary in their own Natures.

The Wages he hath as a Member, and those he receiveth as an Officer, are paid for Services that are very differing; and in the doubt which of them should be preferrably performed, it is likely the greater Salary may direct him, without the further inducements of complying most, where he may expect most advantage by it.

In short, if his dependance is not very great, it will make him a scurvy Officer; if it is great, it will make him a scurvier Member.

XVIII. Men under the scandal of being thought private Pensioners, are too fair a mark to escape being consider'd, in reference to the point in Question.

In case of plain Evidence, it is not to be suppos'd possible, that Men convicted of such a Crime should ever again be Elected.

The difficulty is in determining what is to be done in case of suspicion.

There are suspicions so well grounded, that they may pretend to have the force of proofs, provided the penalty goeth only

to

to the forbearing to Trust, but not extending it so far as to Punish.

There must be some things plain and express to justify the latter, but Circumstances may be sufficient for the former: As where Men have had such sudden Cures of their ill Humours, and opposition to the Court, that it is out of the way of ordinary methods of recovery from such Distempers, which have a much slower progress; it must naturally be imputed to some Specifick that maketh such a quick alteration of the whole Mass of Blood.

Where Men have raised their way of Living, without any visible means to support them in it, a suspicion is justified, even by the Example of the Law, which in cases of this kind, though of an inferior nature, doth upon this foundation not only raise Inferences, but inflict Punishments.

Where Men are immoral, and scandalous in their Lives, and dispense familiarly with the Rules by which the World is Govern'd, for the better preserving the bonds of human Society; it must be a confidence very ill placed, to conclude it impossible for such Men to yield to a Temptation well offer'd and pursu'd; when, the truth is, the habit of such *Bons vivants*, which is the fashionable word, maketh a suspicion so likely, that it is very hard not to believe it to be true.

If there should be nothing but the general Report, even that is not to be neglected.

Common Fame is the only Lyar that deserveth to have some Respect still reserv'd to it; tho she telleth many an Untruth, she often hitteth right, and most especially when she speaketh ill of men.

Her Credit hath sometimes been carried too far, when it hath gone to the divesting men of any thing of which they were possess'd, without more express evidence to justify such a proceeding.

If there was a doubt whether there ever was any Corruption of this kind it would alter the Question; but sure that will not bear the being controverted.

We are told, That *Charles* the Fifth sent over into *England*

1200000

1200000 Crowns to be distributed amongst the Leading Men, to encourage them to carry on Elections.

Here was the Protestant Religion to be bought out for a valuable Consideration according to Law, though not according to Gospel, which exalteth it above any Price that can be set upon it.

Now, except we had reason to believe that the Vertue of the World is improv'd since that time, we can as little doubt that such Temptations may be offered, as that they may be receiv'd.

It will be owned, that there is to be a great tenderness in Suspecting; but it must be allow'd at the same time, that there ought not to be less in Trusting, where the People are so much concern'd; especially, when the Penalty upon the Party suspected goeth no further than a Suspension of that Confidence, which it is necessary to have in those who are to represent the Nation in Parliament.

XIX. I cannot omit the giving a Caution against admitting Men to be chosen, who have Places of any value.

There needeth the less to be said upon this Article, the truth of the Proposition being supported by such plain Arguments.

Sure no Man hath such a plentiful spring of Thought, as that all that floweth from it is too much to be applied to the Business of Parliament.

It is not less sure, that a Member of Parliament, of all others, ought not to be exempted from the Rule, That no Man should serve two Masters.

It doth so split a Man's Thoughts, that no Man can know how to make a fitting Distribution of them to two such differing Capacities.

It exposeth Men to be suspected, and tempted, more than is convenient for the Publick Service, or for the mutual good Opinion of one another which there ought to be in such an Assembly.

It either giveth a real dependance upon the Government, which is inconsistent with the necessity there is, that a Member of Parliament should be disengaged; or at least it hath the

appearance

appearance of it, which maketh them not look like Freemen, though they should have virtue enough to be so.

More Reasons would lessen the Weight of this last, which is, That a Bill to this effect, commonly called the *Self Denying Bill*, pass'd even this last House of Commons.

A greater Demonstration of the irresistible strength of Truth cannot possibly be given ; so that a Copy of that Bill in every County or Burrough, would hardly fail of discouraging such Pretenders from Standing, or at least it would prevent their Success if their own Modesty should not restrain them from attempting it.

XX. If Distinctions may be made upon particular Men, or Remarks fix'd upon their Votes in Parliament, they must be allow'd in relation to those Gentlemen, who for Reasons best known to themselves thought fit to be against the *Triennial Bill*.

The Liberty of Opinion is the thing in the World that ought least to be controll'd, and especially in Parliament.

But as that is an undoubted Assertion, it is not less so, That when Men Sin against their own Light, give a Vote against their own Thought, they must not plead Privilege of Parliament against the being arraigned for it by others, after they are Convicted of it by themselves.

There cannot be a Man, who in his Definition of a House of Commons, will state it to be an Assembly, that for the better redressing of Grievances the People feel, and for the better furnishing such Supplies as they can bear, is to continue, if the King so pleaseth, for his whole Reign.

This could be as little intended, as to throw all into one Hand, and to renounce the Claim to any Liberty, but so much as the Sovereign Authority would allow.

It destroyeth the end of Parliaments, it maketh use of the Letter of the Law to extinguish the Life of it.

It is, in truth, some kind of Disparagement to so plain a thing, that so much has been said and written upon it ; and one may say, It is such an Affront to these Gentlemens Understandings to censure this Vote only as a Mistake, that, as the Age goeth, it is less Discredit to them to call it by its right Name ; and if
that

that is rightly understood by those who are to chuse them, I suppose they will let them exercise their Liberty of Conscience at home, and not make Men their Trustees, who in this Solemn Instance have such an unwillingness to surrender.

It must be own'd, That this Bill hath met with very hard Fortune, and yet that doth not in the least diminish the value of it.

It had in it such a Root of Life, that it might be said, It was not Dead but Sleeped ; and we see that the last Session, it was revived and animated by the Royal Assent, when once fully inform'd of the Consequence, as well as of the Justice of it.

In the mean time, after having told my Opinion, Who ought not to be Chosen :

If I should be ask'd, Who ought to be, my Answer must be, Chuse *Englishmen* ; and when I have said that, to deal honestly, I will not undertake that they are easy to be found.

A

A
Rough Draught
OF A
NEW MODEL
AT
SEA, 1694.

I Will make no other Introduction to the following Discourse, than that as the Importance of our being strong at *Sea*, was ever very great, so in our present Circumstances it is grown to be much greater ; because, as formerly our Force of Shipping contributed greatly to our *Trade* and Safety, so now it is become indispensibly necessary to our very *Being*.

It may be said now to *England, Martha, Martha,* thou art busy about many things, but one thing is necessary. To the Question, What shall we do to be saved in this World ? there is no other Answer but this, Look to your Moate.

The first Article of an *English-mans* Political Creed must be, That he believeth in the Sea, *&c.* without that there needeth no General Council to pronounce him incapable of Salvation here.

We are in an Island, confin'd to it by God Almighty, not as a Penalty but a Grace, and one of the greatest that can be given to Mankind. Happy Confinement, that hath made us Free, Rich, and Quiet ; a fair Portion in this World, and very well worth the preserving ; a Figure that ever hath been envied, and could never be imitated by our Neighbours. Our Situation hath

made

made Greatness abroad by Land Conquests unnatural things to us. It is true, we have made Excursions, and glorious ones too, which make our Names great in History, but they did not last.

Admit the *English* to be Giants in Courage, yet they must not hope to succeed in making War against Heaven, which seemeth to have enjoyed them to acquiesce in being happy within their own Circle. It is no Paradox to say, that *England* hath its Root in the Sea, and a deep one too, from whence it sendeth its Branches into both the *Indies*. We may say further in our present Case, That if *Allegiance* is due to *Protection*, ours to the Sea is due from that Rule, since by that, and by that alone, we are to be protected; and if we have of late suffered Usurpation of other Methods, contrary to the Homage we owe to that which must preserve us, it is time now to restore the *Sea* to its right; and as there is no Repentance effectual without Amendment, so there is not a moment to be lost in the going about it.

It is not pretended to launch into such a Voluminous Treatise, as to set down every thing to which so comprehensive a Subject might lead me; for as the Sea hath little less variety in it than the Land; so the Naval Force of *England* extendeth it self into a great many Branches, each of which are important enough to require a Discourse apart, and peculiarly applied to it: But there must be preference to some Considerations above others, when the weight of them is so visibly Superior that it cannot be contested. It is there, first, that the Foundations are to be laid of our Naval Oeconomy; amongst these, there is one Article which in its own Nature must be allowed to be the Corner-stone of the Building: the Choice of *Officers*, with the *Discipline* and *Encouragement* belonging to them. Upon this Head only, I shall then take the liberty to venture my Opinion into the World, with a real Submission to those, who may offer any thing better for the advantage of the *Publick*.

The first Question then will be, Out of what sort of Men the *Officers* of the *Fleet* are to be chosen; and this immediately leadeth us to the present Controversy between the *Gentlemen* and the *Tarpaulins*.

The

The usual Objections on both sides are too general to be relied upon. Partiality and Common Prejudices direct most Mens Opinions, without entring into the particular Reasons which ought to be the ground of it. There is so much ease in acquiescing in Generals, that the Ignorance of those who cannot distinguish, and the Largeness of those who will not, maketh Men very apt to decline the trouble of stricter Enquiries, which they think too great a price for being in the right, let it be never so valuable.

This maketh them judge in the Lump, and either let their Opinions swim along with the Stream of the World, or give them up wholly to be directed by Success. The effect of this is, that they change their Minds upon every present uneasiness, wanting a steady Foundation upon which their Judgment should be formed. This is a pearching upon the Twigs of things, and not going to the Root. But sure the Matter in question deserveth to be examined in another manner, since so much dependeth upon it.

To state the thing impartially, it must be owned that it seemeth to lye fairest for the *Tarpaulin*: It giveth an Impression that must have so much weight as to make a Man's Opinion lean very much on that side, it carrieth so much Authority with it, it seemeth to be so unquestionable, that those are fittest to Command at Sea, who have not only made it their *Calling*, but their *Element*; that there must naturally be a prejudice to any thing then can be said against it. There must therefore be some Reason extraordinary to support the Argument on the other side, or else the Gentlemen could never enter the Lists against such a violent Objection, which seemeth not to be resisted. I will introduce my Argument with an Assertion, which as I take to be true almost in all Cases, so it is necessary to be explained and inforced in this. The *Assertion* is, that there is hardly a single Proposition to be made, which is not deceitful, and the tying our Reason too close to it, may in many Cases be destructive. Circumstances must come in, and are to be made a part of the Matter of which we are to judge ; positive *Decisions* are always dangerous, more especially in *Politicks*. A Man, who

who will be Master of an Argument, must do like a skilful General, who sendeth Scouts on all sides, to see whether there may not be an Enemy. So he must look round to see what Objections can be made, and not go on in a streight Line, which is the ready way to lead him into a mistake.

Before then, that we conclude what sort of Men are fittest to Command at Sea, a Principle is to be laid down, that there is a differing Consideration to be had of such a Subject-matter, as is in it self distinct and independent, and of such an one as being a Limb of a Body, or a Wheel of a Frame, there is a necessity of suiting it to the rest, and preserving the Harmony of the whole. A Man must not in that Case restrain himself to the separate Consideration of that single Part, but must take care it may fall in and agree with the Shape of the whole Creature, of which it is a Member. According to this Proposition, which I take to be indisputable, it will not I hope appear an Affectation, or an extravagant Fit of unseasonable Politicks, if, before I enter into the particular State of the present Question, I say something of the Government of *England,* and make that the Ground-work of what sort of Men are most proper to be made use of to Command at Sea.

The Forms of Government to which *England* must be subjected, are either *Absolute Monarchy,* a *Commonwealth,* or a *Mixt Monarchy,* as it is now ; with those natural Alterations that the Exigency of Affairs may from time to time suggest. As to Absolute Monarchy, I will not allow my self to be transported into such Invectives, as are generally made against it; neither am I ready to enter into the aggravating Stile of calling every thing *Slavery,* that restraineth Men in any part of their Freedom : One may discern in this, as in most other things, the good and bad of it. We see by too near an Instance, what *France* doth by it ; it doth not only struggle with the rest of *Christendom,* but is in a fair way of giving Law to it.

This is owing in great Measure to a *Despotick* and Undivided Power ; the uncontroulable Authority of the Directive Councils maketh every thing move without Disorder or Opposition, which must give an advantage, that is plain enough of it self, without
being

being proved by the melancholly Experience we have of it at
this time.

I see and admire this; yet I consider at the same time, that
all things of this kind are comparative: That as on one side,
without *Government* Men cannot enjoy what belongeth to them
in particular, nor can a Nation be secure, or preserve it self in
general: So on the other side, the end of *Government* being,
that Mankind should live in some competent State of Freedom,
it is very unnatural to have the *End* destroyed by the *Means* that
were originally made use of to attain it. In this respect something is to be ventured, rather than submit to such a precarious
State of Life, as would make it a Burthen to a reasonable
Creature; and therefore, after I have owned the Advantages in
some kind of an unlimited Government; yet, while they are
attended with so many other discouraging Circumstances, I
cannot think but that they may be bought too dear; and if it
should be so, that it is not possible for a *State* to be *Great* and
Glorious, unless the Subjects are *wretchedly Miserable,* I am not
ashamed to own my low-spirited frailty, in preferring such
a Model of Government, as may agree with the reasonable
Enjoyment of a *Free People,* before such a one by which
Empire is to be extended at such an unnatural Price. Besides
whatever Mens Opinions may be one way or another in the
general Question, there is an Argument in our Case that
shutteth the Door to any Answer to it: *viz.* We cannot subsist under a *Despotick* Power, our very Being would be destroyed
by it; for we are to consider, we are a very little Spot in the
Map of the World, and make a great Figure only by *Trade,*
which is the Creature of Liberty; one destroyed, the other
falleth to the Ground by a natural Consequence that will not
admit a dispute. If we would be measured by our Acres, we
are poor inconsiderable People; we are exalted above our
natural Bounds, by our good Laws, and our excellent Constitution. By this we are not only happy at Home, but considerable
Abroad. Our Situation, our Humour, our Trade, do all concur
to strengthen this Argument. So that all other Reasons must
give

give place to such a one as maketh it out, that there is no Mean between a *Free Nation* and *No Nation*.

We are no more a People, nor *England* can no longer keep its Name, from the moment that our Liberties are extinguish'd; the Vital Strength that should support us being withdrawn, we should then be no more than the Carcass of a Nation, with no other Security than that of *Contempt*; and to subsist upon no other Tenure, than that we should be below the giving Temptation to our stronger Neighbours to devour us. In my Judgment, therefore, there is such a short Decision to be made upon this Subject, that in Relation to *England*, an *Absolute Monarchy* is as unreasonable a thing to be wished, as I hope it will be impossible to be obtained.

It must be considered in the next place, whether *England* is likely to be turn'd into a Commonwealth. It is hard at any time to determine what will be the Shape of the next Revolution, much more at this time would it be inexcusably Arrogant to undertake it. Who can foresee whether it will be from without, or from within, or from both? Whether with or without the Concurrence of the People? Whether regularly produced, or violently imposed? I shall not therefore *Magisterially* declare it impossible that a *Commonwealth* should be settled here; but I may give my humble Opinion, that according to all appearances, it is very improbable.

I will first lay it down for a Principle, That it is not a sound way of arguing, to say, That if it can be made out, that the Form of a *Commonwealth* will best suit with the Interest of the Nation, it must for that reason of necessity prevail.

I will not deny but that *Interest will not lie,* is a right *Maxim,* where ever it is sure to be understood; else one had as good affirm, That no Man in particular, nor Mankind in general, can ever be mistaken. A Nation is a great while before they can see, and generally they must feel first before their Sight is quite cleared. This maketh it so long before they can see their *Interest,* that for the most part it is too late for them to pursue it: If Men must be supposed always to follow their true *Interest,* it must be meant of a New Manufactory of Mankind

by

by God Almighty; there must be some new *Clay*, the old *Stuff* never yet made any such infallible Creature.

This being premis'd, it is to be inquired, Whether instead of inclination, or a leaning towards a *Commonwealth*, there is not in *England* a general dislike to it; if this be so, as I take it to be, by a very great disparity in Numbers, it will be in vain to dispute the *Reason*, whilst *Humour* is against it; allowing the weight that is due to the Argument which may be alledged for it, yet, if the *Herd* is against it, the going about to convince them would have no other effect than to shew that nothing can be more impertinent than good *Reasons*, when they are misplaced or ill-timed.

I must observe, That there must be some previous Dispositions in all great Changes to facilitate and to make way for them: I think it not at all absurd to affirm, That such Resolutions are seldom made at all, except by the general Preparations of Mens Minds they are half made before it is plainly visible that Men go about them.

Though it seemeth to me that this Argument alone maketh all others unnecessary, yet I must take notice that besides what hath been said upon this Subject, there are certain Preliminaries to the first building a *Commonwealth*, some Materials absolutely necessary for the carrying on such a *Fabrick*, which at present are wanting amongst us, I mean *Virtue*, *Morality*, *Diligence*, or at least *Hypocrisy*. Now this Age is so plain dealing, as not to dissemble so far as to an outward Pretence of *Qualities* which seem at present so *Unfashionable*, and under so much Discountenance.

From hence we may draw a plain and natural Inference, That a *Commonwealth* is not fit for us, because we are not fit for a *Commonwealth*.

This being granted, the Supposition of this Form of Government of *England*, with all its Consequences as to the present Question, must be excluded, and *Absolute Monarchy* having been so too by the Reasons at once alledged, it will without further Examination fall to a *Mixt Government*, as we now are. I will not say, that there is never to be any Alteration; the
Constitution

Constitution of the several Parts that concur to make up the Frame of the present Government may be altered in many things, in some for the better, and in others, perhaps for the worse, according as Circumstances shall arise to induce a *Change*, and as Passion and Interest shall have more or less Influence upon the Publick Councils; but still, if it remaineth in the whole so far a *mixt Monarchy*, that there shall be a restraint upon the *Prince* as to the Exercise of a *Despotick Power*, it is enough to make it a Groundwork for the present Question. It appeareth then that a *bounded Monarchy* is that kind of Government which will most probably prevail and continue in *England*; from whence it must follow (as hath been hinted before) that every considerable Part ought to be so composed, as the better to conduce to the preserving the Harmony of the whole Constitution. The *Navy* is of so great Importance, that it would be disparaged by calling it less than the *Life* and *Soul* of Government.

Therefore to apply the Argument to the Subject we are upon; in case the *Officers* be all *Tarpaulins*, it would be in reality too great a tendency to a *Commonwealth*; such a part of the Constitution being *Democratically* disposed may be suspected to endeavour to bring it into that Shape; and where the influence must be so strong, the Supposition will be the more justifiable. In short, if the *Maritime Force*, which is the only thing that can defend us, should be wholly directed by the lower sort of Men, with an intire Exclusion of the *Nobility* and *Gentry*, it will not be easy to answer the Arguments supported by so great a probability, that such a Scheme would not only lean toward a *Democracy*, but directly lead us into it.

Let us now examine the contrary Proposition, *viz. that all Officers should be Gentlemen*.

Here the Objection lieth so fair, of its introducing an *Arbitrary Government*, that it is as little to be answered in that respect, as the former is in the other. *Gentlemen* in a general Definition, will be suspected to lie more than other Men under the Temptations of being made Instruments of unlimited Power; their Relations, their Way of Living, their Tast of the Entertainments of of the *Court,* inspire an Ambition that generally draweth their Inclinations toward it, besides the gratifying of their Interests. Men of Quality are often taken with the Ornaments of Government, the Splendor dazleth them so, as that their Judgments are surprized by it ; and there will be always some that have so little remorse for invading other Mens Liberties, that it maketh them less solicitous to preserve their own.

These things throw them naturally into such a dependance as might give a dangerous Biass ; if they alone were in Command at Sea, it would make that great Wheel turn by an irregular Motion, and instead of being the chief means of preserving the whole Frame, might come to be the chief Instruments to discompose and dissolve it.

The two former exclusive Propositions being necessarily to be excluded in this Question, there remaineth no other Expedient, neither can any other Conclusion be drawn from the Argument as it hath been stated, than that there must be a mixture in the Navy of *Gentlemen* and *Tarpaulins,* as there is in the Constitution of the Government, of *Power* and *Liberty.* This Mixture is not to be so rigorously defined, as to set down the exact Proportion there is to be of each ; the greater or lesser Number must be directed by Circumstances, of which the Government is to Judge, and which make it improper to set such Bounds, as that upon no occasion it shall on either side be lessened or enlarged. It is possible the Men of *Wapping* may think they are injured, by giving them any Partners in the Dominion of the *Sea*; they may take it unkindly to be jostled in their own *Element* by Men of such a different Education, that they may be said to be of another Species; they will be apt to think it an Usurpation upon them, and notwithstanding the Instances that are against them, and which give a kind of Prescription on the other side, they will not easily acquiesce in what they conceive to be a hardship to them.

But I shall in a good measure reconcile my self to them by what follows; *viz.* The *Gentlemen* shall not be capable of bearing Office at *Sea,* except they be *Tarpaulins* too ; that is to say, except they are so trained up by a continued habit of living

at

at *Sea,* that they may have a Right to be admitted free *Denizens* of *Wapping.* Upon this dependeth the whole Matter; and indeed here lieth the difficulty, because the *Gentlemen* brought up under the Connivance of a looser Discipline, and of an easier admittance, will take it heavily to be reduced within the *Fetters* of such a *New Model;* and I conclude, they will be so extreamly averse to that which they call an unreasonable Yoke upon them, that their Original Consent is never to be expected. But if it appeareth to be convenient, and which is more, that it is necessary for the Preservation of the whole, that it should be so ; the Government must be call'd in Aid to suppress these first Boilings of Discontent; the Rules must be imposed with such Authority, and the Execution of them must be so well supported, that by degrees their Impatience will be subdued, and they will concur in an Establishment to which they will every day be more reconciled.

They will find it will take away the Objections which are now thrown upon them, of setting up for Masters without having ever been Apprentices; or at least, without having served out their Time.

Mankind naturally swelleth against Favour and Partiality; their belief of their own Merit maketh Men object them to a prosperous Competitor, even when there is no pretence for it; but when there is the least handle offered, to be sure it will be taken. So, in this Case, when a *Gentleman* is preferr'd at *Sea,* the *Tarpaulin* is very apt to impute it to Friend or Favour: But if that *Gentleman* hath before his Preferment passed through all the Steps which lead to it, so that he smelleth as much of *Pitch* and *Tar,* as those that were *Swadled* in *Sail-Cloath* ; his having an *Escutcheon* will be so far from doing him harm, that it will set him upon the advantage Ground: It will draw a real Respect to his Quality when so supported, and give him an Influence and Authority infinitely superior to that which the *meer Sea-man* can ever pretend to.

When a *Gentleman* hath learned how to *Obey,* he will grow very much fitter to *Command;* his own Memory will advise him not to inflict too rigorous Punishments. He will better resist

HALIFAX   N   the

the Temptations of Authority (which are great) when he reflecteth how much he hath at other times wished it might be gently exercised, when he was liable to the Rigour of it.

When the undistinguish'd *Discipline* of a Ship hath tamed the young Mastership, which is apt to arise from a *Gentleman's* Birth and Education, he then groweth Proud in the right place, and valueth himself first upon knowing his Duty, and then upon doing it.

In plain *English*, Men of *Quality* in their several Degrees must either restore themselves to a better Opinion, both for *Morality* and *Diligence*, or else *Quality* it self will be in danger of being extinguished.

The Original *Gentleman* is almost lost in strictness; when Posterity doth not still further adorn by their Virtue the Escutcheon their Ancestors first got for them by their Merit, they deserve the Penalty of being deprived of it.

To expect that *Quality* alone should waft Men up into *Places* and *Imployments*, is as unreasonable, as to think that a Ship, because it is Carved and Gilded, should be fit to go to *Sea* without *Sails* or *Tackling*. But when a *Gentleman* maketh no other use of his *Quality*, than to incite him the more to his Duty, it will give such a true and settled *Superiority*, as must destroy all Competition from those that are below him.

It is time now to go to the Probationary Qualifications of an *Officer* at *Sea*: And I have some to offer, which I have digested in my Thoughts, I hope impartially, that they may not be Speculative Notions, but things easy and practicable, if the directing Powers will give due Countenance and Incouragement to the Execution of them : But whilst I am going about to set them down, though this little *Essay* was made to no other *End*, than to introduce them, I am upon better Recollection, induced to put a restraint upon my self, and rather retract the Promise I made at the beginning, than by advising the particular Methods by which I conceive the good *End* that is aimed at may be obtained, to incur the Imputation of the thing of the World of which I would least be guilty, which is of anticipating, by my private Opinion, the Judgment of the *Parliament*, or
seeming

seeming out of my slender Stock of Reason to dictate to the Supream Wisdom of the Nation. They will, no doubt, consider the present Establishments for *Discipline* at *Sea,* which are many of them very good, and if well executed, might go a great way in the present Question. But I will not say they are so perfect, but that others may be added to make them more effectual, and that some more Supplemental Expedients may be necessary to compleat what is yet defective : And whenever the *Parliament* shall think fit to take this Matter into their Consideration, I am sure they will not want for their Direction the Auxiliary Reasons of any Man without Doors, much less of one, whose Thoughts are so intirely and unaffectedly resigned to whatever they shall determine in this, or any thing else relating to the Publick.

MAXIMS

MAXIMS

OF

STATE.

1. THAT a Prince who falleth out with *Laws*, breaketh with his best *Friends*.

2. That the exalting his own *Authority* above his *Laws*, is like letting in his *Enemy* to surprize his *Guards*: The *Laws* are the only Guards he can be sure will never run away from him.

3. A *Prince* that will say he can do no Good, except he may do every thing; teacheth the People to say, They are *Slaves*, if they must not do whatever they have a mind to.

4. That *Power* and *Liberty* are like *Heat* and *Moisture*; where they are well mixt, every thing prospers ; where they are single, they are destructive.

5. That *Arbitrary Power* is like most other things that are very hard, they are also very apt to break.

6. That the profit of Places should be measured as they are more or less conducing to the *Publick Service* ; and if Business is more necessary than Splendor, the Instrument of it ought in Proportion to be better paid; that the contrary Method is as impertinent, as it would be to let the Carving of a Ship cost more than all the rest of it.

7. That where the least useful part of the People have the

most

most Credit with the *Prince*, Men will conclude, That the way to get every thing, is to be good for nothing.

8. That an extravagant Gift to one Man, raiseth the Market to every body else; so that in consequence, the unlimited Bounty of an unthinking Prince maketh him a *Beggar*, let him have never so much *Money*.

9. That if ordinary Beggars are *whip'd*, the daily Beggars in fine Cloaths (out of a proportionable Respect to their Quality) ought to be *hanged*.

10. That *Pride* is as loud a Beggar as Want, and a great deal more Sawcy.

11. That a *Prince*, who will give more to Importunity than Merit, had as good set out a Proclamation to all his Loving Subjects, forbidding them to do well, upon the penalty of being undone by it.

12. That a wise *Prince* will not oblige his *Courtiers*, who are *Birds* of *Prey*, so as to disoblige his *People*, who are *Beasts* of *Burthen*.

13. That it is safer for a *Prince* to Judge of *Men* by what they do to one another, than what they do to him.

14. That it is a gross Mistake to think, That a *Knave* between Man and Man, can be honest to a *King*, whom, of all other, Men generally make the least Scruple to deceive.

15. That a *Prince* who can ever trust the *Man* that hath once deceived him, loseth the *Right* of being Faithfully dealt with by any other *Person*.

16. That it is not possible for a *Prince* to find out such an *Honest Knave*, as will let no body else *Cheat* him.

17. That if a *Prince* doth not shew an Aversion to *Knaves*, there will be an Inference that will be very Natural, let it be never so Unmannerly.

18. That a *Prince* who followeth his own Opinion too soon, is in danger of repenting it too late.

19. That it is less dangerous for a *Prince* to mind too much what the *People* say, than too little.

20. That a *Prince* is to take care that the greater part of the People may not be angry at the same time; for though the

first

first beginning of their *Ill Humour* should be against one another, yet if not stopt, it will naturally end in *Anger* against him.

21. That if *Princes* would *Reflect* how much they are in the Power of their *Ministers,* they would be more circumspect in the *Choice* of them.

22. That a wise *Prince* will support good Servants against Mens Anger, and not support ill ones against their Complaint.

23. That *Parties* in a *State* generally, like *Freebooters,* hang out *False Colours*; the pretence is the *Publick Good*; the real *Business* is, to catch *Prizes*; like the *Tartars,* where-ever they succeed, instead of Improving their *Victory,* they presently fall upon the *Baggage.*

24. That a *Prince* may play so long between *Two Parties,* that they may in time join together, and be in earnest with him.

25. That there is more *Dignity* in open *Violence,* than in the unskilful *Cunning* of a *Prince,* who goeth about to *Impose* upon the *People.*

26. That the *People* will ever suspect the *Remedies* for the *Diseases* of the *State,* where they are wholly excluded from seeing how they are prepared.

27. That changing *Hands* without changing *Measures,* is as if a *Drunkard* in a *Dropsey* should change his *Doctors,* and not his *Dyet.*

28. That a *Prince* is to watch that his *Reason* may not be so subdued by his *Nature,* as not to be so much a *Man* of *Peace,* as to be a jest in an *Army*; nor so much a *Man* of *War,* as to be out of his *Element* in his *Council.*

29. That a *Man* who cannot mind his own *Business,* is not to be trusted with the *King's.*

30. That *Quality* alone should only serve to make a shew in the Embroidered Part of the *Government*; but that *Ignorance,* though never so well born, should never be admitted to spoil the *Publick Business.*

31. That he who thinks his *Place* below him, will certainly be below his *Place.*

32. That when a *Princes Example* ceaseth to have the force of

of a *Law*, it is a sure sign that his *Power* is wasting, and that there is but little distance between *Men's* neglecting to *Imitate*, and their refusing to *Obey*.

33. That a *People* may let a *King* fall, yet still remain a *People* ; but if a *King* let his *People* slip from him, he is no longer *King*.

ADVER-

AD V ERTISEMENT.

SInce the Death of the Ingenious Translator of these Essays, an imperfect Transcript of the following Letter was intended for the Press, but having the good fortune to meet with a more correct Copy, I thought my self under a necessity of Publishing it with this Third Edition, not only to do Justice to his Memory, but to the Great Person he Chose for his Patron.

M. G.

A

A Letter sent by his Lordship to Charles Cotton, *Esq.; upon his New Translation and Dedication of* Montaigne's *Essays.*

SIR.

I have too long delay'd my *Thanks* to you for giving me such an obliging *Evidence* of your *Remembrance* : That alone would have been a welcome *Present*, but when join'd with the *Book* in the World I am the best entertain'd with, it raiseth a strong desire in me to be better *known*, where I am sure to be so much *pleased*. I have till now thought *Wit* could not be *Translated*, and do still retain so much of that Opinion, that I believe it impossible, except by one whose *Genius* cometh up to that of the *Author*. You have so kept the Original *Strength* of his *Thought*, that it almost tempts a Man to believe the *Transmigration* of *Souls*, and that his, being us'd to *Hills*, is come into the *Moore-Lands* to Reward us here in *England*, for doing him more Right than his *Country* will afford him. He hath by your means mended his First *Edition* : To transplant and make him *Ours*, is not only a Valuable *Acquisition* to us, but a Just *Censure* of the Critical *Impertinence* of those *French Scribblers* who have taken pains to make little *Cavils* and *Exceptions*, to lessen the Reputation of this great *Man*, whom Nature hath made too big to Confine himself to the Exactness of a Studied *Stile*. He let his *Mind* have its full *Flight*, and sheweth by a generous kind of *Negligence* that he did not Write for Praise, but to give to the World a true Picture of himself and of Mankind. He scorned *affected Periods*, or to please the mistaken Reader with an empty *Chime* of *Words*. He hath no *Affectation* to set himself out, and dependeth wholly upon the

Natural

Natural Force of what is his own, and the Excellent Application of what he borroweth.

You see, Sir, I have kindness enough for *Monsieur de Montaigne* to be your *Rival,* but no Body can pretend to be in equal Competition with you : I do willingly yield, which is no small matter for a Man to do to a more prosperous *Lover* ; and if you will repay this piece of Justice with another, pray believe, that he who can *Translate* such an *Author* without doing him wrong, must not only make me *Glad* but *Proud* of being his

Very humble Servant,

Hallifax.

A

A
CHARACTER
OF
KING *CHARLES* II.

I. *Of his* RELIGION.

A Character differeth from a Picture only in this, every Part of it must be like, but it is not necessary that every Feature should be comprehended in it as in a Picture, only some of the most remarkable.

This Prince at his first entrance into the World had Adversity for his Introducer, which is generally thought to be no ill one, but in his case it proved so, and laid the foundation of most of those Misfortunes or Errors, that were the causes of the great Objections made to him.

The first Effect it had was in relation to his *Religion*.

The ill-bred familiarity of the *Scotch* Divines had given him a distaste of that part of the Protestant Religion. He was left then to the little Remnant of the *Church of England* in the *Fauxbourg St. Germain*; which made such a kind of figure, as might easily be turn'd in such a manner as to make him lose his veneration for it. In a refined Country, where Religion appeared in Pomp and Splendor, the outward appearance of such unfashionable Men was made an Argument against their Religion; and a young Prince not averse to rallery, was the more susceptible of a contempt for it.

The Company he kept, the Men in his Pleasures, and the Arguments of State that he should not appear too much a Protestant, whilst he expected Assistance from a Popish Prince; all these, together with a habit encouraged by an Application

to

to his Pleasures, did so loosen and untie him from his first Impressions, that I take it for granted, after the first Year or two, he was no more a Protestant. If you ask me what he was, my answer must be, that he was of the Religion of a young Prince in his warm Blood, whose Enquiries were more applied to find Arguments against believing, than to lay any settled Foundations for acknowledging Providence, Mysteries, &c. A General Creed, and no very long one, may be presumed to be the utmost Religion of one, whose Age and Inclination could not well spare any Thoughts that did not tend to his Pleasures.

In this kind of Indifference or Unthinkingness, which is too natural in the beginnings of Life to be heavily censured, I will suppose he might pass some considerable part of his Youth. I must presume too that no Occasions were lost, during that Time, to insinuate every thing to bend him towards Popery. Great Art without intermission, against Youth and Easiness, which are seldom upon their guard, must have its Effect. A Man is to be admired if he resisteth, and therefore cannot reasonably be blamed if he yieldeth to them. *When* the critical Minute was, I'll not undertake to determine ; but certainly the inward Conviction doth generally precede the outward Declarations : At what distances, dependeth upon Mens several Complexions and Circumstances ; no stated Period can be fixed.

It will be said that he had not Religion enough to have *Conviction* ; that is a vulgar Error. Conviction indeed is not a proper word but where a Man is convinced by Reason ; but in the common acceptation, it is applied to those who cannot tell why they are so : If Men can be at least as positive in a Mistake as when they are in the right ; they may be as clearly convinced when they do not know why, as when they do.

I must presume that no Man of the King's Age, and his Methods of Life, could possibly give a good reason for changing the Religion in which he was born, let it be what it will. But our Passions are much oftener convinced than our Reason. He had but little Reading, and that tending to his Pleasures more than to his Instruction. In the Library of a young Prince, the

the solemn Folios are not much rumpled, Books of a lighter Digestion have the Dog's Ears.

Some pretend to be very precise in the time of his Reconciling; The Cardinal *de Retz, &c.* I will not enter into it minutely, but whenever it was, it is observable that the Government of *France* did not think it adviseable to discover it openly; upon which such obvious Reflections may be made, that I will not mention them.

Such a Secret can never be put into a place which is so closely stopt, that there shall be no Chinks. Whispers went about, particular Men had Intimations: *Cromwell* had his Advertisements in other things, and this was as well worth his paying for. There was enough said of it to startle a great many, though not universally diffused; So much, that if the Government here, had not crumbled of itself, his Right alone, with that and other clogs upon it, would hardly have thrown it down. I conclude that when he came into *England* he was as certainly a *Roman Catholick,* as that he was a Man of Pleasure; both very consistent by visible Experience.

It is impertinent to give Reasons for Mens changing their Religion. None can give them but themselves, as every Man has quite a different way of arguing: A thing which may very well be accounted for. They are differing kinds of Wit, to be quick to find a *Fault,* and to be capable to find out a *Truth*: There must be industry in the last; the first requires only a lively heat, that catcheth hold of the *weak* side of any thing, but to choose the *strong* one is another Talent. The reason why Men of Wit are often the laziest in their Enquiries is, that their heat carrieth their Thoughts so fast, that they are apt to be tired, and they faint in the drudgery of a continued Application. Have not Men of great Wit in all times permitted their Understandings to give way to their first Impressions? It taketh off from the Diminution when a Man doth not *mind* a thing; and the King had then other Business: The inferior part of the Man was then in Possession, and the Faculties of the Brain, as to serious and painful Enquiries, were laid asleep at least, tho' not extinguished. Careless Men are most subject to Superstition.

Those

Those who do not study Reason enough to make it their Guide, have more Unevenness: As they have Neglects, so they have Starts and Frights; Dreams will serve the turn; Omens and Sicknesses have violent and sudden Effects upon them. Nor is the strength of an Argument so effectual from its intrinsick Force, as by its being well suited to the Temper of the Party.

The *genteel part* of the *Catholick* Religion might tempt a Prince that had more of the fine Gentleman than his governing Capacity required: and the exercise of *Indulgence* to *Sinners* being more frequent in it, than of *inflicting Penance*, might be some recommendation. Mistresses of that Faith are stronger Specificks in this case, than any that are in Physick.

The *Roman Catholicks* complained of his Breach of Promise to them very early.[1] There were broad peepings out, Glimpses so often repeated, that to discerning Eyes it was flaring: In the very first Year there were such Suspicions as produced melancholy shakings of the Head, which were very significant. His unwillingness to *marry* a *Protestant* was remarkable, though both the Catholick and the Christian Crown would have adopted her. Very early in his Youth, when any *German* Princess was proposed, he put off the discourse with Rallery. A thousand little Circumstances were a kind of accumulative Evidence, which in these Cases may be admitted.

Men that were earnest Protestants were under the sharpness of his Displeasure, expressed by Rallery, as well as by other ways. Men near him have made Discoveries from sudden breakings out in Discourse, &c. which shewed there was a Root. It was not the least skilful part of his concealing himself, to make the World think he leaned towards an Indifference in Religion.

He had Sicknesses *before* his Death, in which he did not trouble any Protestant Divines; those who saw him *upon his Death-bed*, saw a great deal.

As to his writing those[2] Papers, he might do it. Though neither

---

[1] Upon the Words of his Declaration.
[2] Two Papers in Defence of the *Roman Catholick* Religion, found in this King's strong Box, in his own hand, and published by King *James* II. afterwards.

neither his Temper nor Education made him very fit to be an Author, yet in this case, (a known Topick so very often repeated) he might write it all himself, and yet not one word of it his own. That Church's Argument doth so agree with Men unwilling to take pains, the Temptation of putting an End to all the trouble of enquiring is so great, that it must be very strong reason that can resist: The King had only his meer natural Faculties, without any Acquisitions to improve them; so that it is no wonder, if an Argument which gave such *Ease* and *Relief* to his Mind, made such an Impression, that with thinking often of it, (as Men are apt to do of every thing they like) he might, by the Effect chiefly of his Memory, put together a few Lines with his own Hand, without any help at the time; in which there was nothing extraordinary, but that one so little inclined to write at all, should prevail with himself to do it with the Solemnity of a Casuist.

II. *His* DISSIMULATION.

ONE great Objection made to him was the concealing himself, and disguising his Thoughts. In this there ought a Latitude to be given; it is a Defect not to have it at all, and a Fault to have it too much. Human Nature will not allow the Mean: like all other things, as soon as ever Men get to do them well, they cannot easily hold from doing them too much. 'Tis the case even in the least things, as singing, &c.

In *France*, he was to dissemble Injuries and Neglects, from one reason; in *England* he was to dissemble too, though for other Causes; A King upon the *Throne* hath as great Temptations (though of another kind) to dissemble, as a King in *Exile*. The King of *France* might have his Times of Dissembling as much with him, as he could have to do it with the King of *France*: So he was in a *School*.

No King can be so little inclined to dissemble but he must needs learn it from his *Subjects*, who every Day give him such

                                                    Lessons

Lessons of it. Dissimulation is like most other Qualities, it hath two Sides; it is necessary, and yet it is dangerous too. To have none at all layeth a Man open to Contempt, to have too much exposeth him to Suspicion, which is only the less dishonourable Inconvenience. If a Man doth not take very great Precautions, he is never so much shewed as when he endeavoureth to hide himself. One Man cannot take more pains to hide himself, than another will do to see into him, especially in the Case of Kings.

It is none of the exalted Faculties of the Mind, since there are Chamber-Maids will do it better than any Prince in Christendom. Men given to dissembling are like Rooks at play, they will cheat for Shillings, they are so used to it. The vulgar Definition of Dissembling is downright Lying; that kind of it which is less ill-bred cometh pretty near it. Only Princes and Persons of Honour must have gentler Words given to their Faults, than the nature of them may in themselves deserve.

Princes dissemble with too many not to have it discovered; no wonder then that He carried it so far that it was discovered. Men compared Notes, and got Evidence; so that those whose Morality would give them leave, took it for an Excuse for serving him ill. Those who knew his Face, fixed their Eyes there; and thought it of more Importance to see, than to hear what he said. His Face was as little a Blab as most Mens, yet though it could not be called a prattling Face, it would sometimes tell Tales to a good Observer. When he thought fit to be angry, he had a very peevish Memory; there was hardly a Blot that escaped him. At the same time that this shewed the Strength of his Dissimulation, it gave warning too; it fitted his present Purpose, but it made a Discovery that put Men more upon their Guard against him. Only Self-flattery furnisheth perpetual Arguments to trust again: The comfortable Opinion Men have of themselves keepeth up Human Society, which would be more than half destroyed without it.

III. *His*

III. *His* AMOURS, MISTRESSES, &c.

IT may be said that his Inclinations to Love were the Effects of Health, and a good Constitution, with as little mixture of the *Seraphick* part as ever Man had: And though from that Foundation Men often raise their Passions; I am apt to think his stayed as much as any Man's ever did in the *lower Region.* This made him like easy Mistresses: They were generally resigned to him while he was abroad, with an implied Bargain. Heroick refined Lovers place a good deal of their Pleasure in the Difficulty, both for the vanity of Conquest, and as a better earnest of their Kindness.

After he was restored, Mistresses were recommended to him; which is no small matter in a *Court,* and not unworthy the Thoughts even of a *Party.* A Mistress either dexterous in herself, or well-instructed by those that are so, may be very useful to her Friends, not only in the immediate Hours of her Ministry, but by her Influences and Insinuations at other times. It was resolved generally by others, whom he should have in his Arms, as well as whom he should have in his Councils. Of a Man who was so capable of choosing, he chose as seldom as any Man that ever lived.

He had more properly, at least in the beginning of his Time, a good Stomach to his Mistresses, than any great Passion for them. His taking them from others was never learnt in a Romance; and indeed fitter for a Philosopher than a Knight-Errant. His Patience for their Frailties shewed him no exact Lover. It is a Heresy according to a true Lover's Creed, ever to forgive an Infidelity, or the Appearance of it. Love of Ease will not do it, where the *Heart* is much engaged; but where mere *Nature* is the Motive, it is possible for a Man to think righter than the common opinion, and to argue, that a Rival taketh away nothing but the Heart, and leaveth all the rest.

In his latter Times he had no *Love,* but insensible Engagements that made it harder than most might apprehend to untie them. The *Politicks* might have their part; a Secret, a Commission, a Confidence in critical Things, though it doth not give a Lease for a precise term of Years, yet there may be Difficulties in dismissing them; there may be no Love all the while; perhaps the contrary.

He was said to be as little constant as they were thought to be. Though he had no Love, he must have some Appetite, or else he could not keep them for meer ease, or for the Love of sauntring; Mistresses are frequently apt to be uneasy; they are in all Respects craving Creatures; so that though the taste of those Joys might be flattened, yet a Man who loved Pleasure so as to be very unwilling to part with it, might (with the Assistance of his *Fancy*, which doth not grow old so fast) reserve some supplemental Entertainments, that might make their personal Service be still of use to him. The Definition of Pleasure, is *what pleaseth*, and if that which grave Men may call a corrupted Fancy, shall adminster any Remedies for putting off mourning for the loss of Youth, who shall blame it?

The *young* Men seldom apply their censure to these Matters; and the *elder* have an Interest to be gentle towards a Mistake, that seemeth to make some kind of amends for their Decays.

He had Wit enough to *suspect*, and he had Wit enough too *not to care*: The Ladies got a great deal more than would have been allowed to be an equal bargain in *Chancery*, for what they did for it; but neither the manner, nor the measure of Pleasure is to be judged by others.

Little Inducements at first grew into strong Reasons by degrees. Men who do not consider Circumstances, but judge at a distance, by a general way of arguing, conclude if a Mistress in some Cases is not immediately turned off, it must needs be that the Gallant is incurably subjected. This will by no means hold in private Men, much less in Princes, who are under more Entanglements, from which they cannot so easily loosen themselves.

His Mistresses were as different in their Humours, as they were in their Looks. They gave Matter of very different Reflections.

tions. The last[1] especially was quite out of the Definition of an ordinary Mistress; the Causes and the Manner of her being first introduced were very different. A very peculiar Distinction was spoken of, some extraordinary Solemnities that might dignify, though not sanctify her Function. Her Chamber was the true Cabinet Council. The King did always by his Councils, as he did sometimes by his Meals; he sat down out of form with the *Queen*, but he supped *below Stairs*. To have the Secrets of a King, who happens to have too many, is to have a King in Chains: He must not only, not part with her, but he must in his own Defence dissemble his dislike: The less kindness he hath, the more he must shew: There is great difference between being *muffled*, and being *tied*: He was the first, not the last. If he had quarelled at some times, besides other Advantages, this Mistress had a powerful *Second* (one may suppose a kind of a *Guarantee*); this to a Man that loved his *Ease*, though his *Age* had not helped, was sufficient.

The thing called *Sauntering*, is a stronger Temptation to Princes than it is to others. The being galled with Importunities, pursued from one Room to another with asking Faces; the dismal Sound of unreasonable Complaints, and ill-grounded Pretences; the Deformity of Fraud ill-disguised; all these would make any Man run away from them; and I used to think it was the Motive for making him walk so fast. So it was more properly taking Sanctuary. To get into a Room, where all Business was to stay at the Door, excepting such as he was disposed to admit, might be very acceptable to a younger Man than he was, and less given to his Ease. He slumbered after Dinner, had the noise of the Company to divert him, without their Solicitations to importune him. In these Hours where he was more unguarded, no doubt the cunning Men of the Court took their times to make their Observations, and there is as little doubt but he made his upon them too: Where men had Chinks he would see through them as soon as

any

[1] The Dutchess of *Portsmouth*.

o 2

any Man about him.   There was much more real Business done there in his Politick, than there was in his personal Capacity, *Stans pede in uno* ; and there was the *French part of the Government,* which was not the least.

In short, without endeavouring to find more Arguments, he was *used* to it.   Men do not care to put off a Habit, nor do often succeed when they go about it.   His was not an *unthinkingness* ; he did not perhaps think so much of his Subjects as they might wish ; but he was far from being wanting to think of himself.

IV. *His* CONDUCT *to his* MINISTERS.

HE lived with his Ministers as he did with his Mistresses ; he used them, but he was not in love with them.   He shewed his Judgment in this, that he cannot properly be said ever to have had a *Favourite,* though some might look so at a distance.   The present use he might have of them, made him throw Favours upon them, which might lead the lookers on into that mistake ; but he tied himself no more to them, than they did to him, which implied a sufficient Liberty on either side.

Perhaps he made *dear Purchases* : If he seldom gave profusely, but where he expected some unreasonable thing, great Rewards were material Evidences against those who received them.

He was *free of access* to them, which was a very gaining Quality.   He had at least as good a Memory for the Faults of his Ministers as for their Services ; and whenever they fell, the whole Inventory came out ; there was not a slip omitted.

That some of his Ministers seemed to have a *Superiority,* did not spring from his Resignation to them, but to his Ease.   He chose rather to be *eclipsed* than to be *troubled.*

His Brother was a Minister, and he had his Jealousies of him.   At the same time that he raised him, he was not displeased

pleased to have him lessened. The cunning Observers found this out, and at the same time that he reigned in the Cabinet, he was very familiarly used at the private Supper.

A Minister turned off is like a Lady's Waiting-Woman, that knoweth all her Washes, and hath a shrewd guess at her Strayings: So there is danger in turning them off, as well as in keeping them.

He had back Stairs to convey *Informations* to him, as well as for other Uses; and though such Informations are sometimes dangerous, (especially to a Prince that will not take the pains necessary to digest them) yet in the main, that humour of *hearing every body against any body*, kept those about him in more awe, than they would have been without it. I do not believe that ever he trusted any Man, or any set of Men so entirely, as not to have some Secrets, in which they had *no share*: As this might make him less well served, so in some degree it might make him the less imposed upon.

You may reckon under this Article his *Female Ministry*; for though he had Ministers of the Council, Ministers of the Cabinet, and Ministers of the Ruelle; the Ruelle was often the *last Appeal*. Those who were not well there, were used because they were *necessary* at the time, not because they were *liked*; so that their Tenure was a little uncertain. His Ministers were to administer Business to him as Doctors do Physick, wrap it up in something to make it *less unpleasant*; some skilful Digressions were so far from being Impertinent, that they could not many times fix him to a fair Audience without them. His *aversion to Formality* made him dislike a *serious Discourse*, if very long, except it was mixed with something to *entertain* him. Some even of the graver sort too, used to carry this very far, and rather than fail, use the coarsest kind of youthful talk.

In general, he was upon pretty *even Terms* with his Ministers, and could as easily bear *their* being *hanged* as some of them could *his* being *abused*.

V. *Of*

V. *Of his* WIT *and* CONVERSATION.

HIS Wit consisted chiefly in the *Quickness* of his *Apprehension*. His Apprehension made him *find Faults,* and that led him to short Sayings upon them, not always equal, but often very good.

By his being abroad, he contracted a Habit of conversing familiarly, which added to his natural Genius, made him very *apt to talk* ; perhaps more than a very nice judgment would approve.

He was apter to make *broad Allusions* upon any thing that gave the least occasion, than was altogether suitable with the very Good-breeding he shewed in most other things. The Company he kept whilst abroad, had so used him to that sort of Dialect, that he was so far from thinking it a Fault or an Indecency, that he made it a matter of Rallery upon those who could not prevail upon themselves to join in it. As a Man who hath a good Stomach loveth generally to talk of Meat, so in the vigour of his Age, he began that style, which by degrees grew so natural to him, that after he ceased to do it out of Pleasure, he continued to do it out of Custom. The Hypocrisy of the former Times inclined Men to think they could not shew too great an Aversion to it, and that helped to encourage this unbounded liberty of Talking, without the Restraints of Decency which were before observed. In his more familiar Conversations with the Ladies, even they must be passive, if they would not enter into it. How far Sounds as well as Objects may have their Effects to raise Inclination, might be an Argument to him to use that Style ; or whether using Liberty at its full stretch, was not the general Inducement without any particular Motives to it.

The manner of that time of *telling Stories,* had drawn him into it ; being commended at first for the Faculty of telling a Tale well, he might insensibly be betrayed to exercise it too often. Stories are dangerous in this, that the best expose a Man most, by being oftenest repeated. It might pass for an

Evidence

Evidence for the Moderns against the Ancients, that it is now wholly left off by all that have any pretence to be distinguished by their good Sense.

He had the Improvements of *Wine*, &c. which made him *pleasant* and *easy in Company*; where he bore his part, and was acceptable even to those who had no other Design than to be merry with him.

The Thing called *Wit*, a Prince may taste, but it is dangerous for him to take too much of it; it hath Allurements which by refining his Thoughts, take off from their *dignity*, in applying them less to the governing part. There is a Charm in Wit, which a Prince must resist: and that to him was no easy matter; it was contesting with Nature upon Terms of Disadvantage.

His Wit was not so ill-natured as to put Men out of countenance. In the case of a King especially, it is more allowable to speak sharply *of* them, than *to* them.

His Wit was not acquired by *Reading*; that which he had above his original Stock by Nature, was from Company, in which he was very capable to observe. He could not so properly be said to have a Wit very much raised, as a plain, gaining, well-bred, recommending kind of Wit.

But of all Men that ever *liked* those who *had Wit*, he could the best *endure* those who had *none*. This leaneth more towards a Satire than a Compliment, in this respect, that he could not only suffer Impertinence, but at sometimes seemed to be pleased with it.

He encouraged some to talk a good deal more with him, than one would have expected from a Man of so good a Taste: He should rather have order'd his Attorney-General to prosecute them for a Misdemeanour, in using Common-sense so scurvily in his Presence. However, if this was a Fault, it is arrogant for any of his Subjects to object to it, since it would look like defying such a piece of Indulgence. He must in some degree loosen the Strength of his Wit, by his Condescension to talk with Men so very unequal to him. Wit must be used to some *Equality*, which may give it Exercise, or else it is apt either to languish, or to grow a little vulgar, by reigning amongst Men

of

of a lower Size, where there is no Awe to keep a Man upon his *guard*.

It fell out rather by Accident than Choice, that his Mistresses were such as did not care that Wit of the best kind should have the Precedence in their Apartments. Sharp and strong Wit will not always be so held in by Good-manners, as not to be a little troublesome in a *Ruelle*. But wherever Impertinence hath Wit enough left to be thankful for being well used, it will not only be admitted, but kindly received; such Charms every thing hath that setteth us off by Comparison.

His *Affability* was a Part, and perhaps not the least, of his Wit.

It is a Quality that must not always spring from the Heart; Mens Pride, as well as their Weakness, maketh them ready to be deceived by it : They are more ready to believe it a Homage paid to their Merit, than a Bait thrown out to deceive them. *Princes* have a particular Advantage.

There was at first as much of Art as Nature in his Affability, but by Habit it became Natural. It is an Error of the better hand, but the *Universality* taketh away a good deal of the Force of it. A Man that hath had a kind Look seconded with engaging Words, whilst he is chewing the Pleasure, if another in his Sight should be received just as kindly, that Equality would presently alter the Relish : The Pride of Mankind will have Distinction; till at last it cometh to Smile for Smile, meaning nothing of either Side; without any kind of Effect; mere Drawing-room Compliments; the *Bow* alone would be better without them. He was under some Disadvantages of this kind, that grew still in proportion as it came by Time to be more known that there was less Signification in those Things than at first was thought.

The Familiarity of his Wit must needs have the Effect of *lessening* the *Distance* fit to be kept to him. The Freedom used to him whilst abroad, was retained by those who used it longer than either they ought to have kept it, or he have suffered it, and others by their Example learned to use the same. A King of *Spain* that will say nothing but *Tiendro cuydado*, will,

to

to the generality, preserve more Respect; an Engine that will speak but sometimes, at the same time that it will draw the Raillery of the Few who judge well, it will create Respect in the ill-judging Generality. Formality is sufficiently revenged upon the World for being so unreasonably laughed at; it is destroyed it is true, but it hath the spiteful Satisfaction of seeing every thing destroyed with it.

His fine Gentlemanship did him no Good, encouraged in it by being too much applauded.

His Wit was better suited to his Condition *before* he was restored than *afterwards*. The Wit of a Gentleman, and that of a crowned Head, ought to be different things. As there is a *Crown Law*, there is a *Crown Wit* too. To use it with Reserve is very good, and very rare. There is a Dignity in doing things *seldom*, even without any other Circumstance. Where Wit will run continually, the Spring is apt to fail; so that it groweth vulgar, and the more it is practised, the more it is debased.

He was so good at finding out other Mens weak Sides, that it made him less intent to cure his own : That generally happeneth. It may be called a treacherous Talent, for it betrayeth a Man to forget to judge himself, by being so eager to censure others : This doth so misguide Men the first Part of their Lives, that the Habit of it is not easily recovered, when the greater Ripeness of their Judgment inclineth them to look more into themselves than into other Men.

Men love to see themselves in the false Looking-glass of other Mens Failings. It maketh a Man think well of himself at the time, and by sending his Thoughts abroad to get Food for Laughing, they are less at leisure to see Faults at home. Men choose rather to make the War in another Country, than to keep all well at home.

VI. *His*

VI. *His* TALENTS, TEMPER, HABITS, *&c.*

HE had a *Mechanical Head,* which appeared in his Inclination to Shipping and Fortification, *&c.* This would make one conclude, that his Thoughts would naturally have been more fixed to Business, if his Pleasures had not drawn them away from it.

He had a very good *Memory,* though he would not always make equal good Use of it. So that if he had accustomed himself to direct his Faculties to his Business, I see no Reason why he might not have been a good deal Master of it. His Chain of *Memory* was longer than his Chain of *Thought*; the first could bear any Burden, the other was tired by being carried on too long; it was fit to ride a Heat, but it had not Wind enough for a long Course.

A very great Memory often forgetteth how much Time is lost by repeating things of no Use. It was one Reason of his talking so much; since a great Memory will always have something to say, and will be discharging itself, whether in or out of Season, if a good Judgment doth not go along with it, to make it stop and turn. One might say of his Memory, that it was a *Beauté Journalière*; Sometimes he would make shrewd Applications, *&c.* at others he would bring things out of it, that never deserved to be laid in it.

He grew by Age into a pretty exact *Distribution* of his *Hours,* both for his Business, Pleasures, and the Exercise for his Health, of which he took as much care as could possibly consist with some Liberties he was resolved to indulge in himself. He walked by his Watch, and when he pulled it out to look upon it, skilful Men would make haste with what they had to say to him.

He was often retained in his *personal* against his *politick* Capacity. He would speak upon those Occasions most dexterously against himself; *Charles Stuart* would be bribed against the *King*; and in the Distinction, he leaned more to his natural Self, than his Character would allow. He would not
suffer

suffer himself to be so much fettered by his Character as was convenient; he was still starting out of it, the Power of Nature was too strong for the Dignity of his Calling, which generally yielded as often as there was a contest.

It was not the best use he made of his *Back-stairs* to admit Men to bribe him against himself, to procure a Defalcation, help a lame Accountant to get off, or side with the Farmers against the Improvement of the Revenue. The King was made the Instrument to defraud the Crown, which is somewhat extraordinary.

That which might tempt him to it probably was, his finding that those about him so often took Money upon those Occasions; so that he thought he might do well at least to be a Partner. He did not take the Money to *hoard* it; there were those at Court who watched those Times, as the *Spaniards* do for the coming in of the *Plate Fleet*. The Beggars of both Sexes helped to empty his Cabinet, and to leave room in them for a new lading upon the next Occasion. These Negotiators played double with him too, when it was for their purpose so to do. He *knew it*, and *went on* still; so he gained his present end, at the time, he was less solicitous to enquire into the Consequences.

He could not properly be said to be either *covetous* or *liberal*; his desire to get was not with an Intention to be rich; and his spending was rather an Easiness in letting Money go, than any premeditated Thought for the Distribution of it. He would do as much to throw off the burden of a present Importunity, as he would to relieve a want.

When once the Aversion to bear Uneasiness taketh place in a Man's Mind, it doth so check all the Passions, that they are dampt into a kind of Indifference; they grow faint and languishing, and come to be subordinate to that fundamental Maxim, of not purchasing any thing at the price of a Difficulty. This made that he had as little Eagerness to oblige, as he had to hurt Men; the Motive of his giving Bounties was rather to make Men less uneasy to him, than more easy to themselves; and yet no ill-nature all this while. He would slide from an

asking

asking Face, and could guess very well. It was throwing a Man off from his Shoulders, that leaned upon them with his whole weight; so that the Party was not gladder to receive, than he was to give. It was a kind of implied bargain; though Men seldom kept it, being so apt to forget the advantage they had received, that they would presume the King would as little remember the good he had done them, so as to make it an Argument against their next Request.

This Principle of making the *love* of *Ease* exercise an entire Sovereignty in his Thoughts, would have been less censured in a private Man, than might be in a Prince. The Consequence of it to the Publick changeth the Nature of that Quality, or else a Philosopher in his private Capacity might say a great deal to justify it. The truth is, a King is to be such a distinct Creature from a Man, that their Thoughts are to be put in quite a differing Shape, and it is such a disquieting task to reconcile them, that Princes might rather expect to be lamented than to be envied, for being in a Station that exposeth them, if they do not do more to answer Mens Expectations than human Nature will allow.

That Men have the less Ease for their loving it so much, is so far from a wonder, that it is a natural Consequence, especially in the case of a Prince. Ease is seldom got without some pains, but it is yet seldomer kept without them. He thought giving would make Men more easy to him, whereas he might have known it would certainly make them more troublesome.

When Men receive Benefits from Princes, they attribute less to his Generosity than to their own Deserts; so that in their own Opinion, their Merit cannot be bounded; by that mistaken Rule, it can as little be satisfied. They would take it for a diminution to have it circumscribed. Merit hath a Thirst upon it that can never be quenched by golden Showers. It is not only still ready, but greedy to receive more. This King *Charles* found in as many Instances as any Prince that ever reigned, because the Easiness of Access introducing the good Success of their first Request, they were the more encouraged to repeat those Importunities, which had been more effectually

stopt

stopt in the Beginning by a short and resolute Denial. But his Nature did not dispose him to that Method, it directed him rather to put off the troublesome Minute for the time, and that being his Inclination, he did not care to struggle with it.

I am of an Opinion, in which I am every Day more confirmed by Observation, that Gratitude is one of those things that cannot be bought. It must be born with Men, or else all the Obligations in the World will not create it. An outward Shew may be made to satisfy Decency, and to prevent Reproach; but a real Sense of a kind thing is a Gift of Nature, and never was, nor can be acquired.

The Love of Ease is an Opiate, it is pleasing for the time, quieteth the Spirits, but it hath its Effects that seldom fail to be most fatal. The immoderate Love of Ease maketh a Man's Mind pay a passive Obedience to any thing that happeneth : It reduceth the Thoughts from having *Desire* to be *content.*

It must be allowed he had a little Over-balance on the well-natured Side, not Vigour enough to be earnest to do a kind Thing, much less to do a harsh one ; but if a hard thing was done to another Man, he did not eat his Supper the worse for it. It was rather a Deadness than Severity of Nature, whether it proceeded from a Dissipation of Spirits, or by the Habit of Living in which he was engaged.

If a King should be born with more Tenderness than might suit with his Office, he would in time be hardned. The Faults of his Subjects make Severity so necessary, that by the frequent Occasions given to use it, it comes to be habitual, and by degrees the Resistance that Nature made at first groweth fainter, till at last it is in a manner quite extinguished.

In short, this Prince might more properly be said to have *Gifts* than *Virtues*, as Affability, Easiness of Living, Inclinations to give, and to forgive : Qualities that flowed from his Nature rather than from his Virtue.

He had not more Application to any thing than the Preservation of his *Health* ; it had an intire Preference to any thing else in his Thoughts, and he might be said without Aggravation to study that with as little Intermission as any Man in the World.

He

He understood it very well, only in this he failed, that he thought it was more reconcilable with his *Pleasures,* than it really was. It is natural to have such a Mind to reconcile these, that 'tis the easier for any Man that goeth about it, to be guilty of that Mistake.

This made him overdo in point of Nourishment, the better to furnish to those Entertainments; and then he thought by great *Exercise* to make Amends, and to prevent the ill Effects of his Blood being too much raised. The Success he had in this Method, whilst he had Youth and Vigour to support him in it, encouraged him to continue it longer than Nature allowed. Age stealeth so insensibly upon us, that we do not think of suiting our way of Reasoning to the several Stages of Life; so insensibly that not being able to pitch upon any *precise Time,* when we cease to be young, we either flatter ourselves that we always continue to be so, or at least forget how much we are mistaken in it.

VII. Conclusion.

AFTER all this, when some rough Strokes of the Pencil have made several Parts of the Picture look a little hard, it is a Justice that would be due to every Man, much more to a Prince, to make some Amends, and to reconcile Men as much as may be to it by the last finishing.

He had as good a Claim to a kind Interpretation as most Men. First as a *Prince* : living and dead, generous and well-bred Men will be gentle to them; next as an *unfortunate Prince* in the beginning of his Time, and a *gentle* one in the rest.

A Prince neither sharpened by his Misfortunes whilst Abroad, nor by his Power when restored, is such a shining Character, that it is a Reproach not to be so dazzled with it, as not to be able to see a Fault in its full Light. It would be a Scandal in this Case to have an exact Memory. And if all who are akin to his Vices, should mourn for him, never Prince would be better attended to his Grave. He is under the Protection of common
Frailty,

Frailty, that must engage Men for their own sakes not to be too severe, where they themselves have so much to answer.

What therefore an angry Philosopher would call *Lewdness*, let frailer Men call a Warmth and Sweetness of the Blood, that would not be confined in the communicating itself; an over-flowing of Good-nature, of which he had such a Stream, that it would not be restrained within the Banks of a crabbed and unsociable Virtue.

If he had sometimes less *Firmness* than might have been wished; let the kindest Reason be given, and if that should be wanting, the best Excuse. I would assign the Cause of it to be his loving at any rate to be *easy*, and his deserving the more to be indulged in it, by his desiring that every body else should be so.

If he sometimes let a *Servant fall*, let it be examined whether he did not *weigh* so much upon his Master, as to give him a fair Excuse. That *Yieldingness*, whatever Foundations it might lay to the Disadvantage of Posterity, was a Specifick to preserve us in Peace for his own Time. If he loved too much to lie upon his own Down-bed of Ease, his Subjects had the Pleasure, during his Reign, of lolling and stretching upon theirs. As a Sword is sooner broken upon a Feather-bed than upon a Table, so his Pliantness broke the blow of a present Mischief much better than a more immediate Resistance would perhaps have done.

Ruin saw this, and therefore removed him first to make way for further Overturnings.

If *he dissembled*; let us remember, first, that he was a King, and that Dissimulation is a Jewel of the Crown; next, that it is very hard for a Man not to do sometimes too much of that, which he concludeth necessary for him to practice. Men should consider, that as there would be no false Dice, if there were no true ones, so if Dissembling is grown universal, it ceaseth to be foul play, having an implied Allowance by the general Practice. He that was so often forced to dissemble in his own Defence, might the better have the privilege sometimes to be the Aggressor, and to deal with Men at their own Weapon.

Subjects

Subjects are apt to be as arbitrary in their *Censure,* as the most assuming Kings can be in their Power. If there might be matter for Objections, there is not less reason for Excuses ; The Defects laid to his Charge, are such as may claim Indulgence from Mankind.

Should no body throw a Stone at his Faults but those who are free from them, there would be but a slender Shower.

What private Man will throw Stones at him because he *loved* ? Or what Prince, because he *dissembled* ?

If he either *trusted,* or *forgave* his *Enemies,* or in some Cases *neglected* his *Friends,* more than could in Strictness be allowed ; let not those Errors be so arraigned as take away the Privilege that seemeth to be due to Princely Frailties. If Princes are under the Misfortune of being accused to govern ill, their Subjects have the less right to fall hard upon them, since they generally so little deserve to be governed well.

The truth is, the Calling of a King, with all its glittering, hath such an unreasonable weight upon it, that they may rather expect to be lamented, than to be envied for being set upon a Pinacle, where they are exposed to Censure, if they do not do more to answer Mens Expectations, than corrupted Nature will allow.

It is but Justice therefore to this Prince, to give all due Softenings to the less shining Parts of his Life ; to offer Flowers and Leaves to hide, instead of using Aggravations to expose them.

Let his Royal Ashes then lie soft upon him, and cover him from harsh and unkind Censures; which though they should not be unjust, can never clear themselves from being indecent.

POLITICAL THOUGHTS

AND

REFLECTIONS.

Of Fundamentals.

EVERY Party, when they find a Maxim for their turn, they presently call it a Fundamental, they think they nail it with a Peg of Iron, whereas in truth they only tie it with a wisp of Straw.

The word soundeth so well that the Impropriety of it hath been the less observed. But as weighty as the word appeareth, no Feather hath been more blown about in the World than this word, *Fundamental.*

It is one of those Mistakes that at sometimes may be of use, but it is a Mistake still.

Fundamental is used as Men use their Friends; commend them when they have need of them, and when they fall out, find a hundred Objections to them.

Fundamental is a Pedestal that Men set every thing upon that they would not have broken. It is a Nail every body would use to fix that which is good for them : for all Men would have that Principle to be immoveable, that serves their use at the time.

Every thing that is created is Mortal, *ergo* all Fundamentals of human Creation will die.

A true Fundamental must be like the Foundation of a House ; if it is undermined the whole House falleth.

The Fundamentals in Divinity have been changed in several Ages of the World.

They have made no difficulty in the several Councils, to destroy and excommunicate Men for asserting Things that at other Times were called Fundamentals.

Philosophy, Astronomy, &c. have changed their Fundamentals as the Men of Art no doubt called them at the time. Motion of the Earth, &c.

Even in Morality one may more properly say, There *should be* Fundamentals allowed, than that there *are* any which in Strictness can be maintained.

However this is the least uncertain Foundation : Fundamental is less improperly applied here than any where else.

Wise and good Men will in all Ages stick to some Fundamentals, look upon them as sacred, and preserve an inviolable Respect for them; but Mankind in general make Morality a more malleable thing than it ought to be.

There is then no certain Fundamental but in *Nature*, and yet *there* are Objections too. It is a Fundamental in Nature that the Son should not kill the Father, and yet the Senate of *Venice* gave a Reward to a Son who brought in his Father's Head, according to a Proclamation.

Salus Populi is an unwritten Law, yet that doth not hinder but that it is sometimes very visible; and as often as it is so, it supersedeth all other Laws which are subordinate Things compared.

The great Punishments upon Self-murder, are Arguments that it was rather a tempting Sin to be discouraged than an unnatural Act.

It is a Fundamental that where a Man intendeth no hurt he should receive none, yet Manslaughter, &c. are Cases of Mercy.

That a Boy under Ten shall not suffer Death, yet where *Malitia supplet ætatem*, otherwise.

That there were Witches—much shaken of late.

That the King is not to be deceived in his Grant—The practical Fundamental the contrary.

That what is given to God cannot be alienated. Yet in practice it is, by Treaties, &c. and even by the Church itself, when they get a better bargain by it.

I can make no other Definition of a true Fundamental than this : *viz.* That whatever a Man hath a desire to do or to hinder,

if

if he hath uncontested and irresistable Power to effect it, that he will certainly do it.

If he thinketh he hath that Power, though he hath it not, he will certainly go about it.

Some would define a Fundamental to be the settling the Laws of Nature and common Equity in such a sort as that they may be well administered: even in this case there can be nothing *fixed*, but it must *vary* for the Good of the whole.

A Constitution cannot make itself; some body made it, not at once but at several times. It is alterable; and by that draweth nearer Perfection; and without suiting itself to differing Times and Circumstances, it could not live. Its Life is prolonged by changing seasonably the several Parts of it at several times.

The Reverence that is given to a Fundamental, in a general unintelligible Notion, would be much better applyed to that *Supremacy or Power* which is set up in every Nation in differing Shapes, that altereth the Constitution as often as the Good of the People requireth it.

Neither *King* nor *People* would now like just the *original Constitution*, without any varyings.

If Kings are only answerable to God, that doth not secure them even in this World; since if God upon the Appeal thinketh fit not to stay, he maketh the People his Instruments.

I am perswaded that where ever any single Man had Power to do himself right upon a *deceitful Trustee*, he would do it. That Thought well digested would go a great way towards the discouraging Invasions upon Rights, &c.

I lay down then as a Fundamental, 1st, that in every Constitution there is *some Power* which neither will nor ought to be bounded.

2. That the King's Prerogative should be as *plain* a thing as the People's Obedience.

3. That a Power which may by parity of Reason destroy the whole Laws, can never be reserved by the Laws.

4. That in all limited Governments it must give the Governor Power to *hurt*, but it can never be so interpreted as to give him

Power

Power to *destroy*, for then in effect it would cease to be a limited Government.

5. That Severity be rare and great; for as *Tacitus* sayeth of *Nero*, 'Frequent Punishments made the People call even his Justice Cruelty.'

6. That it is necessary to make the Instruments of Power easy; for Power is hard enough to be digested by those under it at the best.

7. That the People are never so perfectly backed, but that they will kick and fling if not stroked at seasonable times.

8. That a Prince must think if he loseth his People he can never regain them.

It is both wise and safe to think so.

9. That Kings assuming Prerogative teach the People to do so too.

10. That Prerogative is a Trust.

11. That they are not the *King*'s Laws, nor the *Parliament*'s Laws, but the *Laws of England*, in which after they have passed by the Legislative Power, the People have the *Property*, and the King the *Executive* part.

12. That no Abilities should qualify a noted Knave to be employed in Business. A Knave can by none of his Dexterities make amends for the Scandal he bringeth upon the Crown.

13. That those who will not be bound by the *Laws*, rely upon *Crimes* : a third way was never found in the World to secure any Government.

14. That a Seaman be a Seaman; a Cabinet-Counsellor a Man of Business; an Officer, an Officer.

15. In corrupted Governments the Place is given for the sake of the Man; in good ones the Man is chosen for the sake of the Place.

16. That Crowds at Court are made up of such as would deceive : The *real Worshippers* are few.

17. That *Salus Populi* is the greatest of all Fundamentals, yet not altogether an immoveable one. It is a Fundamental for a Ship to ride at Anchor when it is in Port, but if a Storm cometh the Cable must be cut.

18.

18. *Property* is not a fundamental Right in one Sense, because in the beginning of the World there was none, so that Property itself was an Innovation introduced by Laws.

Property is only secured by trusting it in the best Hands, and those are generally chosen who are least likely to deceive; but if they should, they have a legal Authority to abuse as well as use the Power with which they are trusted, and there is no Fundamental can stand in their way, or be allowed as an Exception to the Authority that was vested in them.

19. *Magna Charta* would fain be made to pass for a Fundamental; and Sir *Edward Coke* would have it, that the Grand Charter was for the most part declaratory of the principal Grounds of the fundamental Laws of *England*.

If that referreth to the Common Law, it must be made out that every thing in *Magna Charta* is always and at all times necessary in itself to be kept, or else the denying a subsequent Parliament the Right of repealing any Law doth by consequence deny the preceding Parliament the Right of making it. But they are fain to say it was only a declarative Law, which is very hard to be proved. Yet suppose it, you must either make the Common Law so stated a thing that all Men know it before-hand, or else universally acquiesce in it whenever it is alledged, from the Affinity it hath to the Law of Nature. Now I would fain know whether the Common Law is capable of being defined, and whether it doth not hover in the Clouds like the Prerogative, and bolteth out like Lightening to be made use of for some particular Occasion? If so, the Government of the World is left to a thing that cannot be defined; and if it cannot be defined, you know not what it is; so that the supream Appeal is, we know not what. We submit to God Almighty though he is incomprehensible, and yet He hath set down His Methods; but for this World, there can be no Government without a stated Rule, and a Supream Power not to be controled neither by the Dead nor the Living.

The Laws under the Protection of the King govern in the ordinary Administration; the extraordinary Power is in Acts
of

of Parliament, from whence there can be no Appeal but to the same Power at another time.

To say a Power is Supream, and not Arbitrary, is not Sense. It is acknowledg'd Supream, and therefore, &c.

If the Common Law is Supream, then those are so who judge what is the Common Law; and if none but the Parliament can judge so, there is an end of the Controversy; there is no *Fundamental*; for the Parliament may judge as they please, that is, they have the Authority, but they may judge against Right, their Power is good, though their Act is ill; no good Man will outwardly resist the one, or inwardly approve the other.

There is then no other Fundamental, but that *every Supream Power must be Arbitrary.*

Fundamental is a Word used by the Laity, as the Word Sacred is by the Clergy, to fix every thing to themselves they have a mind to keep, that nobody else may touch it.

Of Princes.

A PRINCE who will not undergo the Difficulty of Understanding, must undergo the Danger of Trusting.

A wise Prince may gain such an Influence, that his Countenance would be the last Appeal. Where it is not so in some degree, his Authority is precarious.

A Prince must keep up the Power of his Countenance, which is not the least of his Prerogatives.

The Conscience, as well as the Prerogative of a King, must be restrained or loosened as is best for his People.

It may without Scandal be made of stretching Leather, but it must be drawn by a steady Hand.

A King that lets Intercession prevail, will not be long worshipped.

A Prince used to War getteth a military Logick that is not very well suited to the Civil Administration.

If

If he maketh War successfully, he groweth into a Demi-God ; if without Success, the World throweth him as much below Humanity as they had before set him above it.

A Hero must be sometimes allowed to make bold Strokes, without being fettered by strict Reason.

He is to have some generous Irregularities in his Reasoning, or else he will not be a good Thing of his Kind.

PRINCES (*their Rewards of Servants*).

WHEN a Prince giveth any Man a very extravagant Reward, it looketh as if it was rather for an ill thing than a good one.

Both the Giver and Receiver are out of countenance where they are ill suited, and ill applyed.

Serving Princes will make Men proud at first, and humble at last.

Resolving to serve well, and at the same time resolving to please, is generally resolving to do what is not to be done.

A Man that will serve well must often rule the Master so hard that it will hurt him.

It is thought an unsociable Quality in a Court to do ones Duty better than other Men.

Nothing is less forgiven than setting Patterns Men have no mind to follow.

Men are so unwilling to displease a Prince, that it is as dangerous to inform him right, as to serve him wrong.

Where Men get by pleasing, and lose by serving, the choice is so easy that no body can miss it.

PRINCES, *their Secrets.*

MEN are so proud of Princes Secrets, that they will not see the danger of them.

When a Prince trusteth a Man with a dangerous Secret, he would not be sorry to hear the Bell toll for him.

Love

Love of the Subjects to a Prince.

THE Heart of the Subjects yieldeth but a lean Crop where it is not cultivated by a wise Prince.

The Good-will of the Governed will be starved, if it is not fed by the good Conduct of the Governors.

Suffering for Princes.

THOSE who merit because they suffered, are so very angry with those that made them suffer, that though their Services may deserve Employment, their Temper rendereth them unfit for it.

Of Ministers.

THE World dealeth with Ministers of State as they do with ill Fidlers, ready to kick them down Stairs for playing ill, though few of the Fault-finders understand their Musick enough to be good Judges.

A Minister who undertaketh to make his Master very great, if he faileth, is ruin'd for his folly; if he succeedeth, he is feared for his Skill.

A good Statesman may sometimes mistake as much by being too humble as by being too proud: He must take upon him in order to do his Duty, and not in order to the setting himself out.

A Minister is not to plead the King's Command for such things as he may in justice be supposed to have directed.

It is dangerous to serve where the Master hath the Privilege not to be blamed.

It is hard for a Prince to esteem the Parts of a Minister without either envying or fearing them; and less dangerous

for

for a Minister to shew all the Weakness than all the Strength of his Understanding.

There are so many things necessary to make up a good Minister, that no wonder there are so few of them in the World.

There is hardly a rasher thing, than for a Man to venture to be a good Minister.

A Minister of State must have a Spirit of liberal Oeconomy, not a restrained Frugality.

He must enlarge his Family-Soul, and suit it to the bigger Compass of a Kingdom.

A Prince should be asked, why he *will* do a thing, but not why he *hath* done it.

If the Boys were to choose a School-master, it should be one that would not whip them ; the same thing if the Courtiers were to choose a Minister.

They would have a great many Play-days, no Rods, and leave to rob Orchards.—The Parallel will hold.

Wicked MINISTERS.

A Cunning Minister will engage his Master to begin with a small wrong Step, which will insensibly engage him in a great one.

A Man that hath the Patience to go by Steps, may deceive one much wiser than himself.

State-business is a cruel Trade ; Good-nature is a Bungler in it.

Instruments of STATE-MINISTERS.

MEN in Business are in as much danger from those that work under them, as from those that work against them.
                                                                When

When the Instruments bend under the Weight of their Business, it is like a weak-legg'd Horse that brings his Rider down with him.

As when they are too weak they let a Man fall, so when they are too strong they throw him off.

If Men of Business did not forget how apt their Tools are to break or fail, they would shut up Shop.

They must use things called *Men* under them, who will spoil the best Scheme that can be drawn by Human Understanding.

Tools that are blunt cannot cut at all, and those that are sharp are apt to cut in the wrong place.

Great difference between a good Tool and a good Workman.

When the Tools will be Workmen they cut their own Fingers, and every body's else.

Of the People.

THERE is more Strength in *Union* than in *Number*; witness the People that in all Ages have been scurvily used, because they could so seldom agree to do themselves Right.

The more the weaker, may be as good a Proverb as, The more the merrier.

A People can no more stand without Government than a Child can go without Leading-Strings : as old and as big as a Nation is, it can't go by itself, and must be led.   The *Numbers* that make its Strength, are at the same time the Cause of its Weakness and Incapacity of Acting.

Men have so *discovered themselves* to *one another,* that Union is become a mere Word, in reality impracticable.

They trust, or suspect, not upon Reason but ill-grounded Fame ; they would be at ease, saved, protected, *&c.* and give nothing for it.

The lower Sort of Men must be indulged the Consolation of finding fault with those above them ; without that, they would be so melancholy, that it would be dangerous, considering their Numbers.

They

They are too many to be told of their Mistakes, and for that Reason they are never to be cured of them.

The Body of the People are generally either so dead that they cannot move, or so mad that they cannot be reclaimed : to be neither all in a Flame, nor quite cold, requireth more Reason than great Numbers can ever attain.

The People can seldom agree to move together against a Government, but they can to sit still and let it be undone.

Those that will be Martyrs for the People, must expect to be repayed only by their *Vanity*, or their *Virtue*.

A Man that will head the Mob is like a Bull let loose, tyed about with Squibs and Crackers.

He must be half mad that goeth about it, yet at some times shall be too hard for all the wise Men in a Kingdom : For though good Sense speaketh against Madness, yet it is out of Countenance whenever it meets it.

It would be a greater Reproach to the People that their *Favour* is short-liv'd, if their *Malice* was not so too.

The Thoughts of the People have no regular Motion, they come out by Starts.

There is an accumulative Cruelty in a number of Men, though none in particular are ill-natured.

The angry Buzz of a Multitude is one of the bloodiest Noises in the World.

Of Government.

AN exact Administration, and good choice of proper Instruments doth insensibly make the Government in a manner absolute without assuming it.

The best Definition of the best Government is, that it hath no Inconveniences but such as are supportable; but Inconveniences there must be.

The Interest of the Governors and the Governed is in reality the same, but by Mistakes on both Sides it is generally very differing.

differing. He who is a Courtier by Trade, and the Country Gentleman who will be popular, right or wrong, help to keep up this unreasonable Distinction.

There are as many apt to be angry at being well, as at being ill governed. For most Men to be well governed must be scurvily used.

As Mankind is made, the keeping it in order is an ill-natured Office.

It is like a great Galley where the Officers must be whipping with little Intermission, if they will do their Duty.

It is in a disorderly Government as in a River, the lightest Things swim at the top.

A Nation is best to be judged by the Government it is under at the time. Mankind is moulded to good or ill, according as the Power over it is well or ill directed. A Nation is a Mass of Dough, it is the Government that kneadeth it into Form.

Where Learning and Trade flourish in a Nation, they produce so much Knowledge, and That so much Equality among Men, that the Greatness of Dependencies is lost, but the Nation in general will be the better for it : For if the Government be wise, it is the more easily governed ; if not, the bad Government is the more easily overturned, by Mens being more united against it than when they depended upon great Men ; who might sooner be gained over and weakend by being divided.

There is more reason for allowing *Luxury* in a Military Government than in another ; the perpetual Exercise of War not only excuseth but recommendeth the Entertainments in the Winter. In another it groweth into a Habit of uninterrupted Expences and idle Follies, and the Consequences of them to a Nation become irrecoverable.

CLERGY.

IF the Clergy did not live like temporal Men, all the Power of Princes could not bring them under the temporal Jurisdiction.

They

They who may be said to be of God Almighty's Houshold, should shew by their Lives that he hath a well disciplined Family.

The Clergy in this Sense, of Divine Institution ; that God hath made Mankind so weak that it must be deceived.

RELIGION.

IT is a strange thing that the way to save Mens Souls should be such a cunning Trade, as to require a skilful Master.

The time spent in praying to God, might be better employed in deserving well from him.

Men think praying the easier Task of the two, and therefore choose it.

The People would not believe in God at all, if they were not permitted to believe wrong in him.

The several Sorts of Religion in the World are little more than so many spiritual Monopolies.

If their Interests could be reconciled, their Opinions would be so too.

Men pretend to serve God Almighty who doth not need it, but make use of him because they need him.

Factions are like Pirates that set out false Colours ; when they come near a Booty Religion is put under Deck.

Most Mens Anger about Religion is as if two Men should quarrel for a Lady they neither of them care for.

Of PREROGATIVE, POWER *and* LIBERTY.

A Prerogative that tendeth to the Dissolution of all Laws must be void in itself, *felo de se* ; for a Prerogative is a Law. The reason of any Law is, that no Man's Will should be a Law.

The

The King is the Life of the Law, and cannot have a Prerogative that is mortal to it.

The Law is to have a Soul in it, or it is a dead thing. The King is by his Sovereign Power to add Warmth and Vigour to the meaning of the Law. We are by no means to imagine there is such an Antipathy between them, that the Prerogative, like a Basilisk, is to kill the Law, whenever it looks upon it.

The Prince hath very rarely use of his Prerogative, but hath constantly a great Advantage by the Laws.

They attribute to the Pope indeed, that all the Laws of the Church are in his Breast; but then he hath the Holy Ghost for his learned Counsel, &c.

The People's Obedience must be *plain*, and without *Evasions*. The Prince's Prerogative should be so too.

King *Charles the First* made this Answer to the Petition of Right, (to the Observation whereof he held himself obliged in Conscience, as well as of his Prerogative.) ' That the People's ' Liberties strengthen the King's Prerogative, and the King's ' Prerogative is to defend the People's Liberties.'

That Prince's Declarations allow the Original of Government to come from the People. Prerogative never yet pretended to repealing.

The first ground of Prerogative was to enable the Prince to do *good*, not to do *every thing*.

If the ground of a King's desire of Power be his assurance of himself that he will do no hurt by it; is it not an Argument for Subjects to desire to *keep* that which they will never *abuse*?

It must not be such a Prerogative as giveth the Government the Rickets; all the Nourishment to go to the upper part, and the lower starved.

As a Prince is in danger who calleth a stronger than himself to his Assistance; so when Prerogative useth *Necessity* for an Argument, it calleth in a stronger thing than itself. The same Reason may overturn it. Necessity too is so plain a thing, that every body sees it, so that the Magistrate hath no great privilege in being the Judge of it. Necessity therefore is a dangerous Argument for Princes, since (wherever it is real) it constitutes every

every Man a Magistrate, and gives as great a Power of dispensing to every private Man, as a Prince can claim.

It is not so proper to say that *Prerogative* justifieth *Force*, as that *Force* supporteth *Prerogative*. They have not been such constant Friends but that they have had terrible *Fallings* out.

All Powers are of God; and between *Permission* and *Appointment*, well considered, there is no real difference.

In a limited Monarchy, Prerogative and Liberty are as jealous of one another as any two neighbouring States can be of their respective Incroachments.

They ought not to part for small Bickerings, and must bear little Jealousies without breaking for them.

Power is so apt to be insolent, and Liberty to be saucy, that they are very seldom upon good Terms.

They are both so quarrelsome that they will not easily enter into a fair Treaty. For indeed it is hard to bring them together; they ever quarrel at a distance.

Power and Liberty are respectively managed in the World in a manner not suitable to their Value and Dignity.

They are both so abused that it justifieth the Satires that are generally made upon them. And

They are so in Possession of being misapplied, that instead of censuring their being abused, it is more reasonable to wonder whenever they are *not* so.

They are perpetually wrestling, and have had their Turns when they have been thrown, to have their Bones broken by it.

If they were not both apt to be out of Breath, there would be no living.

If Prerogative will urge Reason to support it, it must bear Reason when it resisteth it.

It is a Diminution instead of a Glory, to be above treating upon equal Terms with Reason.

If the People were designed to be the sole Property of the supream Magistrate, sure God would have made them of a differing and subordinate Species; as he hath the Beasts, that by the Inferiority of their Nature they might the better submit to the Dominion of Mankind.

If

If none were to have Liberty but those who understand what it is, there would not be many freed Men in the World.

When the People contend for their Liberty, they seldom get any thing by their Victory but new Masters.

Liberty can neither be got, nor kept, but by so much Care, that Mankind generally are unwilling to give the Price for it. And therefore, in the Contest between Ease and Liberty, the first hath generally prevailed.

Of Laws.

LAWS are generally not understood by three Sorts of Persons, *viz.* by those that make them, by those that execute them, and by those that suffer, if they break them.

Men seldom understand any Laws but those they *feel*.

Precepts, like Fomentations, must be rubbed into us; and with a rough Hand too.

If the Laws could speak for themselves, they would complain of the Lawyers in the first Place.

There is more Learning now required to explain a Law made, than went to the making it.

The Law hath so many Contradictions, and Varyings from itself, that the Law may not improperly be called a Law-breaker.

It is become too changeable a thing to be defined: it is made little less a *Mystery* than the *Gospel*.

The Clergy and the Lawyers, like the Free-Masons, may be supposed to take an Oath not to tell the Secret.

The Men of Law have a Biass to their calling in the Interpretations they make of the Law.

Of Parliaments.

THE Parliaments are so altered from their original Constitution, that between the Court and the Country, the House, instead of being united, is like Troops of a contrary Party facing one another, and watching their Advantage.

Even the well-meaning Men who have good Sense too, have
their

their Difficulties in an Assembly; what they offer honestly for a good End, will be skilfully improved for an ill one.

It is strange that a gross Mistake should live a Minute in an Assembly; one would expect that it should be immediately stifled by their discerning Faculties. But Practice convinceth that a Mistake is no where better entertained.

In Parliaments, Men wrangle in behalf of Liberty, that do as little care for it, as they deserve it.

Where the People in Parliament give a good deal of Money in exchange for any thing from the Crown, a wise Prince can hardly have an ill bargain. The present Gift begetteth more ; it is a Politick kind of Generation ; and whenever a Parliament does not bring forth, it is the Unskilfulness of the Government, that is the cause of the Miscarriage.

Parliaments would bind and limit one another, and enact that such and such things shall not be made *Precedents*. There is not a word of Sense in this Language, which yet is to be understood the Sense of the Nation, and is printed as solemnly as if it was Sense.

Of PARTIES.

THE best Party is but a kind of a Conspiracy against the rest of the Nation. They put every body else out of their Protection. Like the *Jews* to the *Gentiles*, all others are the Offscowrings of the World.

Men value themselves upon their Principles, so as to neglect Practice, Abilities, Industry, &c.

Party cutteth off one half of the World from the other, so that the mutual Improvement of Mens Understanding by conversing, &c. is lost, and Men are half undone, when they lose the advantage of knowing what their Enemies think of them.

It is like Faith without Works; They take it for a Dispensation from all other Duties, which is the worst kind of *dispensing Power*.

It groweth to be the Master Thought; the Eagerness against one another at home, being a nearer Object, extinguisheth that which we ought to have against our foreign Enemies; and few Mens Understandings can get above overvaluing the Danger that is nearest, in comparison of that more remote.

It turneth all Thought into talking instead of doing. Men get a habit of being unuseful to the Publick by turning in a Circle of Wrangling and Railing, which they cannot get out of: And it may be remarked, that a *speculative* Coxcomb is not only unuseful, but mischievous : A *practical* Coxcomb under discipline may be made use of.

It maketh a Man thrust his Understanding into a Corner, and confine it till by degrees he destroys it.

Party is generally an Effect of Wantonness, Peace, and Plenty, which beget Humour, Pride, *&c.* and that is called Zeal and publick Spirit.

They forget insensibly that there is any body in the World but themselves, by keeping no other Company; so they miscalculate cruelly. And thus Parties mistake their Strength by the same reason that private Men overvalue themselves; for we by finding fault with others, build up a partial Esteem of ourselves upon the Foundation of their Mistakes: So Men in Parties find faults with those in the Administration, not without reason, but forget that they would be exposed to the same Objections, and perhaps greater, if it was their Adversary's turn to have the fault-finding part.

There are Men who shine in a Faction, and make a Figure by Opposition, who would stand in a worse light, if they had the Preferments they struggle for.

It looketh so like *Courage* (but nothing that is like is the same) to go to the *Extream,* that Men are carried away with it, and blown up out of their Senses by the wind of popular Applause.

That which looketh *bold* is a great Object that the People can discern ; But that which is *wise* is not so easily seen : It is
one

one part of it that it is not seen, but at the *End* of a Design. Those who are disposed to be wise too late, are apt to be valiant too early.

Most Men enter into a Party rashly, and retreat from it as shamefully. As they encourage one another at first, so they betray one another at last: And because every Qualification is capable of being corrupted by the Excess, they fall upon the extream, to fix mutual Reproaches upon one another.

Party is little less than an Inquisition, where Men are under such a Discipline in carrying on the common Cause, as leaves no Liberty of private Opinion.

It is hard to produce an Instance where a Party did ever succeed against a Government, except they had a good handle given them.

No original Party ever prevailed in a turn; it brought up *something else*, but the first Projectors were thrown off.

If there are two Parties, a Man ought to adhere to that which he disliketh least, though in the whole he doth not approve it: For whilst he doth not list himself in one or the other Party, he is looked upon as such a Straggler, that he is fallen upon by both. Therefore a Man under such a Misfortune of Singularity, is neither to provoke the World, nor disquiet himself, by taking any particular Station.

It becometh him to live in the Shade, and keep his Mistakes from giving Offence; but if they are his Opinions, he cannot put them off as he doth his Cloaths. Happy those who are convinced so as to be of the general Opinions.

Ignorance maketh most Men go into a Party, and Shame keepeth them from getting out of it.

More Men hurt others they do not know why than for any reason.

If there was any Party entirely composed of honest Men, it would certainly prevail; but both the honest Men and the Knaves resolve to turn one another off when the Business is done.

They by turns defame all *England*, so nobody can be employed that hath not been branded: There are few Things so criminal as a Place.

Of

Of COURTS.

THE Court may be said to be a Company of well-bred fashionable Beggars.

At Court, if a Man hath too much Pride to be a Creature, he had better stay at home: A Man who will rise at Court must begin, by creeping upon All-four: A Place at Court, like a Place in Heaven, is to be got by being much upon *one's Knees.*

There are hardly two Creatures of a more differing Species than the same Man, when he is pretending to a Place, and when he is in Possession of it.

Mens Industry is spent in receiving the Rents of a Place, there is little left for discharging the Duty of it.

Some Places have such a corrupting Influence upon the Man, that it is a supernatural thing to resist it.

Some Places lye so fair to entertain Corruption, that it looketh like renouncing a due Perquisite, not to go into it.

If a getting Fool would keep out of Business, he would grow richer in a Court than a Man of Sense.

One would wonder that in a Court where there is so little Kindness, there should be so much *whispering.*

Men must brag of kind Letters from Court, at the same time that they do not believe one Word of them.

Men at Court think so much of their own Cunning, that they forget other Mens.

After a Revolution, You see the *same Men* in the Drawing-room, and within a Week the same *Flatterers.*

Of PUNISHMENT.

WHEREVER a Government knows *when* to *show* the Rod, it will not often be put to *use* it. But between the want of Skill, and the want of Honesty, Faults generally either escape Punishment, or are mended to no Purpose.

Men

Men are not hang'd for stealing Horses, but that Horses may not be stolen.

Wherever a Knave is not punished, an honest Man is laugh'd at.

A Cheat to the Publick is thought infamous, and yet to accuse him is not thought an honourable part. What a Paradox! 'Tis an ill Method, to make the Aggravation of the Crime a Security against the Punishment; so that the Danger is not to *rob*, but not to *rob enough*.

Treason must not be *inlayed Work* of *several Pieces*, it must be an entire Piece of itself. *Accumulative* in that case is a murdering Word, that carrieth Injustice, and no Sense in it.

An *Inference*, though never so rational, should go no farther than to justify a *Suspicion*, not so far as to inflict a *Punishment*. Nothing is so apt to break with Stretching, as an *Inference*; and nothing so ridiculous, as to see how Fools will abuse one.

MORAL

Moral Thoughts.
and
Reflections.

Of the World.

IT is from the Shortness of Thought, that Men imagine there is any great Variety in the World.

Time hath thrown a Vail upon the Faults of former Ages, or else we should see the same Deformities we condemn in the present Times.

When a Man looketh upon the Rules that are made, he will think there can be no Faults in the World; and when he looketh upon the Faults, there are so many he will be tempted to think there are no Rules.

They are not to be reconciled, otherwise than by concluding that which is called *Frailty* is the incurable *Nature* of Mankind.

A Man that understandeth the World must be weary of it; and a Man who doth not, for that Reason ought not to be pleased with it.

The Uncertainty of what is to come, is such a dark Cloud, that neither Reason nor Religion can quite break through it; and the Condition of Mankind is to be weary of what we do know, and afraid of what we do not.

The World is beholden to *generous Mistakes* for the greatest Part of the Good that is done in it.

Our *Vices* and *Virtues* couple with one another, and get Children that resemble both their Parents.

If a Man can hardly inquire into a Thing he undervalueth, how can a Man of good Sense take pains to understand the World?

To understand the World, and to like it, are two things not easily to be reconciled.

That

That which is called an *Able Man* is a great Over-valuer of the World, and all that belongeth to it.

All that can be said of him is, that he maketh the best of the General Mistake.

It is the Fools and the Knaves that make the Wheels of the World turn. *They* are *the World*; those few who have Sense or Honesty sneak up and down single, but never go in Herds.

To be too much *troubled* is a worse way of over-valuing the World than the being too much *pleased*.

A Man that steps aside from the World, and hath leisure to observe it without Interest or Design, thinks all Mankind as mad as they think him, for not agreeing with them in their Mistakes.

Of AMBITION.

THE serious Folly of wise Men in *over-valuing the World*, is as contemptible as any thing they think fit to censure.

The first Mistake belonging to Business is the going into it.

Men make it such a Point of Honour to be fit for Business, that they forget to examine whether Business is fit for a Man of Sense.

There is Reason to think the most celebrated Philosophers would have been Bunglers at Business; but the Reason is because they despised it.

It is not a Reproach but a Compliment to Learning, to say, that *Great Scholars* are less fit for Business; since the truth is, Business is so much a lower thing than Learning, that a Man used to the last cannot easily bring his Stomach down to the first.

The Government of the World is a great thing; but it is a very coarse one too, compared with the Fineness of Speculative Knowledge.

The Dependance of a great Man upon a greater, is a Subjection that lower Men cannot easily comprehend.

Ambition

Ambition hath no Mean, it is either upon *all four* or upon *Tiptoes*.

Nothing can be humbler than Ambition, when it is so disposed.

Popularity is a Crime from the Moment it is sought; it is only a Virtue where Men have it whether they will or no.

It is generally an Appeal to the People from the Sentence given by Men of Sense against them.

It is stepping very low to get very high.

Men by Habit make irregular Stretches of Power, without discerning the Consequence and Extent of them.

Eagerness is apt to overlook Consequences, it is loth to be stopt in its Career ; for when Men are in great haste, they see only in a straight Line.

Of Cunning *and* Knavery.

CUNNING is so apt to grow into Knavery, that an honest Man will avoid the Temptation of it. But Men in this Age are half bribed by the Ambition of circumventing, without any other encouragements. So proud of the Character of being *able* Men, that they do not care to have their Dexterity confined.

In this Age, when it is said of a Man, He knows *how to live*, it may be imply'd he is not very honest.

An honest Man must lose so many Occasions of Getting, that the World will hardly allow him the Character of an Able one.

There is however more *Wit* requisite to be an honest Man, than there is to be a Knave.

The most necessary thing in the World, and yet the least usual, is to reflect that those we deal with, may know how to be as arrant Knaves as ourselves.

The Eagerness of a Knave maketh him often as catchable, as Ignorance maketh a Fool.

No Man is so much a Fool as not to have Wit enough sometimes

times to be a Knave; nor any so cunning a Knave, as not to have the Weakness sometimes to play the Fool.

The Mixture of Fool and Knave, maketh up the parti-coloured Creatures that make all the Bustle in the World.

There is not so pleasant a Quarry, as a Knave taken in a Net of his own making.

A Knave leaneth sometimes *so hard* upon his Impudence, that it breaketh and lets him fall.

Knavery is in such *perpetual Motion,* that it hath not always Leisure to look to its own Steps; 'tis like sliding upon Scates, no Motion so smooth or swift, but none gives so terrible a *Fall*.

A Knave loveth *Self* so heartily, that he is apt to over-strain it: by never thinking he can get enough, he gets so much less. His Thought is like Wine that fretteth with too much fermenting.

The Knaves in every Government are a kind of Corporation; and though they fall out with one another, like all Beasts of Prey, yet upon occasion they unite to support the common Cause.

It cannot be said to be such a Corporation as the Bank of *England,* but they are a numerous and formidable Body, scarce to be resisted; but the Point is, they can never rely upon one another.

Knaves go chain'd to one another like Slaves in the Gallies, and cannot easily untie themselves from their Company. Their Promises and Honour indeed do not hinder them, but other intangling Circumstances keep 'em from breaking loose.

If Knaves had not foolish Memories, they would never trust one another so often as they do.

Present Interest, like present Love, maketh all other Friendship look cold to it, but it faileth in the holding.

When one Knave betrayeth another, the one is not to be blamed, nor the other to be pitied.

When they complain of one another as if they were honest Men, they ought to be laugh'd at as if they were Fools.

There are some Cunning-men who yet can scarce be called Rational Creatures; yet they are often more successful than

Men

Men of Sense, because those they have to deal with are upon a looser Guard; and their Simplicity maketh their Knavery unsuspected.

There is no such thing as a venial Sin against Morality, no such thing as a small Knavery: He that carries a small Crime easily, will carry it on when it grows to be an Ox. But the little Knaves are the greater of the two, because they have less the Excuse of Temptation.

Knavery is so humble, and Merit so proud, that the latter is thrown down because it cannot stoop.

Of FOLLY and FOOLS.

THERE are five Orders of Fools, as of Building: 1. The Blockhead, 2. Coxcomb, 3. Vain Blockhead, 4. Grave Coxcomb, and 5. The Half-witted Fellow; this last is of the Composite Order.

The Follies of grave Men have the Precedence of all others, a ridiculous Dignity, that gives them a Right to be laughed at in the first place.

As the masculine Wit is the strongest, so the masculine Impertinence is the greatest.

The Consequence of a Half-Wit is a Half-Will, there is not Strength enough in the Thought to carry it to the End.

A Fool is naturally recommended to our Kindness by setting us off by the Comparison. Men are grateful to Fools for giving them the Pleasure of contemning them.

But Folly hath a long Tail that is not seen at first: for every single Folly hath a Root, out of which more are ready to sprout; and a Fool hath so unlimited a Power of mistaking, that a Man of Sense can never comprehend to what degree it may extend.

There are some Fools so low, that they are preferred when they are laught at. Their being named putteth them in the List of Men, which is more than belongeth to them.

One

One should no more laugh at a contemptible Fool, than at a dead Fly.

The Dissimulation of a Fool should come within the Statute of Stabbing. It giveth no Warning.

A Fool will be rude from the Moment he is allowed to be familiar; he can make no other use of Freedom than to be unmannerly.

Weak Men are apt to be *cruel*, because they stick at nothing that may repair the ill Effect of their Mistakes.

Folly is often more cruel in the Consequence, than Malice can be in the Intent.

Many a Man is murthered by the well-meant Mistakes of his unthinking Friends.

A weak Friend, if he will be kind, ought to go no farther than Wishes; if he proffereth either to say, or to do, it is dangerous.

A Man had as good go to Bed to a Razor, as to be intimate with a foolish Friend.

Mistaken Kindness is little less dangerous than premeditated Malice.

A Man hath not the Relief of being angry at the Blows of a mistaken Friend.

A busy Fool is fitter to be shut up than a downright Madman.

A Man that hath only Wit enough not to do Hurt, committeth a Sin if he aimeth at doing Good.

His passive Understanding must not pretend to be active.

It is a Sin against Nature for such a Man to be meddling.

It is hard to find a Blockhead so wise as to be upon the Defensive; he will be sallying, and then he is sure to be ill used.

If a dull Fool can make a Vow and keep it, never to speak his own Sense, or do his own Business, he may pass a great while for a rational Creature.

A Blockhead is as ridiculous when he talketh, as a Goose is when it flieth.

The grating a Gridiron is not a worse Noise, than the jingling of Words is to a Man of Sense.

It

It is Ill-manners to silence a Fool, and Cruelty to let him go on.

Most Men make little other use of their Speech than to give evidence against their own Understanding.

A great Talker may be a Man of Sense, but he cannot be one, who will venture to rely upon him.

There is so much Danger in Talking, that a Man strictly wise can hardly be called a sociable Creature.

The great Expence of Words is laid out in *setting ourselves out,* or *deceiving* others ; to *convince* them requireth but a few.

Many Words are always either suspicious or ridiculous.

A Fool hath no Dialogue within himself, the first Thought carrieth him without the Reply of a second.

A Fool will admire or like nothing that he understands, a Man of Sense nothing but what he understands.

Wise Men gain, and poor Men live, by the Superfluities of Fools.

Till Follies become ruinous, the World is better with than it would be without them.

A Fool is angry that he is the Food of a Knave, forgetting that it is the End of his Creation.

Of HOPE.

HOPE is a kind Cheat; in the Minute of our Disappointment we are angry, but upon the whole matter there is no Pleasure without it.

It is so much a pleasanter thing than Truth to the greatest Part of the World, that it hath all their Kindness, the other only hath their Respect.

Hope is generally a wrong Guide, though it is very good Company by the way. It brusheth through Hedge and Ditch till it cometh to a great Leap, and there it is apt to fall and break its Bones.

It

It would be well if Hopes carried Men only to the top of the Hill, without throwing them afterwards down the Precipice.

The Hopes of a Fool are blind Guides, those of a Man of Sense doubt often of their Way.

Men should do with their Hopes as they do with tame Fowl, cut their Wings that they may not fly over the Wall.

A *hoping* Fool hath such terrible Falls, that his Brains are turned, though not cured by them.

The *Hopes* of a Fool are Bullets he throws into the Air, that fall down again and break his Skull.

There can be no entire Disappointment to a wise Man, because he maketh it a Cause of succeeding another time. A Fool is so unreasonably raised by his *Hopes,* that he is half dead by a Disappointment: his mistaken Fancy draweth him so high, that when he falleth, he is sure to break his Bones.

Of ANGER.

ANGER is a better Sign of the Heart than of the Head ; it is a breaking out of the Disease of Honesty. Just Anger may be as dangerous as it could be if there was no Provocation to it ; for a Knave is not so nice a Casuist but that he will ruin, if he can, any Man that blameth him.

Where Ill-nature is not predominant, Anger will be short-breathed, it cannot hold out a long Course. Hatred can be tired and cloyed as well as Love : for our Spirits, like our Limbs, are tired with being long in one Posture.

There is a Dignity in Good-sense that is offended and defaced by Anger.

Anger is never without an Argument, but seldom with a good one.

Anger raiseth Invention but it overheateth the Oven.

Anger, like Drink, raiseth a great deal of unmannerly Wit.

True Wit must come by Drops ; Anger throweth it out in a Stream, and then it is not likely to be of the best kind.

Ill Language punisheth Anger by drawing a Contempt upon it.

Of

Of APOLOGIES

IT is a dangerous Task to answer Objections, because they are helped by the Malice of Mankind.

A bold Accusation doth at first draw such a general Attention, that it gets the World on its side.

To a Man who hath a mind to find a Fault, an Excuse generally giveth farther hold.

Explaining is generally half confessing.

Innocence hath a very short Style.

When a Jealousy of any kind is once raised, it is as often provoked as cured by any Arguments, let them be never so reasonable.

When Laziness letteth things alone, it is a Disease; but when Skill doth it, it is a Vertue.

Malice may help a Fool to aggravate, but there must be *Skill* to know how to extenuate.

To lessen an Object that at the first Sight giveth Offence, requireth a dexterous Hand : There must be Strength as well as Skill to take off the Weight of the first Impression.

When a Man is very unfortunate, it looketh like a saucy thing in him to justify himself.

A Man must stoop sometimes to his ill Star, but he must never lie down to it.

The Vindications Men make of themselves to *Posterity* would hardly be supported by Good-Sense, if they were not of some Advantage to their own Families.

The defending an ill Thing is more criminal than the doing it, because it wanteth the Excuse of its not being premeditated.

An Advocate for Injustice is like a Bawd that is worse than her Client who committeth the Sin.

There is hardly any Man so strict as not to vary a little from Truth when he is to make an Excuse.

Not telling all the Truth is hiding it, and that is comforting or abetting a Lye.

A long Vindication is seldom a skilful one.

Long doth at least imply *Doubtful* in such a Case.

A

A Fool should avoid the making an Excuse, as much as the committing a Fault; for a Fool's Excuse is always a second Fault : and whenever he will undertake either to hide or mend a thing, he proclaimeth and spoileth it.

Of MALICE *and* ENVY.

MALICE is a greater Magnifying-Glass than Kindness.

Malice is of a low Stature, but it hath very long Arms. It often reacheth into the next World, Death itself is not a Bar to it.

Malice, like Lust, when it is at the Height, doth not know Shame.

If it did not sometimes cut itself with its own Edge, it would destroy the World.

Malice can mistake by being *keen* as well as by being *dull.*

When Malice groweth *critical,* it loseth its Credit.

It must go under the Disguise of Plainness, or else it is exposed.

Anger may have some Excuse for being blind, but Malice none : for Malice hath time to look before it.

When Malice is overgrown, it cometh to be the highest degree of Impertinence.   For that reason, it must not be fed and pampered, which is apt to make it play the fool.   But where it is wise and steady, there is no Precaution, that can be quite Proof against it.

Ill-will is seldom cured on a sudden, it must go off by degrees, by insensible Transpiration.

Malice may be sometimes out of Breath, Envy never.   A Man may make Peace with Hatred, but never with Envy.

No Passion is better heard by our will, than that of Envy : No Passion is admitted to have Audience with less Exception.

Envy taketh the Shape of *Flattery,* and that maketh Men hug it so close, that they cannot part with it.

The

The sure way to be commended is to get into a Condition of being pitied. For Envy will not give its leave to commend a Man, till he is miserable.

A Man is undone, when Envy will not vouchsafe to look upon him.

Yet after all, Envy doth Virtue as much good as hurt, by provoking it to appear. Nay, it forcibly draweth out, and inviteth Virtue, by giving it a Mind to be revenged of it.

Of Vanity.

THE World is nothing but Vanity cut out into several Shapes.

Men often *mistake* themselves, but they never *forget* themselves.

A Man must not so entirely fall out with Vanity, as not to take its Assistance in the doing great Things.

Vanity is like some Men who are very useful, if they are kept under ; and else not to be endured.

A little Vanity may be allowed in a Man's Train, but it must not sit down at Table with him.

Without some Share of it, Mens Talents would be buried like Ore in a Mine unwrought.

Men would be less eager to gain Knowledge, if they did not hope to set themselves out by it.

It sheweth the Narrowness of our Nature, that a Man that intendeth any one thing extreamly, hath not Thought enough left for any thing else.

Our Pride maketh us over-value our Stock of Thought, so as to trade much beyond what it is able to make good.

Many aspire to learn what they can never comprehend, as others pretend to teach what they themselves do not know.

The Vanity of teaching often tempteth a Man to forget he is a Blockhead.

Self-conceit driveth away the suspecting how scurvily others think of us.

Vanity

Vanity cannot be a Friend to Truth, because it is restrained by it; and Vanity is so impatiently desirous of shewing itself, that it cannot bear the being crossed.

There is a Degree of Vanity that recommendeth; if it goeth further, it exposeth.

So much as to stir the Blood to do commendable Things, but not so much as to possess the Brain, and turn it round.

There are as many that are blown up by the Wind of Vanity, as are carried away by the Stream of Interest.

Every body hath not Wit enough to Act out of Interest, but every body hath little enough to do it out of Vanity.

Some Mens Heads are as easily blown away as their Hats.

If the commending others well, did not recommend ourselves, there would be few Panegyricks.

Mens Vanity will often dispose them to be commended into very troublesome Employments.

The desiring to be remember'd when we are dead, is to so little purpose, that it is fit Men should, as they generally are, be disappointed in it. Nevertheless, the desire of leaving a good Name behind us is so honourable to ourselves, and so useful to the World, that good Sense must not be heard against it.

Heraldry is one of those foolish Things that may yet be too much despised.

The Contempt of Scutcheons is as much a Disease in this Age, as the over-valuing them was in former Times.

There is a good Use to be made of the most contemptible Things, and an ill one of those that are the most valuable.

Of Money.

IF Men considered how many Things there are that Riches cannot buy, they would not be so fond of them.

The Things to be bought with Money, are such as least deserve the giving a Price for them.

Wit and Money are so apt to be abused, that Men generally make a shift to be the worse for them.

Money in a Fool's Hand exposeth him worse than a pyed Coat.

Money hath too great a Preference given to it by States, as well as by particular Men.

Men are more the Sinews of War than Money.

The third part of an Army must be destroyed, before a good one can be made out of it.

They who are of opinion that Money will do every thing, may very well be suspected to do every thing for Money.

False LEARNING.

A Little Learning *misleadeth*, and a great deal often *stupifieth* the Understanding.

Great Reading without applying it, is like Corn *heaped* that is not *stirred*, it groweth musty.

A learned Coxcomb dyeth his Mistakes in so much a deeper Colour : A wrong kind of Learning serveth only to embroider his Errors.

A Man that hath read without Judgment, is like a Gun charged with Goose-shot, let loose upon the Company.

He is only well furnished with Materials to expose himself, and to mortify those he liveth with.

The reading of the greatest Scholars, if put into a Limbeck, might be distilled into a small quantity of *Essence*.

The Reading of most Men, is like a Wardrobe of old Cloaths that are seldom used.

Weak Men are the worse for the good Sense they read in Books, because it furnisheth them only with more Matter to mistake.

Of COMPANY.

MEN that cannot entertain themselves want somebody, though they care for nobody.

An impertinent Fellow is never in the right, but in his being weary of *himself*.

By

By that time Men are fit for Company, they see the Objections to it.

The Company of a Fool is dangerous as well as tedious.

It is flattering some Men to endure them.

Present Punishment attendeth the Fault.

A *following* Wit will be welcome in most Companies; A *leading* one lieth too heavy for Envy to bear.

Out-doing is so near reproaching, that it will generally be thought very ill Company.

Any thing that shineth doth in some measure tarnish every thing that standeth next to it.

Keeping much Company generally endeth in playing the Fool or the Knave with them.

Of FRIENDSHIP.

FRIENDSHIP cometh oftener by Chance than by Choice, which maketh it generally so uncertain.

It is a Mistake to say a Friend can be bought.

A Man may buy a good Turn, but he cannot buy the Heart that doth it.

Friendship cannot live with Ceremony, nor without Civility.

There must be a nice Diet observed to keep Friendship from falling sick; nay, there is more Skill necessary to keep a Friend, than there is to reclaim an Enemy.

Those Friends who are above Interest are seldom above Jealousy.

It is a Misfortune for a Man not to have a Friend in the World, but for that reason he shall have no Enemy.

In the Commerce of the World, Men struggle little less with their Friends, than they do with their Enemies.

Esteem ought to be the ground of *Kindness,* and yet there are no Friends that seldomer meet.

Kindness is apt to be as *afraid* of Esteem, as that is to be *ashamed* of Kindness.

Our Kindness is greatest to those that will do what we would have them, in which our Esteem cannot always go along.

Miscellaneous Thoughts

AND

REFLECTIONS.

Of Advice and Correction. THE Rule *of doing as we would be done by*, is never less observed than it is in telling others their Faults. But Men intend more to shew others that they are free from the Fault, than to dissuade them from committing it.

They are so pleased with the prudent Shape of an Adviser, that it raiseth the value they have of themselves, whilst they are about it.

Certainly, to give Advice to a Friend, either asked or unasked, is so far from a Fault, that it is a Duty; but if a Man love to give Advice, it is a sure sign that he himself wanteth it.

A Man whilst he is advising putteth his Understanding upon Tiptoes, and is unwilling to bring it down again.

A weak Man had rather *be thought* to know, than *know*, and that maketh him so impatient to be told of a Mistake.

He who will not be the better for other Mens Faults, hath no cure left for his own.

But he that can probe himself to cure his own Faults, will seldom need either the Surgery of his Friends or of his Enemies.

Of Alterations. IN a corrupted Age the putting the World in order would breed Confusion.

A rooted Disease must be *stroaked away*, rather than *kicked away*.

As soon as Men have Understanding enough to find a Fault, they have enough to see the danger of mending it.

Desiring to have any thing mended, is venturing to have it spoiled: To know when to let Things alone, is a high pitch of good

good Sense. But a Fool hath an Eagerness, like a Monkey in a Glass Shop, to break every thing in the handling.

Curing and *Mending* are generally meer Words of Art not to be relied upon. They are set out in Bills, but the *Mountebanks* only get by them.

GREAT Bashfulness is oftener an Effect of Pride than of Modesty. *Bashful-ness.*

Modesty is oftner mistaken than any other Virtue.

WISE Venturing is the most commendable Part of human Prudence. *Boldness.*

It is the upper Story of Prudence, whereas perpetual Caution is a kind of under-ground Wisdom that doth not care to see the Light.

It is best for great Men to shoot over, and for lesser Men to shoot short.

MEN who borrow their Opinions can never repay their Debts. They are Beggars by Nature, and can therefore never get a Stock to grow rich upon. *Borrow-ers of Opi-nions.*

A Man who hath not a distinguishing Head, is safest by not minding what any body sayeth.

He had better trust to his own Opinion, than spoil another Man's for want of apprehending it.

IT is some kind of Scandal not to bear with the Faults of an honest Man. *Candour.*

It is not loving Honesty enough to allow it distinguishing Privileges.

There are some decent Faults which may pretend to be in the lower Rank of Virtues; and surely where Honour or Gratitude are the Motives, Censure must be a good deal silenced.

MEN must be saved in this World by their Want of Faith. *Of Cau-tion and Suspicion.*

A Man that getteth Care into his Thoughts, cannot properly be said to trade without a Stock.

Care and right Thought will produce Crops all the Year without staying for the Seasons.

A Man is to go about his own Business as if he had not a Friend in the World to help him in it.

He

He that relieth upon himself will be oppressed by others with Offers of their Service.

All are apt to shrink from those that lean upon them.

If Men would think how often their own Words are thrown at their Heads, they would less often let them go out of their Mouths.

Mens Words are Bullets that their Enemies take up and make use of against them.

A Man watches himself best when others watch him too.

It is as necessary for us to suppress our Reason when it offendeth, as our Mistakes when they expose us.

In an unreasonable Age, a Man's Reason let loose would undo him.

A wise Man will do with his Reason as a Miser doth with his Money, hoard it, but be very sparing in the Expence of it.

A Man that should call every thing by its right Name, would hardly pass the Streets without being knock'd down as a common Enemy.

A Man cannot be more in the Wrong than to own without Distinction the being in the Right.

When a Man is very kind or very angry, there is no sure Guard but Silence upon that Subject.

A Man's Understanding is easily shoved out of its Place by warm Thoughts of any kind.

We are not so much Masters of our Heat as to have enough to warm our Thoughts, and not so much as to set them on fire.

A great Enemy is a great Object that inviteth Precaution, which maketh him less dangerous than a mean one.

An old Man concludeth from his knowing Mankind, that they know him too, and that maketh him very wary.

On the other hand, it must be allowed, that a Man's being deceived by Knaves hath often this ill Effect, that it maketh him too jealous of honest Men.

The Mind, like the Body, is subject to be hurt by every thing it taketh for a Remedy.

There are some such very great Foreseers, that they grow into the Vanity of pretending to see where nothing is to be seen.

He

He that will see at too great a distance, will sometimes mistake a Bush for a Horse: The Prospect of a wise Man will be bounded.

A Man may so overdo it in looking too far before him, that he may stumble the more for it.

And, to conclude, He that leaveth nothing to Chance will do few things ill, but he will do very few things.

Suspicion is rather a Virtue than a Fault, as long as it doth like a Dog that *watcheth*, and doth *not bite*.

A wise Man, in trusting another, must not rely upon his *Promise* against his *Nature*.

Early Suspicion is often an Injury, and late Suspicion is always a Folly.

A wise Man will keep his Suspicions muzzled, but he will keep them awake.

There can no Rules be given to Suspicion, no more than to Love.

Suspicion taketh Root, and beareth Fruit, from the moment it is planted.

Suspicion seldom wanteth Food to keep it up in Health and Vigour. It feedeth upon every thing it seeth, and is not curious in its Diet.

Suspicion doth not grow up to an Injury till it breaketh out.

When our Suspicion of another Man is once discovered by him, there ought to be an end of all further Commerce.

He that is never suspected, is either very much esteemed, or very much despised.

A Man's *Interest* is not a sufficient Ground to suspect him, if his *Nature* doth not concur in it.

A weak Man hath less Suspicion than a wise one, but when he hath it, he is less easily cured.

The Remedies as often increase the Disease, as they do allay it; and a Fool valueth himself upon suspecting at a venture.

MANY Men *swallow* the being cheated, but no Man could *Cheats*. ever endure to *chew* it.

Few Men would be deceived, if their Conceit of themselves did not help the Skill of those that go about it.

COMPLAINING

Complaint.   COMPLAINING is a Contempt upon ones self :
It is an ill Sign both of a Man's Head and of his Heart.

A Man throweth himself down whilst he complaineth ; and when a Man throweth himself down, no body careth to take him up again.

Content.   CONTENT layeth Pleasure, nay Virtue, in a Slumber, with few and faint Intermissions.

It is to the Mind, like Moss to a Tree, it bindeth it up so as to stop its Growth.

Converts.   THE Impudence of a Bawd is Modesty, compared with that of a Convert.

A Convert hath so much to do to gain Credit, that a Man is to think well before he changeth.

Desires.   MEN generally state their Wants by their Fancy, and not by their Reason.

The poor young Children are whipt and beaten by the old ones, who are much more inexcusably impertinent.

Not having things, is a more proper Expression for a Man of Sense than his wanting them.

Where Sense is wanting, every thing is wanting.

A Man of Sense can hardly want, but for his Friends and Children that have none.

Most Men let their Wishes run away with them.

They have no mind to stop them in their Career, the Motion is so pleasing.

To desire what belongeth to another Man is Misprision of Robbery.

Men are commanded not to covet, because when they do they are very apt to take.

Difficulty.   A DIFFICULTY raiseth the Spirits of a great Man, he hath a mind to wrestle with it, and give it a Fall.

A Man's Mind must be very low, if the Difficulty doth not make a part of his Pleasure.

The Pride of Compassing may more than compare with the Pleasure of Enjoying.

Dissem-
bling.   NOTHING so ridiculous as a false Philosopher, and nothing so rare as a true one.

Men

Men take more pains to hide than to mend themselves.

MENS Pride, as well as their Weakness, disposeth them to *Dreams.* rely upon Dreams, from their thinking themselves of such Importance as to have Warning of what is to befal them.

The Enquiry into a Dream is another Dream.

IT is a piece of Arrogance to dare to be drunk, because a Man *Drunken-* sheweth himself without a Vail. *ness.*

THE best way to suppose what may come, is to remember *Expe-* what is past. *rience.*

The best Qualification of a Prophet is to have a good Memory.

Experience maketh more Prophets than Revelation.

The Knowledge that is got without Pains, is kept without Pleasure.

The Struggling for Knowledge hath a Pleasure in it like that of Wrestling with a fine Woman.

EXTREMITY is always ill, that which is good cannot live *Extremes.* a Moment with it.

Any body that is Fool enough will be safe in the World, and any body that can be Knave enough will be rich in it.

The generality of the World falleth into an insufficient *Mean* that exposeth them more than an *Extreme* on either Side.

THOUGH Memory and Invention are not upon good Terms, *Faculties* yet when the first is loaded, the other is stifled. *of the* *Mind.*

The Memory hath Claws by which it holdeth fast; but it hath no Wings, like the Invention, to enable it to fly.

Some Mens Memory is like a Box, where a Man should mingle his Jewels with his old Shoes.

There ought to be a great Difference between the Memory and the Stomach; the last is to admit every thing, the former should have the Faculty of Rejecting.

It is a nice Mean between letting the Thought languish for want of Exercise, and tiring it by giving it too much.

A Man may dwell so long upon a Thought, that it may take him Prisoner.

The hardest thing in the World is to give the Thoughts due Liberty, and yet retain them in due Discipline.

They

They are Libertines that are apt to abuse Freedom, and do not well know how to bear Restraint.

A Man that excels in any one thing has a kind of arbitrary Power over all that hear him upon that Subject, and no Man's Life is too short to know any one thing perfectly.

The modern Wit is rather to set Men out, than to make them of any Use.

Some Men have acted Courage who had it not; but no Man can act Wit, if Nature doth not teach him his Part. True Wit is always revenged upon any false Pretender that meddleth with it.

Wit is the only thing that Men are willing to think they can ever have enough of.

There is a happy Pitch of Ignorance that a Man of Sense might pray for.

A Man that hath true Wit will have Honour too, not only to adorn, but to support it.

Families. THE building up a Family is a Manufacture very little above the building a House of Cards.

Time and Accidents are sure to furnish a Blast to blow it down.

No House wanteth new Tiling so often as a Family wants Repairing.

The Desire of having Children is as much the Effect of Vanity as of Good-nature.

We think our Children a Part of ourselves, though as they grow up they might very well undeceive us.

Men love their Children, not because they are promising Plants, but because they are theirs.

They cannot discredit the Plant, without disparaging the Soil out of which it came.

Pride in this, as in many other things, is often mistaken for Love.

As Children make a Man poor in one Sense, so in another they inforce Care, and that begetteth Riches.

Love is presently out of Breath when it is to go up Hill, from the Children to the Parents.

'TIS

'TIS good to have Men in Awe, but dangerous to have them *Fear.* afraid of us.

The Mean is so nice, that the hitting upon it is oftner the Effect of Chance than of Skill.

A Degree of Fear sharpeneth, the Excess of it stupifieth.

It is as scandalous not to fear at some times, as it can be to be afraid at others.

FOLLY begets Want, and Want Flattery; so that Flattery, *Flattery.* with all its Wit, is the Grandchild of Folly.

Were it not for Bunglers in the manner of doing it, hardly any Man would ever find out he was laughed at.

And yet, generally speaking, a Trowel is a more effectual Instrument than a Pencil for Flattery.

Men generally do so love the Taste of Flattery, their Stomach can never be overcharged with it.

There is a Right Reverend Flattery that hath the Precedence of all other Kinds of it.

This Mitred Flattery is of all others the most exalted. It ever groweth in proportion, and keepeth pace with Power. There is a noble Stroke of it in the Articles sent to Princess *Mary* from *Henry* VIII. 'Such is his Majesty's *Gracious and* '*Divine Nature*—shewing Mercy to such as *repentantly cry and* '*call* for the same.'

FORGETTING is oftner an Aggravation than an Excuse. *Forgetful-* The Memory will seldom be unmannerly but where it is *ness.* unkind.

THERE needeth little Care to *polish* the Understanding; *Good-* if true Means were used to *strengthen* it, it will polish itself. *manners.*

Good-manners is such a Part of Good-sense, that they cannot be divided; but that which a Fool calleth Good-breeding is the most unmannerly thing in the World.

Right Good-manners require so much Sense, that there is hardly any such thing in the World.

GOOD-NATURE is rather acted than practised in the *Good-* World. *nature.*

Good-nature to others is an inseparable Part of Justice.

GOOD-WILL, like Grace, floweth where it listeth. *Good-will.*

Men

Men mean so very well to themselves, that they forget to mean well to any body else.

Heat. GOOD-SENSE will allow of some intermitting Fevers, but then the Fit must be short.

Honesty. HE that can be quite indifferent when he seeth another Man injured, hath a lukewarm Honesty that a wise Man will not depend upon.

He that is not concerned when he seeth an ill thing done to another, will not be very eager to do a good one himself.

Hypocrisy. THERE is so much Wit necessary to make a skilful Hypocrite, that the Faculty is fallen amongst Bunglers, who make it ridiculous.

Injuries. AN Injury may more properly be said to be postponed, than to be forgiven.

The Memory of it is never so subdued, but that it hath always Life in it.

The Memory of an Enemy admitteth no decay but Age.

Could we know what Men are most apt to remember, we might know what they are most apt to do.

It is a general Fault that we dislike Men only for the Injuries they do to us, and not for those they do to Mankind. Yet it will be hard to give a good Reason why a Man who hath done a deliberate Injury to one, will not do it to another.

The Memory and the Conscience never did, nor never will agree about forgiving Injuries.

Nature is Second to the Memory, and Religion to the Conscience.

When the Seconds fight, the latter is generally disarmed.

Integrity. A MAN in a corrupted Age must make a Secret of his Integrity, or else he will be looked upon as a common Enemy.

He must engage his Friends not to speak of it; for he setteth himself for a Mark to be ill used.

Justice. AS far as keeping distance is a sign of Respect, Mankind hath a great deal for Justice.

They make up in Ceremony what they want in Good-will to it.

Where

Where the Generality are Offenders, Justice cometh to be Cruelty.

TO Love, and to be in Love with any thing, are Things as differing, as good Sense and Impertinence. *To Love, and be in Love differ-*

When we once go beyond bare liking, we are in danger of *ferent.* parting with Good-Sense; and it is not easy for Good-Sense to get so far as liking.

WHEN by habit a Man cometh to have a bargaining Soul, *Lucre.* its Wings are cut, so that it can never soar.

It bindeth Reason an Apprentice to Gain, and instead of a Director, maketh it a Drudge.

THE being kind to a Lyar, is abetting a Treason against *Lying.* Mankind.

A Man is to inform the first Magistrate, that he may be clap'd up.

Lies are embroidered with Promises and Excuses.

A known Lyar should be outlawed in a well ordered Government.

A Man that renounceth Truth, runneth away from his trial in the World.

The use of Talking is almost lost in the World by the habit of Lying.

A Man that doth not tell all the Truth, ought to be hanged for a Clipper.

Half the Truth is often as arrant a Lye, as can be made.

It is the more dexterous, but not the less criminal kind of Lying.

NAMES to Men of Sense are no more than Fig-leaves; to the *Names.* generality they are thick Coverings that hide the Nature of Things from them.

Fools turn Good-Sense upon its Head, they take Names for Things, and Things only for Names.

IT is a general Mistake to think the Men we like are good *Partia-* for every thing, and those we do not, good for nothing. *lity.*

A MAN who is Master of Patience, is Master of every thing else. *Patience.*

He that can tell how to bear in the right Place, is Master of every body he dealeth with.

POSITIVE

Positive-ness. POSITIVE is the Perfection of Coxcomb, he is then come to his full Growth.

Prospe-rity. IT sheweth Mens Nature, that when they are pampered in any kind, they are very apt to play jadish Tricks.

One of the Tricks of any Creature that is wanton, is to kick what is next them.

Quiet. EVERY thing that doth us good is so apt to do us hurt too, that it is a strong Argument for Men to be quiet.

If Men would think more, they would act less.

The greatest Part of the Business of the World, is the Effect of not thinking.

Reason and Pas-sion. MOST Men put their Reason out to Service to their Will.

The Master and the Man are perpetually falling out.

A third Man will hazard a beating, if he goes about to part them.

Nothing hath an uglier Look to us than Reason, when it is not of our side.

We quarrel so often with it, that it maketh us afraid to come near it.

A Man that doth not use his Reason, is a tame Beast; a Man that abuses it, is a wild one.

Reputa-tion. IT is a self-flattering Contradiction, that wise Men despise the Opinion of Fools, and yet are proud of having their Esteem.

Self-love. SELF-LOVE rightly defined, is far from being a Fault.

A Man that loveth himself right, will do every thing else right.

Shame. A MAN who doth not think he is punished when he is blamed, is too much hardened to be ever reformed.

The Court of Shame hath of late lost much of its Jurisdiction. It ought by right both to judge in the first Instance, and to exclude all Appeals from it.

Shame is a Disease of the last Age, this seemeth to be cured of it.

Singula-rity. SINGULARITY may be good Sense at home, but it must not go much abroad.

It is a Commendation to be that which a crowd of mistaken Fools call Singular.

There

There can hardly be a severer thing said to a Man in this Age, than that he is like the rest of the World.

SLANDER would not stick, if it had not always something *Slander.* to lay hold of.

A Man who can allow himself the Liberty to slander, hath the World too much at his Mercy.

But the Man that despiseth Slander deserveth it.

SPEAKERS in Publick should take more Pains to hold in *Speakers in Publick.* their Invention than to raise it.

Invention is apt to make such Sallies, that it cannot secure its Retreat.

He that will not make a Blot, will be pretty sure in his time to give a Stroke.

A patient Hearer is a sure Speaker.

Men are angry when others do not hear them, yet they have more Reason to be afraid when they do.

MISPENDING a Man's time is a kind of *self-homicide*, it is *Time the loss of it.* making Life to be of no use.

TRUTH is not only stifled by Ignorance, but concealed out *Truth.* of Caution or Interest; so if it had not a Root of Immortality, it must have been long since extinguished.

THE most useful Part of Wisdom is for a Man to give *Wisdom.* a good guess, what others think of him.

It is a dangerous thing to guess partially, and a melancholy thing to guess right.

Nothing would more contribute to make a Man wise, than to have always an Enemy in his view.

A wise Man may have more Enemies than a weak one, but he will not so much feel the weight of them. Indeed the being wise doth either make Men our Friends, or discourage them from being our Enemies.

Wisdom is only a comparative Quality, it will not bear a single Definition.

A MAN hath too little Heat, or Wit, or Courage, if he hath *Youth.* not sometimes more than he should.

Just enough of a good thing is always too little.

Long Life giveth more Marks to shoot at, and therefore old

Men

Men are less well thought of, than those who have not been so long upon the Stage.

Other Mens Memories retain the ill, whilst the good Things done by an old Man, easily slip out of them.

Old Men have in some degree their Reprisals upon younger, by making nicer Observations upon them, by virtue of their Experience.

FINIS.

Oxford : Horace Hart, Printer to the University